POEM PORTRAITS

BOOKS BY JAMES J. METCALFE

Love Portraits

My Rosary of Rhymes

Poem Portraits

More Poem Portraits

Garden In My Heart

James J. Metcalfe's Poems for Children

Poem Portraits

A COLLECTION OF VERSE

by

JAMES J. METCALFE

Garden City Books

GARDEN CITY, NEW YORK

DEDICATION

I dedicate this book of verse . . . To you, my loving wife . . . For all the inspiration you . . . Have given me in life . . . To both of you, my precious sons . . . And you, my daughter dear . . . Because you youngsters are the ones . . . Who bring me so much cheer . . . The four of you together are . . . My four-leaf clover bright . . . And you are every lucky star . . . I wish upon at night . . . You are the story of my pride . . . My faith and courage strong . . . And every moment at your side . . . Becomes a sweeter song . . . You make my life a joy to live . . . And help my dreams come true . . . And so with all my heart I give . . . These lines to each of you.

Foreword

IF the poetry of Ovid, Shakespeare, Keats, Longfellow and others whose works involve no copyright payments would sell newspapers, you'd be reading the strumming of their lyres along with such current intelligence as the odds paid at the horse tracks, who shot whom and where, when and—possibly—why, and other tales of triumphs and distresses in this naughty world.

And if the lines of Millay, Auden and other moderns who have distilled verse in the moonshine would sell papers, managing editors and circulation managers would clamor to get the bards on the editorial budget. But the product of this array of past and present genius doesn't make newspaper circulation as James Metcalfe's verse does.

So, by the definite and unanswerable appraisal of newspaper sales figures Metcalfe is America's foremost poet today. Jim sings those simple little songs that echo the thoughts in the hearts of millions of mute Miltons.

In the long, sleek chauffeur-driven limousines and in the crowded streetcars and buses—in the rooms of the cliff-dwellers in huge cities and in those houses where windows shine cheerfully as your train or plane passes in the night—Jim's verse rains a gentle shower on the soul.

Jim, who was born in Berlin, Germany, on September 16, 1906, received his early education at the University of Notre Dame and his law degree at Loyola University, Chicago—the hard way, in night school. He walked off with all sorts of scholastic honors in oratory. At 14 he turned out his first bit of rhyme and rhythm but poetry was strictly a sideline with him in the years that followed—four years in the Federal Bureau of Investigation and nine years of investigating for the United States Department of Agriculture, interspersed with two years of reporting, feature writing and picture-desk work for the Chicago *Times*.

As a G-man, Metcalfe was in on the killing of John Dillinger. As a reporter, he won the National Headliners Club silver plaque for his undercover work in exposing the German and German-American Bunds.

Yes, Jim has been around, and in getting around and meeting all types of humanity he has always looked past the outside and into their hearts.

He's out-smarted and out-fought the toughest, fought for and lifted the spirits of the weary and troubled, and he shares with the multitude of those who have dreams and hopes for their loved ones the dreams and hopes he has for his own delightful family. His pen often turns to that family—wife Lillian, who was born in Norway; Jimmie and Donnie, products of Chicago, and the little princess, Kristina Maria, a native Texan and mighty proud of it. Their home is in Dallas.

Jim's verse looks and reads so easy that it wins the finest of all tributes: "That's just what I was thinking. Why didn't I write that?"

Those of us in newspaper work who know how Jim Metcalfe's verse has brought light and wholesomeness into the papers we help to make, and who know him as one of the best of the strong and kindly characters we've ever met, are proud of him. We are happy that we can present him to our mutual friends, the public.

HERB GRAFFIS
Sun-Times
Chicago

Contents by Subject

ix

OCCUPATION

xiv

POEM PORTRAITS

ALBUM OF DREAMS

Between the covers of this book . . . We keep the golden past
. . . When we were only youngsters and . . . The world was wide
and vast . . . And every season, each in turn . . . That saw us laugh
and play . . . And fall in love and join our hearts . . . Upon that
wedding day . . . The pictures of our honeymoon . . . And other
trips we took . . . And of the home where now I rest . . . While you
keep house and cook . . . The picnics and the parties and . . . The
friends who came to call . . . And everything that meant to us . . .
Just anything at all . . . And as the years go rolling by . . . I only
hope that we . . . Compile a dozen other books . . . As dear to
you and me.

FINAL GRADE

In school the youth is graded on . . . His answers right or wrong
. . . In sports a lot depends upon . . . His being weak or strong . . .
And later on when he begins . . . To earn his daily bread . . . His
score is always one that wins . . . If he can keep his head . . . He
gets a rating from his boss . . . According to the way . . . The profit
overcomes the loss . . . Throughout his working day . . . But more
important to his name . . . Is how he lives his life . . . And whether
he can gather fame . . . And stay away from strife . . . His mark is
not the bright or dim . . . That money represents . . . But whether
friends repose in him . . . Their faith and confidence.

TELL ME YOU LOVE ME

I do not know what thoughts of me . . . Are in your heart today
. . . But there is just one sentiment . . . I long to have you say . . .
I want to hear you whisper that . . . You are in love with me
. . . And you will always feel the same . . . Wherever you may
be . . . Because I am in love with you . . . And in the stars that
rise . . . I see the soft reflection of . . . Your wistful, friendly eyes
. . . Because the flowers in the sun . . . And every sky of blue . . .
Remind me of the happiness . . . That I have had with you . . .
And in the valley of my dreams . . . I look for every sign . . . That
might reveal the way you feel . . . About this heart of mine.

GOD IS MY GUIDE

This evening as I wander home . . . My heart is worn with care
. . . And in my loneliness I have . . . A feeling of despair . . . I
wonder if tomorrow will . . . Be better than today . . . Or whether
it will be the same . . . Along my weary way . . . And yet I know
my God is there . . . To guide and comfort me . . . With promises of happiness . . . For all eternity . . . I know that He is at my
side . . . Wherever I may go . . . Beneath the sun and silver stars
. . . And in the winds that blow . . . So why should I be sorrowful
. . . Or ever have a doubt . . . When God is always at my side . . .
To love and help me out?

LETTER

A letter is a simple thing . . . That anyone can write . . . And
one that takes so little time . . . From any day or night . . . And
yet it means so much to those . . . Who get the mail we send . . .
As customer or merchant or . . . As relative or friend . . . Because
it demonstrates to them . . . How thoughtfully we live . . . And
that we feel a message is . . . The least that we can give . . . It
shows our willingness to keep . . . In touch with those we know
. . . And that we do remember them . . . No matter where we
go . . . A letter is a simple thing . . . Of paper and of ink . . .
Designed to tell the addressee . . . Whatever thoughts we think.

DOCTOR

The doctor is a learned man . . . As anyone can tell . . . He does
however much he can . . . To make our bodies well . . . He di-
agnoses all our ills . . . With patience and with care . . . Pre-
scribes a tonic or some pills . . . And plenty of fresh air . . . He
treats our bruises and our cuts . . . And mends each broken bone
. . . He drives through rain and muddy ruts . . . When called by
telephone . . . He helps the baby to arrive . . . And grow in health
and weight . . . He wants the world to stay alive . . . And illness
to abate . . . He is an understanding man . . . Who tells us what
to eat . . . And who does everything he can . . . To keep us on
our feet.

FRIENDLY WORLD

The world is such a friendly place . . . In which to spend my
time . . . That I am never bothered by . . . The scenery or clime
. . . I know that everywhere I go . . . I merely look around . . .
And happily another friend . . . Is somewhere to be found . . . A
friend I have not met before . . . And do not call by name . . . But
who is understanding and . . . Is helpful just the same . . . A
friend who has not heard of me . . . And yet who is at hand . . .
As real as any neighbor in . . . The most familiar land . . . And so
no matter where I go . . . I do not mind the place . . . Because I
know that I shall find . . . Another friendly face.

LUNCH ECONOMY

I like to give my order for . . . The lunch I want to eat . . . And
leisurely enjoy it with . . . The office friends I meet . . . But now
the cost of living and . . . Especially of food . . . Has obviously
risen to . . . The point of being rude . . . And so in order not to
go . . . Financially berserk . . . I have decided after this . . . To
bring my lunch to work . . . I may not take much time to eat . . .
Or share it with a friend . . . But I am sure that I shall be . . . Successful in the end . . . I shall not have to bother what . . . To order
every day . . . And when I get through eating, there . . . Will be
no check to pay.

PATRIOTIC PRIDE

The finest thing that we can have . . . Is patriotic pride . . . And
it is something we should show . . . And never try to hide . . . We
should salute the Stars and Stripes . . . And never be afraid
. . . To stand up instantly each time . . . We hear our anthem
played . . . We should be loyal to the core . . . And bravely confident . . . And we should speak respectfully . . . About our government . . . Because we owe at least this much . . . To our United
States . . . Where we abide in comfort and . . . In freedom from
all hates . . . And being patriotic is . . . A mighty easy way . . .
To demonstrate our gratitude . . . For all we have today.

MY SLIPPERS

My slippers wait for me all day . . . In their accustomed place
. . . While I am at the office with . . . A pair of shoes that lace . . .
Until I come back home again . . . By trolley or beside . . . My
wifely chauffeur, who so oft . . . Provides me with a ride . . . And
then my slippers go to work . . . And take me by the feet . . .
Conveying me from room to room . . . To each selected seat . . .
They are so warm and cozy and . . . They fit so nice and snug
. . . There is not space remaining for . . . The very smallest bug
. . . And when I take them off at night . . . And crawl in bed once
more . . . They stand in constant readiness . . . Upon the cold,
hard floor.

NO REGRETS

Sometimes I meditate upon . . . The days of long ago . . . The
pleasures and the plans and all . . . The friends I used to know . . ,
I carefully compare them with . . . My fortunes of today . . . To
see if I am better off . . . For what I put away . . . Because as I
grow older I . . . Forever change my mind . . . And I decide that
certain things . . . Are better left behind . . . But later on I wonder
if . . . I took the proper path . . . Or if I may be forced to face
. . . A mournful aftermath . . . Although I must acknowledge
that . . . I never have as yet . . . Encountered any reason for . . .
The tiniest regret.

NO MATTER WHERE

Though I may never see you, dear . . . Though I may never say
. . . The thoughts that whisper to my heart . . . And fill my soul
each day . . . I shall not cease to love you more . . . Than anything
I know . . . Or any other one I meet . . . No matter where I go
. . . I shall not cease to hold you high . . . In genuine esteem . . .
Or fail to find your loveliness . . . In any happy dream . . . I shall
not see the silver stars . . . That cover all the skies . . . Without
I shall imagine I . . . Am gazing in your eyes . . . I shall not stand
upon a shore . . . Or sail a single sea . . . Without the wish that
you were mine . . . And you were there with me.

4

HUMBLY COURAGEOUS

God always wants us to be meek . . . And humble in His sight
. . . But also to be strong of heart . . . And brave enough to
fight . . . To overcome temptation and . . . To conquer every sin
. . . And brook no interference in . . . Our earnestness to win . . .
He longs to see our courage in . . . Whatever we may do . . . Especially the fortitude . . . Of being good and true . . . The fear-
lessness of being kind . . . And generous to all . . . The gallantry
of helping those . . . Who struggle and who fall . . . God wants
us to be humble in . . . Acknowledging His aid . . . But in all
other things to be . . . Resolved and unafraid.

AFTERNOON RAIN

I do not mind the morning rain . . . That washes off the skies
. . . Or rain that patters in the night . . . When I have closed my
eyes . . . But usually I do not like . . . The melancholy tune . . .
That marks a steady drizzle in . . . The idle afternoon . . . Be-
cause it always makes me feel . . . A little lonely then . . . And
always makes we wish the rain . . . Would go away again . . . It
fills me with discouragement . . . It turns my hopes to fears . . .
And somehow in the afternoon . . . The raindrops look like tears
. . . I do not mind a shower in . . . The morning or at night . . .
But in the afternoon I long . . . To see the heavens bright.

WAITRESS

The waitress is a lady fair . . . Done up in apron strings . . .
Who tries to take your order while . . . You talk of other things
. . . She lingers patiently as you . . . Peruse the bill of fare . . .
And tells you what you cannot have . . . Because it is not there
. . . She brings the dishes one by one . . . And calmly sets them
down . . . Not caring if your name is Joe . . . Or if you claim
renown . . . She stands aside and watches you . . . So she can be
right there . . . In case you call to her or wave . . . Your finger in
the air . . . She caters to your every wish . . . And seldom makes
a slip . . . And when you go she looks to see . . . If you have left
a tip.

ALL GOOD WISHES

I send my compliments today . . . With friendship warm and true . . . I hope success will come your way . . . In everything you do . . . I wish you all the luck you need . . . And after that some more . . . I hope your path will always lead . . . To some inviting door . . . I hope the skies look clear and bright . . . Wherever you may be . . . I hope there will be stars at night . . . To keep you company . . . I hope the future will unfold . . . Whatever you would win . . . I hope you find your pot of gold . . . I hope your ship comes in . . . May love bestow its magic touch . . . And all your dreams be sweet . . . I wish you health, I hope so much . . . Your life will be complete.

TRADE MARK

A trade mark is the name by which . . . An article is known . . . And that which brings about a sale . . . Wherever it is shown . . . But in addition it reflects . . . The manufacturer's pride . . . In something that has proved itself . . . Each time it has been tried . . . It promises the buyer that . . . The product is the best . . . Or anyway it is at least . . . As good as all the rest . . . It satisfies the customer . . . That it is bound to please . . . And it is quite significant . . . Of high-grade qualities . . . Indeed the trade mark is a thing . . . That means a lot in life . . . Especially to every man's . . . Discriminating wife.

HOMECOMING

Our circumstances made us move . . . And sell the house we had . . . But we are going home again . . . And we are mighty glad . . . The trip to other parts was quite . . . A fascinating change . . . But Texas is our paradise . . . And our familiar range . . . So we are going home again . . . To all the friends we know . . . Where zero is a temperature . . . It never gets below . . . Where hearts are warm and handshakes firm . . . And smiles forever last . . . While loneliness and tears belong . . . To some forgotten past . . . We're on our way to Dallas and . . . The moment we arrive . . . We will be wonderfully content . . . And glad to be alive.

FROWN

I never like to see a frown . . . Because it seems to me . . . It turns the facial muscles down . . . To fashion misery . . . Because it fills the human face . . . With wrinkles large and small . . . That neither show becoming grace . . . Nor look polite at all . . . A frown reflects internal pain . . . Or what is worse than that . . . It tolerates with great disdain . . . What it is pointing at . . . And many times a frown portrays . . . A prejudice or pride . . . That life affords no common ways . . . To cover or to hide . . . It is a sort of social wall . . . That signifies a doubt . . . And it is something we would all . . . Be better off without.

MY BASHFUL PLEA

I am a bashful person and . . . I only wish that you . . . Would give me some encouragement . . . In what I want to do . . . I want to call you darling and . . . I want to let you know . . . I think about you all the time . . . And everywhere I go . . . I want to say I love you and . . . If ever it could be . . . To kiss your lips and someday soon . . . To have you marry me . . . I want to make a home for you . . . And see that you are gay . . . With all the sunshine in my heart . . . To keep the clouds away . . . But I am just so bashful that . . . I know not what to do . . . And that is why I wish I had . . . A little help from you.

PRAYER FOR HONESTY

O Lord, may I be honest in . . . Whatever things I do . . . And most of all, O Lord, I want . . . To be that way with You . . . I want to strive for fairness in . . . My dealings everywhere . . . And be forever satisfied . . . To have my equal share . . . To speak and walk in truthfulness . . . That I may be sincere . . . And thus courageously go forth . . . With never any fear . . . Let me not be deceitful, Lord . . . For vanity or pride . . . Or yet to camouflage some deed . . . That I may want to hide . . . But help me now, O Lord, to keep . . . My life an open book . . . Upon whose pages everyone . . . Is always free to look.

INVITATION

I like to be invited to . . . An evening with a friend . . . And many folks are lavish with . . . The offers they extend . . . But all too often they present . . . Their courtesies to me . . . Without a special welcome to . . . Their hospitality . . . Their words are very general . . . And never contemplate . . . A definite or tentative . . . Or any kind of date . . . They simply say, "Come over when . . . You have the time to spare" . . . And thus they leave their friendly thoughts . . . Suspended in the air . . . I like to be invited but . . . I also like to know . . . At least approximately when . . . I may prepare to go.

ACTOR

An actor has no easy life . . . But he must work a lot . . . And when his time to play begins . . . He's really on the spot . . . He has to use his hands and feet . . . And move his lips and eyes . . . And thousands are the sentences . . . He has to memorize . . . He must be ready with a smile . . . Or look a little sad . . . He must be frightened, nonchalant . . . Hysterical or mad . . . And it is not enough for him . . . To offer tears and laughs . . . For he must shake the public's hand . . . And furnish autographs . . . His agent or director is . . . Forever on the phone . . . And so no matter where he goes . . . His life is not his own.

RARE FRIEND

It is no easy thing to find . . . A friend along the way . . . I mean the friend whose smile extends . . . Beyond a single day . . . Who does not merely shake your hand . . . And say a quick hello . . . Before he vanishes among . . . The little winds that blow . . . But on the more important side . . . I have in mind the one . . . Who thinks of you from early dawn . . . Until the day is done . . . Who has a word of cheerful praise . . . For everything you do . . . And when misfortune turns the tide . . . Is still a friend to you . . . The kind of friend whose attitude . . . Is never dark or cold . . . But who is always loyal and . . . Who has a heart of gold.

8

WHATEVER WEATHER

I wish I could explain to you . . . The reason for the rain . . . It
is because you comfort me . . . And soothe my every pain . . . I
wish that I could tell you why . . . The snow is always white . . .
It is a symbol of the way . . . You help me through the night
. . . The sun is just another sign . . . That draws me close to
you . . . Because when I am at your side . . . The sky is always
blue . . . And when the wind is blowing and . . . I wander on the
street . . . You are the only one on earth . . . I ever care to meet
. . . And so the weather may be grand . . . Or somewhat poor or
fair . . . But you are still the only one . . . For whom I ever care.

PRAYER IN REVIEW

Almighty God, another year . . . Is drawing to a close . . . And
during it the world has had . . . Its wonders and its woes . . . We
won the wars of East and West . . . And everything they meant
. . . Though You saw fit to take away . . . Our faithful President . . . We had our hardships and we had . . . Our heartaches
to endure . . . But most of them are over and . . . The peace appears secure . . . The atom bomb was introduced . . . With all its
deadly might . . . And yet it helped immeasurably . . . To ter-
minate the fight . . . And while our hearts are still in doubt . . .
About each coming dawn . . . We thank You, God, for giving us
. . . The strength to carry on.

FARMER'S SATURDAY

He's up at dawn and does his chores . . . Like any other day . . .
But after that the old routine . . . Takes on a different sway . . . He
gets his wife and youngsters and . . . They all drive into town . . .
To see what folks are doing and . . . If things are up or down
. . . The missus does the shopping while . . . The daughter finds
a beau . . . And Junior buys a ticket to . . . The Wild West picture show . . . But pa just stands around and talks . . . To everyone he sees . . . Or joins the crowd around the man . . . Who's
selling remedies . . . And when it's dark they head for home . . .
And all along the way . . . They swap the sights and gossip
of . . . Another Saturday.

HUSBAND

He is the man who takes a vow . . . To love and honor her . . . And do however much he can . . . To make her happier . . . He is the Mr. of the house . . . (If not the master too) . . . And he must be prepared to pay . . . Whatever bills come due . . . For him there is no real success . . . Or glory in this life . . . Unless it brings some happiness . . . To his devoted wife . . . He may not be the smartest or . . . The strongest man of all . . . He may not have a handsome face . . . Or measure very tall . . . He may not be a millionaire . . . As cash determines worth . . . But always in her heart he is . . . The grandest man on earth.

WIFE

A wife is one who cleans your house . . . And cooks the things you eat . . . Who darns your sox and mends your shirts . . . To keep you looking neat . . . Who manages to pay the bills . . . And lay some cash aside . . . With half as much as you put out . . . To have your needs supplied . . . She is the one who listens to . . . Your troubles of the day . . . But as for worries of her own . . . Has nothing much to say . . . Who calls you strong and handsome and . . . Adores your healthy tan . . . And lets you think you are the boss . . . And quite a clever man . . . She praises your accomplishments . . . And always tries to please . . . While you forget her birthdays and . . . Your anniversaries.

HEALTHY MIND

We need a healthy body to . . . Endure our daily grind . . . But more than that we ought to have . . . A young and healthy mind . . . Because the mind controls the flesh . . . And doctors often tell . . . How rightful thinking plays its part . . . To keep the body well . . . Our thoughts should always hold a place . . . Upon the highest plane . . . And contemplate the glory of . . . The greatest goal to gain . . . They should be bright and wholesome and . . . Encouraging and true . . . Not just to keep us healthy but . . . To help our neighbor too . . . And whether there are many things . . . Or few that we expect . . . A healthy mind is always sure . . . Of honor and respect.

PUBLICITY

In nearly every walk of life . . . Wherever we may be . . . There is a wealth of worthiness . . . In good publicity . . . A picture or a story as . . . Related by the press . . . Or any oral version of . . . Our glory and success . . . Because we should not try to hide . . . The lamp that we have lit . . . As long as there are others who . . . May learn and benefit . . . Our own example may be just . . . What others need to know . . . To fill them with the confidence . . . To carry on and grow . . . Publicity can help the cause . . . Of every neighborhood . . . If it is handled right and it . . . Is factual and good.

OUR FIGHTING FLAG

Old Glory flies supreme today . . . Wherever breezes blow . . . Supremely proud in hurling back . . . The challenge of the foe . . . Supremely proud in conquering . . . Steel walls and armored heights . . . Courageously, unyieldingly . . . Defending human rights . . . Old Glory with its stars and stripes . . . Of red and white and blue . . . The symbol of democracy . . . A champion through and through . . . A banner born of freedom and . . . Baptized in hero's blood . . . Undaunted by the ravages . . . Of fire and of flood . . . Old Glory, bright and beautiful . . . Supreme in peace and war . . . May God protect our flag and may . . . It fly for evermore!

FOOTBALL

The varsity is on the field . . . The crowd is in the stands . . . And everywhere this college sport . . . Receives applauding hands . . . The quarterback calls signals and . . . The players start to run . . . And cleats go digging in the turf . . . Until the final gun . . . The kickoff and the quick return . . . A sweep around the end . . . Another try at center and . . . A line that will not bend . . . It is a game of skill and wit . . . For amateur and pro . . . That glorifies the passing arm . . . And educated toe . . . A game in which the touchdown is . . . A most important score . . . But character and fairness are . . . The things that mean much more.

NEWS PHOTOGRAPHER

He risks his life to picture life . . . Upon a camera plate . . . For him all things pass hurriedly . . . The deadlines never wait . . . By land, by sea and air he goes . . . To "bring 'em back alive" . . . A riot scene, a pretty girl . . . A record-breaking drive . . . A robber flees, a fire roars . . . A plane comes crashing down . . . The Moneybags are Reno-bound . . . The circus comes to town . . . The weatherman turns somersaults . . . A dropkick wins the game . . . And Maizie plunges 20 floors . . . To gain post-mortem fame . . . However life may move along . . . The lens is everywhere . . . And when the paper hits the street . . . We find the picture there.

FRIENDSHIP VALUE

If there is anything I need . . . I call upon a friend . . To see if it is something he . . . Can bring to me or send . . . And if there is a service I . . . Am certain he can do . . . I ask him to be good enough . . . To undertake it, too . . . Because I always ask myself . . . What is a friendship worth . . . Unless it really brings about . . . Some benefit on earth? . . . Why cultivate acquaintances . . . And be in constant doubt . . . When I am up against a wall . . . That they will help me out? . . . And whether I am poor myself . . . Or I have wealth and fame . . . If I am called upon I shall . . . Expect to do the same.

OFFICE BOY

The office boy is one who does . . . A hundred things a day . . . To sort of help around the place . . . Where people get their pay . . . He fills up all the inkwells and . . . He dusts the desks and chairs . . . Distributes mail and gathers up . . . Completed questionnaires . . . He runs the errands for the firm . . . And often he must fly . . . To bring the boss some cigarets . . . Or get his favorite pie . . . His salary is very small . . . But he is always told . . . How others started out that way . . . To write their names in gold . . . And so he pays attention to . . . His duty and his dress . . . If he intends at all to climb . . . The ladder to success.

WE SHALL GIVE THANKS

Some day these lads who fight so well . . . With battleships and
guns . . . Will tell their glowing stories to . . . Their daughters
and their sons . . . Some day they will be happy in . . . A home to
call their own . . . And never after that will they . . . Be going on
alone . . . The Government will honor them . . . With praise and
higher ranks . . . With gold and silver medals and . . . The
people's deepest thanks . . . And those that do not touch again
. . . The safety of our shore . . . Will have their sacred names en-
shrined . . . In hearts for evermore . . . And we who shall recall
the deeds . . . Of those courageous ones . . . Shall pay our homage
to their wives . . . Their mothers and their sons.

HER TAKING WAYS

Kristina takes my pencil and . . . My paper and my glue . . .
And anything she thinks she needs . . . For what she wants to do
. . . She simply helps herself to all . . . The articles she sees . . .
Without advance permission and . . . Without formalities . . . Of
course I make allowances . . . For she is only three . . . But now
and then I wish she would . . . Respect my property . . . Because
when I have need of them . . . And when I look around . . . The
items indispensable . . . Are nowhere to be found . . . And when
I ask her where they are . . . A smile is on her face . . . And it is
plain that she does not . . . Recall the hiding-place.

IF I WERE WEALTHY

If I were wealthy and I had . . . All things at my command . . .
I think that I would try to do . . . Some good throughout the land
. . . I would contribute something of . . . My money and my time
. . . Beyond a meager moment and . . . The fraction of a dime . . .
I would give all the hours and . . . The cash I had to spare . . . To
do as much as possible . . . For people everywhere . . . Not just
because I would not need . . . The income or the days . . . But
just because I could befriend . . . The world in many ways . . .
And after all what greater joy . . . Can anybody gain . . . Than
sharing his umbrella with . . . A neighbor in the rain?

FOREVER YOURS

I walked among the stars tonight . . . And saw you standing there
. . . Your wistful eyes with beauty bright . . . Beneath your flowing
hair . . . You were so perfect, so divine . . . But you were human
too . . . Because I took your hand in mine . . . And whispered love
to you . . . We lingered through the hours long . . . And leaned
against the sky . . . While in the magic of a song . . . Our dreams
went drifting by . . . I kissed your lovely lips and then . . . I promised with my heart . . . I would return to you again . . . And we
would never part . . . And though the stars may disappear . . . And
I may walk alone . . . I shall be yours forever, dear . . . Forever,
dear, your own.

I MUST BELIEVE

I must believe in God because . . . There is no other way . . .
That I am able to explain . . . Why I am here today . . . There is
no other reason for . . . The mystery of me . . . The mind that
plans, the heart that loves . . . The soul of memory . . . There is
no answer in a book . . . Or in the changing sky . . . Except that
God created me . . . And only He knows why . . . I must believe
in God because . . . I see so many signs . . . That indicate my life
is just . . . A part of His designs . . . So many signs that point the
way . . . To choose the right from wrong . . . And how to walk
in faith and hope . . . And keep my courage strong.

ROAD SALESMAN

He has to travel day and night . . . To earn his loaf of bread . . .
And take a chance that he will have . . . A place to rest his head
. . . His business is to call upon . . . The merchants low and high
. . . And try to sell the ones who think . . . They do not want to
buy . . . His bags are filled with samples and . . . The ads that he
displays . . . To introduce his product and . . . To catch the
buyer's gaze . . . Some people think that all he does . . . Is roam
around for fun . . . But actually he has a job . . . And tries to get
it done . . . And while he may be happy and . . . Content at times
to roam . . . He usually is lonely and . . . He longs to be back
home.

JUNIOR HIGH

When grammar school is put away . . . We breathe a happy sigh
. . . And eagerly we turn our steps . . . To tackle junior high . . .
And there we study harder as . . . We find ourselves in touch . . .
With social science, languages . . . Geography and such . . . Our
English is improved some more . . . And if we study shop . . . We
learn to make a lot of things . . . Before we reach the top . . .
And then there is gymnasium with . . . Its exercise and play . . .
To build our strength and keep us in . . . Good health from day
to day . . . But soon our song is ended and . . . Again we say
good-by . . . As passing grades advance our names . . . From
junior high to high.

LIGHTS OUT

My wife and I agree that when . . . We go to bed at night . . .
The last one to retire must . . . Extinguish every light . . . And
that is only common sense . . . As anyone can see . . . Because it
keeps the light bill low . . . And saves on energy . . . But somehow
it appears to me . . . That ever since we wed . . . I have been
slower than my wife . . . In getting into bed . . . And that would
be all right except . . . That when the lights are out . . . I have to
feel my way and then . . . I stumble all about . . . And what con-
fuses me the most . . . And really makes me sore . . . Is tripping
over shoes and things . . . She leaves upon the floor.

APRIL IN MY HEART

Why do I think of April when . . . September is at hand . . .
And summer gives a parting touch . . . Of beauty to the land?
. . . Why do I look for flowers now . . . And listen for the rain . . .
As though my heart were hoping for . . . Some magical refrain?
. . . I walk upon the velvet grass . . . And gaze up at the trees . . .
And everywhere I find a world . . . Of endless memories . . . I
know it is September but . . . The calendar is wrong . . . I see
the skies of April and . . . In April I belong . . . I feel the breezes
blowing and . . . The rain about to start . . . September may be
here but it . . . Is April in my heart.

ACROSS THE SEA

I gave a message to the wind . . . To take across the sea . . . And now I hear the faint reply . . . The wind is bringing me . . . It is the answer to the prayer . . . I said so many times . . . It is the echo of the clock . . . That sounds its silvery chimes . . . And now I know as surely as . . . The sun that sets each day . . . There is a certain someone who . . . Will never turn away . . . There is a gorgeous rainbow and . . . There is a pot of gold . . . And love is something beautiful . . . That never grows too old . . . And though our happy hours may . . . Be short and very few . . . Our love will be eternal and . . . Our dreams will all come true.

TO YOU, O GOD

To You, O God, I dedicate . . . My every thought and deed . . . My struggle for existence and . . . My effort to succeed . . . The friendships that I call my own . . . The pleasures of each day . . . And everything of happiness . . . That comes along my way . . . To You I dedicate my tears . . . Each sorrow and regret . . . The things that I remember and . . . The ones that I forget . . . My home and all my property . . . My most determined schemes . . . Whatever words I choose to speak . . . And all my many dreams . . . Each goal that I attain, O God . . . Each error that I make . . . To You I dedicate my life . . . And every breath I take.

BARBECUE

When I am really hungry and . . . I have a pennies few . . . I like to treat my stomach to . . . A tasty barbecue . . . A sandwich filled with beef or ham . . . Or chicken soft and brown . . . Fresh pie and then some coffee or . . . Some milk to wash it down . . . It seems to add a zest to life . . . And makes me feel more fit . . . Particularly if the meat . . . Is roasted in a pit . . . Some people crave filet mignon . . . Or oysters on the shell . . . But I prefer the barbecue . . . With its delicious smell . . . And while I do not claim to be . . . A connoisseur of food . . . I recommend the sandwich that . . . Is richly barbecued.

CONTRACTOR

He builds a house from ground to roof . . . With stone or brick
or wood . . . In keeping with the general style . . . Throughout
the neighborhood . . . He puts up walls and he installs . . . The
windows and the doors . . . And after he has sanded them . . .
He polishes the floors . . . His task is not an easy one . . . For he
must supervise . . . The many different jobs in which . . . His
workers specialize . . . He has to keep his books and pay . . .
The wages that are due . . . And even when the house is built
. . . His labor is not through . . . Because he has to sell the place
. . . And figure out finance . . . Unless some wealthy person
buys . . . The building in advance.

MY SILENT FRIENDS

I often wonder out of all . . . The friends I ever made . . . How
many met misfortune and . . . How many made the grade . . .
A few of them have written notes . . . And some have called on
me . . . But many seem to go their way . . . Alone and silently
. . . Perhaps they have acquired all . . . They ever hoped to get . . .
Or maybe things went wrong for them . . . And they are deep in
debt . . . I only wish within my heart . . . That all of them were
here . . . So I could praise their victories . . . Or add a little cheer
. . . I only wish that I could see . . . The sunshine of their smiles
. . . And share their good companionship . . . Along the many
miles.

SOME BUSY LADY

Although I have not written, I . . . Have NOT forgotten you
. . . But actually I have been RUSHED . . . With other things to
do . . . You see, I have to WORK each day . . . And take some
time to EAT . . . And then there are some people whom . . . I
SIMPLY have to meet . . . I MUST go shopping and I MUST
. . . Have someone do my hair . . . And at the movies I relax . . .
(SOME rest is only fair!) . . . At home I have to read a bit . . . To
stimulate my MIND . . . And Sunday is the ONLY day . . .
For sleeping late, I find . . . So you can SEE how many things
. . . I REALLY have to do . . . But these few lines should prove
that I . . . Have not forgotten YOU!

MEN OF THE AIR

They rise from the ground with their silvery wings . . . And the
spirit of youth in their eyes . . . To challenge the foe from above
and below . . . And conquer the enemy skies . . . They soar from
their ship on the tossing sea . . . And head for the hostile craft . . .
They bank and they dive with their guns alive . . . To victory fore
and aft . . . And the sun goes down and the moon comes up . . .
But theirs are the endless flights . . . And the constant strain till
the final plane . . . Is caught in their faithful sights . . . Whatever
the odds, they never give up . . . As long as their bullets last . . .
They never turn back in the face of flak . . . Or the thunderous
cannon blast . . . Their song is the tune of the motor's roar . . .
And the wind when it rushes by . . . As they carry through to their
rendezvous . . . With their targets in the sky.

KRISTINA'S DOLLY

I see a tiny rocking chair . . . Beside the fireplace . . . And on it
sits a dolly with . . . A very pretty face . . . She does not say a
single word . . . She does not even stir . . . And yet I know she
wants to have . . . Kristina comfort her . . . She wants our little
girl to come . . . And pick her up and play . . . And put her in
the buggy for . . . A pleasant stroll today . . . She wants to watch
Kristina and . . . To listen to her speak . . . And have her pat and
hug her and . . . To kiss her on the cheek . . . And then she
wants Kristina dear . . . To take her into bed . . . So she will be
in all the dreams . . . That fill her curly head.

THE UNCONCERNED

Some people think the world was made . . . For other folks to
run . . . And they are not concerned about . . . The way the job
is done . . . They do not let it bother them . . . Or ever interfere
. . . With anything that promises . . . A peaceful atmosphere . . .
They do not realize what a mess . . . We would be in today . . . If
every other creature were . . . Inclined to feel that way . . . It never
dawns on them at all . . . That they are needed too . . . To figure
out the future and . . . To see the struggle through . . . That
we must work together as . . . An undivided team . . . If we would
be successful and . . . Fulfill our every dream.

HIGHEST MATHEMATICS

If I could count the silver stars . . . And strike a total true . . . I
know that in that figure they . . . Would all add up to you . . .
And then if I subtracted some . . . The figure might be less
. . . But nothing could reduce the sum . . . Of all your loveliness . . . I could divide them by the moon . . . And yet I know
the count . . . So far as it reflected you . . . Would be the same
amount . . . Or I could multiply each one . . . A thousand times
by three . . . And it would just begin to show . . . How much you
mean to me . . . By algebra, geometry . . . Or anything I try . . .
The answer is that you surpass . . . The beauty of the sky.

A DAD'S PRAYER

Almighty Father, help me be . . . A good and loving dad . . .
That my dear children may enjoy . . . The blessings I have had
. . . Give me the wisdom I should use . . . To teach them right
from wrong . . . And how to keep on going when . . . The road
is rough and long . . . To do the duty that is theirs . . . Until its
very end . . . To look for lasting beauty and . . . Appreciate a
friend . . . Endow me with the grace I need . . . To mold their
gentle youth . . . According to the measurements . . . Of loyalty
and truth . . . Enable me to comfort them . . . Whenever they are
sad . . . And O my Father, grant that they . . . Will always love
their dad.

OLD SONGS

The simple songs of years gone by . . . Come back to me today
. . . Reminding me of happiness . . . I had along the way . . . The
songs I sang when I was young . . . And life was bright and new
. . . The melodies that made me cry . . . When I was feeling
blue . . . They are a sort of diary . . . Of dreams that I have known
. . . Wherever I have wandered and . . . The changing winds have
blown . . . And now they all come back to me . . . Like ghosts
of yesteryears . . . To paint their picture of the past . . . With all
its smiles and tears . . . The simple songs, the sweeter songs . . .
Of years and years gone by . . . That fill my heart with memories
. . . And leave a lonely sigh.

MAYOR

The mayor of a city is . . . The same as any king . . . Except he does not have the right . . . To rule on everything . . . He usually has aldermen . . . Who vote the way they feel . . . Or else a city manager . . . Who handles every deal . . . While he receives the visitors . . . Of fortune and of fame . . . And always tries to publicize . . . The city's noble name . . . He has to speak at banquets and . . . To keep from being late . . . Whenever there is anything . . . The people celebrate . . . His name is carved in stone or bronze . . . Wherever projects start . . . And by his faithful service he . . . Can win the city's heart.

MY LOYAL FRIENDS

My greatest treasures are the friends . . . Who always are the same . . . In poverty or plenty and . . . In humbleness or fame . . . Who comfort me when skies are gray . . . And everything goes wrong . . . And counsel me to try again . . . With courage new and strong . . . They are the ones whose kindly words . . . So much inspire me . . . To live a better life each day . . . And practice charity . . . In every way they show that they . . . Are generous and true . . . And any favor I may ask . . . They are prepared to do . . . And someday I may search the world . . . For riches I have known . . . But I shall never be without . . . The friends I call my own.

BUSINESS AIRS

Some people think it pays them well . . . To put on business airs . . . And play up their importance in . . . The handling of affairs . . . Their secretaries bar the doors . . . And make their callers wait . . . And if they should be out to lunch . . . They always come back late . . . They talk in condescending tones . . . As though their every deed . . . Donated great ability . . . To serve a vital need . . . But people who are actually . . . Important on this earth . . . Are those who need no business airs . . . To demonstrate their worth . . . They are the ones who work and who . . . Are really busy but . . . Whose hearts are always open and . . . Whose doors are never shut.

OUR YOUNG SOLDIERS

Our soldiers are so very young . . . For what they have to do
. . . Their sweetest songs are still unsung . . . Their memories are
few . . . And yet their strength of flesh and mind . . . Surpasses
you and me . . . And they are just the daring kind . . . To bring
us victory . . . They have the stamina and they . . . Believe in
what is right . . . They know we have to live the way . . . They
carry out the fight . . . They know the tide is theirs to stem . . .
And turn against the foe . . . And we sincerely honor them . . .
Wherever bugles blow . . . They are the lads of younger years
. . . They are the loyal sons . . . Who put aside their smiles and
tears . . . For bayonets and guns.

LETTER TO SANTA

Our youngsters now are jotting down . . . The things they hope
to see . . . When Santa Claus leaves packages . . . Around the
Christmas tree . . . Their lists are long with shiny toys . . . Bright
dolls and candy sticks . . . With story books and countless games
. . . Including magic tricks . . . Of course our daughter cannot
write . . . Or even print her name . . . But she picks up her pencil
and . . . She scribbles just the same . . . While her big brothers
fill her mind . . . With glowing tales of gold . . . Assuring her of
wondrous gifts . . . That Santa's bag will hold . . . And all in all
we figure that . . . Old Santa's fame will dim . . . Unless he brings
enough to them . . . To keep their faith in him.

COMPLAINERS

Some creatures constantly complain . . . Throughout the day and
night . . . As though the world were upside down . . . With nothing ever right . . . They criticize the government . . . And what
their neighbors do . . . And every plan the people try . . . To see
their struggle through . . . When times are good they grumble at
. . . The prices on display . . . And when depressions come they
groan . . . About their meager pay . . . They gripe whenever any
road . . . Is just a little rough . . . And when they get a lucky break
. . . It never brings enough . . . They growl about the weather
and . . . Consistently bemoan . . . The world and all its foolish
faults . . . Except of course their own.

MARRIAGE BOND

The marriage bond is more than just . . . A ticket for a meal . . .
It is supposed to represent . . . A 50–50 deal . . . It is a partnership
of love . . . That centers in the heart . . . And constantly requires
each . . . To play an equal part . . . It contemplates a deep respect
. . . And willingness to share . . . The tears and troubles either
one . . . Is called upon to bear . . . The marriage bond is meant to
be . . . An everlasting tie . . . Eternal as the silver stars . . . That
decorate the sky . . . It is a miracle to match . . . The glory of the
sun . . . By which a promise is pronounced . . . And two become
as one.

GOD, GIVE ME STRENGTH

God, give me strength to live and love . . . And fight for what
is right . . . And let me have the courage to . . . Endure the haunt-
ing night . . . Let not the sun go down too soon . . . Lest I should
lose the way . . . Let not the rain break forth, let not . . . A cloud
be gray today . . . Let youth and hope impel me toward . . . The
goal of all I seek . . . And let there be some wisdom in . . . Whatever words I speak . . . God, grant that all my music may . . .
Be soft and gay and good . . . And of the beauty that is bright
. . . And bravely understood . . . And give me grace, that I may
give . . . What gratitude I can . . . For every inspiration in . . .
The faith of fellow-man.

WILL ROGERS OF CLAREMORE

In Claremore on a sloping hill . . . His name is carved in stone'
. . . And there the rope and saddle are . . . That once he called
his own . . . And all the other articles . . . However small they be
. . . That give his greatness back to us . . . In living memory . . .
It's well we do to honor him . . . This Oklahoma son . . . Who
waged a war on worldly woes . . . Without a sword or gun . . .
Whose only weapon was his wit . . . Whose only aim was joy . . .
The happiness of every man . . . And every girl and boy . . . He
never spoke an unkind word . . . Or raised his hand to strike . . .
Instead he said, "I never met . . . A man I didn't like."

ALL FOR THE BEST

Sometimes the sky is overcast . . . And I am feeling blue . . .
And as the hours wander by . . . I know not what to do . . . And
sometimes there is tragedy . . . To meet me at the door . . . And I
must wonder whether life . . . Is worth my fighting for . . . But
always there is some way out . . . And I have come to know
. . . That brighter things will comfort me . . . In just a day or so
. . . And I have learned that what is past . . . Was purposeful
and good . . . But in my bed of bitterness . . . It was misunderstood . . . There is a certain destiny . . . In every human quest . . .
Because when anything goes wrong . . . It happens for the best.

UNHANDY HUSBAND

I envy him who paints his house . . . And him who makes repairs
. . . As well as every gentleman . . . Who varnishes the stairs . . .
Who fixes locks, erects a fence . . . And makes a shelf or two . . .
And does what any artisan . . . Is qualified to do . . . For I am
not a handy man . . . I never studied shop . . . And where that
special knowledge starts . . . I am compelled to stop . . . And
that is why my lovely wife . . . Who knows much more than I
. . . Informs me that she should have wed . . . A more ingenious
guy . . . But I am just a writer who . . . Confesses to the sin . . .
That all his hands can fashion is . . . The doghouse he is in.

I LIKE YOUR VOICE

I like to hear you talk to me . . . And I adore the way . . . Your
eager eyes become more bright . . . With every word you say . . .
Your beautiful expressions are . . . Like music to my ears . . . And
when you speak of something sad . . . My heart is moved to tears
. . . Your phrases are forever kind . . . And gentle as can be . . .
And I behold the sunshine when . . . You whisper joyfully . . . I
like your merry laughter and . . . The softness of your sigh . . .
But I would never, never want . . . To hear you say good-by . . . I
like to listen to your voice . . . So friendly and sincere . . . And
most of all when you declare . . . "I love you truly, dear."

23

CHOICEST PRAYER

The little prayer we say in church . . . Is beautiful and good . . .
And surely up in Heaven it . . . Is heard and understood . . . It is
a prayer but it is not . . . The best that we can give . . . Because
the choicest prayer of all . . . Is how we try to live . . . Our daily
deed of charity . . . The favor for a friend . . . The frank apology
that brings . . . A quarrel to an end . . . The noble sacrifice we
make . . . That someone else may smile . . . The sympathy
whereby we show . . . That life is worth the while . . . These are
the things that really count . . . However one compares . . . And
these by every measurement . . . Are quite the choicest prayers.

WELCOME RAIN

The rain is drumming on my door . . . And on the window
pane . . . In every corner of the house . . . I hear its sad refrain
. . . It has a way of echoing . . . A melancholy sound . . . Perhaps
because it takes away . . . The sunshine all around . . . And yet I
know that it is meant . . . To makes the flowers grow . . . And
always it is needed for . . . The crops the farmers sow . . . It
brings relief in summer and . . . It washes off the street . . . And
it provides a playground for . . . The children's naked feet . . .
And so I listen to it pour . . . And watch it drench the sod . . . And
welcome it because it is . . . The handiwork of God.

POLITICIAN

The politician is a man . . . With quite a charming flare . . .
Whose wide vocabulary fills . . . The regions of the air . . . Whose
specialty is promises . . . However great or small . . . Who understands the country's ills . . . And how to cure them all . . . A smile
is on his features and . . . Cigars are in his hand . . . Particularly
at the polls . . . When votes are in demand . . . He uses every arti-
fice . . . To win the ballot match . . . Although he must beware
the law . . . That bears the name of Hatch . . . And while his
practices result . . . In many storms and hates . . . It must be said
that he maintains . . . Our great United States.

WEST POINT CADET

He is the college student in . . . A uniform of gray . . . Whose
dream in life is to become . . . A general some day . . . He wants to
serve his country as . . . A soldier tried and true . . . And leave his
name to history . . . In red and white and blue . . . He longs to be
an officer . . . With character complete . . . And every inch a
gentleman . . . Wherever people meet . . . He builds his body and
his mind . . . In every way he can . . . Because he wants to gradu-
ate . . . And show he is a man . . . And when that final day arrives
. . . And he is on parade . . . He holds his head up high because
. . . He knows he made the grade.

WONDERFUL FRIEND

A friend is like a visitor . . . Who never goes away . . . But who
does not impose on you . . . Or seem to overstay . . . He brings
a smile and he becomes . . . A most important part . . . Of all
the plans and hopes and dreams . . . That fill your mind and heart
. . . He offers his suggestions and . . . The help that he can give
. . . Without attempting to disturb . . . The way you want to
live . . . A friend is like a brother who . . . Is always on your side
. . . And speaks of your accomplishments . . . With pleasure
and with pride . . . Who only wants your friendship and . . . Who
never makes demands . . . Who sympathizes when you grieve . . .
And always understands.

SITUATION NOT WANTED

I'm glad I'm not the President . . . Of these United States . . .
The guiding hand of government . . . And all it contemplates
. . . I'm glad I do not have to judge . . . The merits of each bill . . .
To dicker with and try to budge . . . The boys upon the Hill
. . . To keep the White House running right . . . Peruse the flood
of mail . . . Attempt to ease the farmer's plight . . . Adjust the
labor scale . . . To pick the ones who are the best . . . For more
important posts . . . To honor each distinguished guest . . . And
drink a thousand toasts . . . I'm glad I do not have to deal . . .
With all the nation's souls . . . And worry over how they feel
. . . When they invade the polls.

AT EARLY DAWN

I always like the morning best . . . When it is barely dawn . . .
Before the shadows vanish and . . . The last small star is gone
. . . For that is when I contemplate . . . My labor and my play . . .
And take an inventory of . . . My dreams of yesterday . . . And
that is when I look ahead . . . And wonder what will be . . .
And whether there is such a thing . . . As fate or destiny . . . It is
the hour when my heart . . . Is filled with hope and prayer . . .
But never any fear of life . . . To haunt me anywhere . . . Because
the sky is changing and . . . It is the end of night . . . And that is
when my courage and . . . My faith are new and bright.

YOUR SPECIAL DAY

I love you each and every day . . . But on this special one . . . I
thank you and I honor you . . . For all that you have done . . .
Because it is your birthday and . . . It seems the proper time
. . . To tell you of my gratitude . . . If only in a rhyme . . . I love
you, darling, for your faith . . . And for your friendly smile . . .
Your words of true encouragement . . . That make my life worth
while . . . Your willingness to share with me . . . The bitter and
the sweet . . . And do however much you can . . . To make my
world complete . . . Believe me, darling, when I say . . . My heart
belongs to you . . . And may this birthday be the one . . . When
all your dreams come true.

BOOKKEEPING WIFE

I used to keep the records of . . . My monetary life . . . But
finally I handed them . . . To my beloved wife . . . The state-
ments and the canceled checks . . . And all the notes I kept . . .
Because at keeping books she said . . . That she was quite adept
. . . Well, I heard nothing more from her . . . For 30 days or so
. . . But just about that time she had . . . An awful tale of woe . . .
She said she had the stubs and checks . . . Completely figured out
. . . But not the balance in the bank . . . Or how it came about . . .
And so she turned the records back . . . As pretty as you please
. . . And now once more I have to see . . . That everything
agrees.

A GOOD NAME

Let us not seek enormous wealth . . . Or popular acclaim . . .
But let us be content to have . . . A good and honest name . . . For
money has a narrow use . . . And it can only bring . . . The pleasure of the power we . . . Possess in purchasing . . . While fame
was never made to last . . . Except in history books . . . Where
now and then in after years . . . The weary student looks . . .
But worthiness of character . . . Is boundless as the sea . . . And
timeless as the sands that run . . . Throughout eternity . . . And
wealth and fame may touch the stars . . . And disappear again
. . . But virtue lives forever in . . . The hearts of fellow-men.

I KNOW YOU, LORD

Lord, I have never seen Your face . . . Or held Your loving
hand . . . And yet I feel Your presence here . . . And all throughout the land . . . I have not heard Your gentle voice . . . But
everywhere I go . . . I listen to the sacred words . . . That You
would have me know . . . I have not visited Your home . . . And
dined with You as such . . . But in the churches You have built . . .
I try to keep in touch . . . For somehow in my humble heart . . . I
understand You are . . . As real and present as the sun . . . The
moon and every star . . . As near as any neighbor and . . . As
close as any kin . . . My master, friend and guardian . . . Against
the way of sin.

MY DICTIONARY

My dictionary guides me to . . . The words I want to use . . .
And thousands are the synonyms . . . That I am free to choose
. . . It teaches me the proper way . . . To spell and to pronounce
. . . And just which definition is . . . The one that really counts
. . . It shows the derivations and . . . Its pages are replete . . . With
adjectives and adverbs from . . . The ballroom to the street . . . My
dictionary is a book . . . I could not do without . . . Because it
helps me speak and write . . . And settles every doubt . . . But I
should read it more if I . . . Would really get along . . . For when
I trust my memory . . . I usually go wrong.

27

VOICE FROM THE WEST

Berlin is yours and Europe now . . . Is free from shell and flak . . . This war is over and I wish . . . I could be going back . . . I wish that I were still alive . . . To celebrate this day . . . To drink a toast to victory . . . And join you while you pray . . . You are entitled to your songs . . . You have a right to cheer . . . And I don't want to spoil your fun . . . Or draw a single tear . . . But don't forget that while the war . . . With Germany is won . . . There is another job ahead . . . Before your work is done . . . I won't be going there to help . . . My buddies beat Japan . . . But you, I know, will do your part . . . For every fighting man . . . I know you'll make the planes and tanks . . . And buy the bonds to win . . . I know you'll crack up Tokyo . . . The way you did Berlin . . . I wish I could be there myself . . . To fire one more shot . . . Now it's your job—so get in there . . . And give it all you've got.

PICKING UP

My wife is always fussing at . . . The children and myself . . . Because we do not hang up clothes . . . Or put things on the shelf . . . She says we are a lazy bunch . . . And that she spends each day . . . In picking up the articles . . . We leave in disarray . . . Our sons are careless with their coats . . . Their schoolbooks and their toys . . . And our young daughter does her best . . . To duplicate the boys . . . My desk is cluttered up and there . . . Are marks upon the floor . . . While someone used a crayon bright . . . To decorate the door . . . Although we try to argue that . . . It's all a part of life . . . We never quite convince my dear . . . Uncompromising wife.

WHAT GOAL TO GAIN?

Sometimes I wonder if the goal . . . I started to attain . . . Is what I want and whether it . . . Is worth my while to gain . . . I do not mean that I oppose . . . The labor I must do . . . Or that I do not think I have . . . The will to carry through . . . But merely that I ask myself . . . If life can offer me . . . The fullness and the final fruits . . . Of opportunity . . . I wonder whether any goal . . . Is worth my fighting for . . . And if it really holds success . . . And happiness in store . . . And then again it seems to me . . . There is no tear or smile . . . That does not have its own reward . . . And prove itself worth while.

FOREVER, LOVE

I shall love you today and tomorrow, my love . . . And in all the tomorrows there are . . . I shall love you as long as there lingers a song . . . And the sky has a single star . . . In the spring when the wind is a gentle breeze . . . And the rain and the roses are here . . . In the summery days when the friendly rays . . . Of the golden sun appear . . . In the lonely lap of the autumn months . . . Where the beautiful leaves must fall . . . And again in the night when the fields are white . . . In the folds of their wintry shawl . . . I shall love you while ever a mountain stands . . . And the waves of the ocean pass . . . And until the sands of the farthest lands . . . Have run through the hour-glass . . . I shall love you as much as my heart can love . . . Wherever, my love, you are . . . I shall love you as long as there lingers a song . . . And the sky has a single star.

HELP ME, O LORD

Help me, O Lord, to go through life . . . With faith and courage strong . . . And give me all the grace I need . . . To keep from doing wrong . . . Enable me to be myself . . . And never let me boast . . . When I become the honored guest . . . Or act the gracious host . . . I want to walk the righteous path . . . And be sincere and true . . . In every word and every thought . . . And everything I do . . . Let not temptation lead me to . . . The ugliness of sin . . . But let me guard the beauty of . . . My eagerness to win . . . Help me, O Lord, to live my life . . . According to Your way . . . And never let me hesitate . . . Or ever go astray.

WRITING A LETTER

The way to write a letter that . . . Will please the addressee . . . Is not to speak of startling news . . . Or tell of tragedy . . . But just to paint the picture of . . . Our ordinary day . . . And how we spend the moments of . . . Our time at work and play . . . What Mrs. Jones revealed to us . . . Across the garden fence . . . And how someone enabled us . . . To save a small expense . . . The baby's tooth, a promised raise . . . The weather warm or cool . . . An evening out to dine and dance . . . And Junior's grades in school . . . The little things from day to day . . . Are those that mean the most . . . In any letter we prepare . . . That we intend to post.

29

WORST WORM

The creature most detestable . . . Of all the worms on earth . . .
Is he who tries with all his might . . . To undermine your
worth . . . Who takes the favors you bestow . . . And then behind
your back . . . Declares that brains and competence . . . Are qualities you lack . . . He smiles and bows and lets you think . . . That
he admires you . . . When underhanded deeds are all . . . He ever
wants to do . . . His jealousy is obvious . . . And it is also plain
. . . That in your job he never would . . . Be equal to the strain
. . . But still he tries to bluff his way . . . And glorify his worth . . .
To prove he is the lowest form . . . Of all the worms on earth.

MUSIC IN MY HEART

My heart is filled with magic strains . . . Of music old and new
. . . And all of them are melodies . . . Reminding me of you . . .
Reminding me of April when . . . The wind was in your hair . . .
And every time the sun came out . . . A rainbow lingered there
. . . Reminding me of winter nights . . . When snow was on the
ground . . . While we divided happiness . . . And passed the stars
around . . . And oh, the songs we used to sing . . . When life was
young and sweet . . . And autumn leaves were fashioning . . . A
carpet for our feet . . . My heart is filled with love's refrain . . . So
old and yet so new . . . The soft, enchanting melody . . . Of yesteryear and you.

HAVE YOU A HOME?

Have you a home to call your own? . . . A place to sleep and
eat . . . Where happiness and peace prevail . . . And friends forever meet? . . . Have you a place to talk out loud . . . And share
your greatest schemes . . . With one who thinks the world of
you . . . And understands your dreams? . . . A place where children run about . . . And give their laughter gay . . . To everything
of consequence . . . That occupies the day? . . . Have you a home
where things go wrong . . . But somehow every night . . . You get
them straightened out again . . . And life is still all right? . . . Because if you have all of this . . . You have the very best . . . Your
life is quite complete and you . . . Can do without the rest.

AVERAGE READER

He reads the paper every day . . . In order not to lose . . . His knowledge of the way the world . . . Considers current news . . . He wants to learn how people live . . . Around the globe today . . . And whether things are quite as bad . . . As some reporters say . . . He scans conflicting articles . . . About this day and age . . . And carefully compares them with . . . The editorial page . . . He may not get to be as smart . . . As some who come and go . . . But he discovers many things . . . He never used to know . . . And all in all it seems that he . . . Is qualified to choose . . . Between the propaganda and . . . The strictly honest news.

COAL MINER

The miner makes his living at . . . The bottom of a hole . . . Where he extracts a substance that . . . Is known to us as coal . . . He tunnels down into the earth . . . To earn his daily bread . . . And all his moves are guided by . . . The lamp upon his head . . . His work is mighty strenuous . . . His pay is not the best . . . And when his shift is at an end . . . He does deserve a rest . . . We seldom recognize his worth . . . Or stop to think that he . . . Is furnishing the fuel for . . . The nation's family . . . It sure would warm his heart to know . . . That when we warmed our feet . . . We did not think of his address . . . As some forgotten street.

NAVY WIFE'S PRAYER

I look at the stars in their silvery light . . . And I know that they shine on the sea . . . And I know that they shine over harbor and cove . . . Wherever your ship may be . . . So I ask them to carry my prayer to God . . . And to summon a special star . . . To serve as a sentinel over the spot . . . Where you and your vessel are . . . My prayer to God is a prayer for you . . . And the courage that wins renown . . . That your shells may fly to their target's eye . . . And your ship may never go down . . . That the dawn will come with a golden sun . . . On a calm and gentle sea . . . And nothing will happen to interfere . . . With your final victory . . . And I pray that when all of your duty is done . . . And silent are all the alarms . . . Your ship will be anchored and you will be safe . . . Forever again in my arms.

FRIENDLY SMILE

Of all the old and new delights . . . That make this life worth
while . . . I think that none gives greater joy . . . Than just a
friendly smile . . . A smile that seems to say hello . . . And how
are you today . . . And sort of picks your troubles up . . . And
pushes them away . . . It is a greeting fit for kings . . . Yet always
it is free . . . And it belongs to every class . . . Of social company
. . . A friendly smile relieves the strain . . . Wherever strangers
meet . . . And as it praises victory . . . It comforts in defeat . . .
It is the kind of handshake that . . . Will penetrate a glove . . .
And now and then it lights the flame . . . That kindles into love.

KRISTINA'S GRACE

The other night at supper when . . . We all sat down to pray . . .
I asked our small Kristina dear . . . To fold her hands that way
. . . And right away she folded them . . . And with a solemn
face . . . She listened so attentively . . . While Jimmie said the
grace . . . My wife and I exchanged a smile . . . That meant that
we were proud . . . And both our boys were quick to praise . . .
Their sister right out loud . . . The meal went on as usual . . . But
every now and then . . . Kristina dear would clasp her hands . . .
And start to pray again . . . And now we know not what to do
. . . At mealtime every day . . . Because our baby daughter loves
. . . To fold her hands and pray.

THE THINGS I WANT

These are the things I want in life . . . The sun when I arise . . .
The dewdrops on the flowers and . . . The slowly moving skies
. . . The rivers and the rushing rains . . . The cold of ice and
snow . . . The green, dark woods, the fertile fields . . . Where
gentle breezes blow . . . The winding road of stone and dust . . .
The picket fence of white . . . The cottage with a friendly day . . .
And warm, familiar night . . . The toasting blaze of heavy logs
. . . The smell of cooking food . . . The coziness of slippers and
. . . A yawning, sleepy mood . . . The hours for companion-
ship . . . In music old and new . . . The window full of silver
stars . . . And time to dream with you.

BILLFOLD

It's just a piece of leather in . . . A certain manner bound . . . To hold the things a man believes . . . He has to haul around . . . Like cards that show his membership . . . In union, club or press . . . His auto registration and . . . His residence address . . . A rent receipt, a postage stamp . . . The record of a loan . . . The name of some blonde baby and . . . The number of her phone . . . A snapshot of his fiancee . . . His mother or his wife . . . Or of a little fellow who . . . Is everything in life . . . And as for keeping money, well . . . You know the dope on that . . . It bulges out on payday, but . . . The next A.M. it's flat.

GAS STATION MAN

The gentlemen who service cars . . . Along the winding miles . . . Are known throughout the country for . . . Their warm and friendly smiles . . . They are prepared to furnish you . . . With gasoline and oil . . . And fill your radiator so . . . It will not start to boil . . . They sell their products and their parts . . . But many things are free . . . Like washing glass and checking on . . . The wheels and battery . . . From early dawn till late at night . . . They work in grease and grime . . . To give you driving comfort and . . . To save you precious time . . . And while financially they may . . . Be doing very well . . . It is in courtesy that they . . . Invariably excel.

FRIENDSHIP LASTS

Acquaintances are pleasant and . . . Companionship is fun . . . But I am sure that friendship is . . . The only lasting one . . . I may enjoy the company . . . Of somebody I meet . . . Upon a bus or trolley or . . . Along a busy street . . . Or I may use the telephone . . . And say a fond hello . . . To someone I have never seen . . . Or incidentally know . . . But mere acquaintances are like . . . The ships that pass at night . . . And they have left my mind as soon . . . As they are out of sight . . . While friendship is enduring and . . . An everlasting part . . . Of everything that brightens life . . . And warms the human heart.

STRICTLY CASH

I do not like to borrow and . . . I do not like to lend . . . Because
they both are dangerous . . . And I may lose a friend . . . I do not
like to borrow books . . . Or any other thing . . . Because until I
pay my debts . . . I keep on worrying . . . And when it comes to
lending, well . . . I worry just as much . . . About the borrowers
with whom . . . I try to keep in touch . . . I know it is a benefit
. . . To have a rating good . . . With all the credit agencies . . .
And in the neighborhood . . . But I am happier and I . . . Am
free from strain and stress . . . If I can fully manage with . . .
Whatever I possess.

LET US HELP THEM

Our men are coming home today . . . From every foreign shore
. . . To put away the uniforms . . . That make them think of
war . . . They have been hungry for their homes . . . And all
their loved ones here . . . Who helped so much to keep their
faith . . . Their courage and good cheer . . . And all they want or
ask for now . . . Is just the chance to be . . . The ordinary citizens
. . . Of their community . . . They want to take their places in . . .
The world they used to know . . . And walk in peaceful happiness
. . . Wherever they may go . . . So let us be considerate . . . And
help them all we can . . . And thereby give our gratitude . . . To
every service man.

JUST ANOTHER DAY

This date is not as tragic as . . . The one we used to know . . .
Because the tax on income is . . . Deducted as we go . . . Accord-
ingly the chances are . . . We do not have a debt . . . And there
may be a refund that . . . We are supposed to get . . . Unless of
course the year before . . . We sold a house or two . . . Or made
some other profit when . . . The tax was not yet due . . . Or if we
had an income and . . . No cash was taken out . . . And March
15th was something we . . . Were not concerned about . . . But
otherwise we have no fear . . . Of what we have to pay . . . And
this historic date is just . . . An ordinary day.

MY MORNING PRAYER

O Lord, if I am good today . . . And live according to Your way . . . And if my being good, O Lord . . . Will gain me any small reward . . . I ask You to remember her . . . My loving wife and comforter . . . And every hour and moment bless . . . Her life with health and happiness . . . For she deserves them more than I . . . Considering the years gone by . . . Considering how she has been . . . My courage and my will to win . . . How she has sacrificed for me . . . And stood beside me faithfully . . . O Lord, be gracious to my wife . . . I love her even more than life.

PLAN FOR TOMORROW

Tomorrow is a special day . . . Because it is unspent . . . And so it offers all its time . . . For us to be content . . . It has not even made a start . . . And therefore it is free . . . For us to use in any way . . . To keep us company . . . We may devote its hours to . . . A very worthy cause . . . Or figure every minute as . . . Another chance to pause . . . In any case we ought to stop . . . And think of it today . . . And try to measure out our work . . . With time enough for play . . . We ought to make a schedule for . . . Our labor and our rest . . . So every second will be one . . . In which we do our best.

TIRE OF YOU?

How could I tire of you, dear . . . When every day it seems . . . That you become a deeper part . . . Of my endearing dreams? . . . How could I weary of your words . . . When they inspire me . . . To goals of greater worthiness . . . And nobler victory? . . . You are forever in my heart . . . Wherever I may go . . . And in your kind companionship . . . My happy hours grow . . . I want to do so much for you . . . I know not where to start . . . To prove that I adore you, dear . . . With all my loving heart . . . And you are so completely in . . . My every thought sincere . . . I could not ever find the time . . . To tire of you, dear.

UNHAPPY HOSTESS

Consider now how miserable . . . A fellow's wife must feel . . . Who plans and works the whole day long . . . To make a special meal . . . Who buys the choicest groceries . . . Regardless of expense . . . And slaves beside the oven where . . . The heat is so intense . . . The wife who sets the table and . . . Who does her very best . . . To please the appetite of one . . . Who is an honored guest . . . And then who hears that guest describe . . . The places near and far . . . Where he has had delicious steaks . . . Champagne and caviar . . . The guest who knows his restaurants . . . And how their dishes rate . . . But never has a compliment . . . For what is on his plate.

NO BETTER FRIEND

The day is warm with sunshine and . . . The sky is extra blue . . . Because in all the world I have . . . No better friend than you . . . Because you always greet me with . . . A kindly word and smile . . . And in a dozen different ways . . . You make my life worth while . . . You comfort me whenever I . . . Have any fears to hide . . . And when my heart is sad I know . . . That you are at my side . . . I look to you for counsel and . . . The courage that I need . . . As well as inspiration for . . . My every daily deed . . . And all the stars are silver-bright . . . When night is young and new . . . Because I know in everything . . . I can depend on you.

JOKE

A joke is something humorous . . . That makes a person laugh . . . And has a way of telling him . . . To cut his tears in half . . . It may describe the tall or small . . . The skinny or the fat . . . And it may draw a thousand smiles . . . Or fall forever flat . . . One kind is known as practical . . . And while it may be fun . . . It sometimes brings about regret . . . That it was ever done . . . A joke is just a story that . . . Is whispered to a friend . . . Who many times would sigh relief . . . If it would ever end . . . There are a million jokes on earth . . . But whether false or true . . . The only one you may resent . . . Is one that is on you.

MOTHER DEAR

Dear Mother, you are part of me . . . And I am part of you . . .
And you are part of everything . . . I ever think or do . . . And out
of all the parts of life . . . I am or hope to be . . . I need not tell
you, Mother dear . . . You are the best in me . . . You are the
sweetest of my songs . . . The truest of my friends . . . You are
the sunshine in my heart . . . The dream that never ends . . . You
are the hand that comforts me . . . The smile that lifts me up . . .
And you are all the sugar at . . . The bottom of my cup . . . Oh,
Mother dear, there are some things . . . I cannot write or say . . .
But all my love and gratitude . . . Go out to you today!

TOO QUICK TO JUDGE

Some people are too quick to judge . . . And eager to condemn
. . . The faults of others that they feel . . . Do not belong to them
. . . They think they are so righteous in . . . Their attitude toward
life . . . And that they know the only way . . . To settle every
strife . . . But if the truth were known, perhaps . . . Their sins
would be the same . . . And some of them might even have . . . A
greater cause for shame . . . In any case there is the fact . . . That
they are doing wrong . . . By trying to advise the world . . . How
it should get along . . . They should not be so quick to judge . . .
Or eager to condemn . . . Because some day a judgment may . . .
Be catching up with them.

SOME MORNING

Some morning when the golden sun . . . Adorns a sky of blue
. . . And all the world is beautiful . . . I want to walk with you
. . . I want you to behold the charm . . . Of nature's magic art . . .
And listen to the song of love . . . That echoes in my heart . . . I
want to take the path that winds . . . Among the flowers fair
. . . And offer you whatever things . . . I have the right to share
. . . My worldly goods, my silent thoughts . . . The silver stars that
gleam . . . The promise of tomorrow and . . . My everlasting
dream . . . I want to whisper all my plans . . . And what I hope
to be . . . And then I want to ask you, dear . . . To share your
life with me.

LET US GIVE THANKS

Let us be humble in our hearts . . . And most sincerely say . . .
A word of gratitude to God . . . On this Thanksgiving Day . . .
Let us be grateful for our health . . . And for the strength of
mind . . . To serve our neighbors of the world . . . By being good
and kind . . . For all the peace and friendship that . . . Prevail
on land and sea . . . And for the common happiness . . . Of opportunity . . . Let us be thankful for our homes . . . Our children
near and far . . . And every little dream that tries . . . To touch
a silver star . . . Let us give gratitude to God . . . For every song
we sing . . . And for the wondrous beauty and . . . The joy of
everything.

BOOKSTORE

The bookstore is a place to browse . . . For something good to
read . . . About a certain character . . . Economy or creed . . . It
is the house of fiction and . . . Of poetry and such . . . Including
all the fairy tales . . . The children like so much . . . And usually
its counters and . . . Its windows will display . . . The plain and
fancy greetings cards . . . For every special day . . . As well as pens
and pencils and . . . Some stationery bright . . . And volumes of
instructions on . . . The proper way to write . . . The bookstore
is a dreamland where . . . The would-be author sees . . . A pub-
lished work that bears his name . . . And brings him royalties.

ARCHITECT

He is the man who shapes the plan . . . For every wall and floor
. . . For every ceiling, porch and roof . . . Each window and each
door . . . He dreams of cozy cottages . . . And buildings that will
rise . . . Until they tower in the dawn . . . To touch the very skies
. . . Upon a paper sheet he draws . . . The beautiful designs . . .
To build the temple of his faith . . . In everything divine . . . He
molds the magic masterpiece . . . Of dwellings high and low . . .
To guard against inclemencies . . . Wherever winds may blow . . .
And well he knows that his success . . . And how he fills his purse
. . . Are products of the Architect . . . Of all the universe.

MY FRIENDS

My files are filled with names of friends . . . Whom I have come to know . . . Along the many winding paths . . . Where I have chanced to go . . . Especially the genial ones . . . Who help me on my way . . . With true encouragement and with . . . The kindly things they say . . . Whose smiles of golden sunshine are . . . The answer to my tears . . . And form the perfect rainbow bright . . . That never disappears . . . I keep a faithful register . . . Of each familiar name . . . Without regard to worldly wealth . . . Or anything of fame . . . Because no matter who they are . . . Or where the rainbow ends . . . The only thing important is . . . That they are all my friends.

OFFICE MANAGER

This most peculiar animal . . . Invariably is one . . . That likes to take the credit for . . . Whatever work is done . . . That frowns on you when you are late . . . And sneers at your excuse . . . While figuring some special way . . . To multiply abuse . . . Of course there are exceptions and . . . Occasions when you find . . . An office manager who is . . . Considerate and kind . . . But usually this creature feels . . . Important as can be . . . And quite the business model of . . . Supreme efficiency . . . And what is even worse is that . . . For all its lack of wit . . . This most peculiar animal . . . Will get away with it.

KINDERGARTEN

The kindergarten is the place . . . Where little children go . . . To learn to be together while . . . Their little bodies grow . . . They cut and paste and try to draw . . . And play with blocks and rings . . . They look at pretty picture books . . . And other pleasant things . . . But also they are taught to say . . . Good-morning and good-night . . . And other words and phrases that . . . Are friendly and polite . . . They learn the need for cleanliness . . . And neatness in their dress . . . And many ways by which to bring . . . Their parents happiness . . . And while they may not master how . . . To add up two and two . . . They do discover life in school . . . Is interesting and new.

SLEEPING LATE

On Sundays and on Saturdays . . . I like to celebrate . . . By staying in my cozy bed . . . And sleeping somewhat late . . . And always I look forward to . . . The closing of the week . . . And to the solid comfort of . . . A pleasant slumber streak . . . But when the sun is barely up . . . My wife is wide awake . . . And getting breakfast ready, she . . . Insists that I partake . . . So I get up and have a bite . . . And back to bed I go . . . And then she starts to clean the house . . . And play the radio . . . The children shout and play and they . . . Are loud as they can be . . . And you can just imagine how . . . Much sleep there is for me!

THANKS FOR THE DATE

I want to thank you for the date . . . We had the other night . . . It made the moon look larger and . . . The stars seemed twice as bright . . . I do not know when I was quite . . . So happy and content . . . Or when I understood so well . . . What friendship really meant . . . You were so good and kind to me . . . And in your charming smile . . . I felt that everything in life . . . Was wonderfully worth while . . . You made me very happy though . . . You made me wonder too . . . If I did anything to bring . . . Some happiness to you . . . So would you tell me how you liked . . . Our date beneath the moon? . . . And if you please, I wish you would . . . Inform me very soon.

CUP OF LIFE

Life is full of beauty . . . Life is truly gay . . . If we do our duty . . . If we stop to play . . . Life is like the weather . . . Sun and rain and snow . . . Calling us together . . . Everywhere we go . . . Counting off the hours . . . Drifting with the sky . . . Gathering the flowers . . . Never asking why . . . Life is like tomorrow . . . Never here today . . . Drinking of a sorrow . . . That has passed away . . . Teeming with desire . . . Hoping for the best . . . Stirring up the fire . . . Looking for a guest . . . Dreaming of a treasure . . . Hidden in the sea . . . Searching for a pleasure . . . Locked in memory.

PRAYER FOR WAR DADS

O God, The Father of all men . . . Hear now the humble prayer
. . . We older dads are saying for . . . The young dads over there
. . . The valiant men in uniform . . . On battlefield afar . . . Who
fight for freedom and for all . . . The better things there are . . .
Whose children are the dreams of peace . . . That fill their valleys
green . . . Their sons and daughters—some of whom . . . They
have not even seen . . . Dear God, give them Your special care
. . . Watch over them today . . . And bring them safely home
again . . . We do beseech and pray . . . That they may kiss the
trembling lips . . . Of reunited joy . . . And listen to the laughter
of . . . A little girl or boy.

VOTER

The voter is a citizen . . . Who has the right to say . . . What he
believes should happen on . . . The next election day . . . He is the
humble little man . . . Whose buttonhole is worn . . . By those
who talk of candidates . . . With eagerness or scorn . . . He hears
the public rallies and . . . He sees the rising foam . . . Of office
arguments and those . . . That permeate the home . . . He listens
to the radio . . . And reads the printed news . . . And half his mail
is literature . . . On how he ought to choose . . . But when the time
arrives to pay . . . His polling place respects . . . He is the only
one to say . . . Where he shall put his X.

YOU'RE WELCOME

A "thank you" for a favor is . . . The least we all expect . . . And
by established custom it . . . Is socially correct . . . But we who
do the favor for . . . The friend who is in need . . . Should also
let him know that he . . . Is welcome to the deed . . . Not just
because the rules declare . . . It is the thing to do . . . But to assure
him that our thoughts . . . Are generous and true . . . To let him
know that we are glad . . . To help him all we can . . . And that
we find it comforting . . . To serve our fellow-man . . . And so
when thanks are said to us . . . For any courtesy . . . We ought
to say "Indeed you are . . . As welcome as can be."

41

LET ME BE KIND

If ever I am called upon . . . To help my brother out . . . Let me be kind and generous . . . Beyond the slightest doubt . . . Let me be ready to assist . . . In every way I can . . . And be of faithful service to . . . My friendly fellow-man . . . Let me pursue the path of God . . . And go to each address . . . Of those unfortunate who are . . . The poor and penniless . . . For what have I to gain on earth . . . Unless I learn to care? . . . Unless I love my brother with . . . A willingness to share? . . . The glory of the greatest fame . . . And all that wealth can be . . . Are only as a grain of sand . . . Compared to charity.

PAYDAY

It may be monthly or it may . . . Be every week or two . . . But payday is the part of life . . . That most appeals to you . . . For then you get your wages, less . . . Whatever you must pay . . . For income tax and for the time . . . When all your hair is gray . . . Yes, payday is the day to smile . . . With cash enough to spend . . . For rent and food, amusements and . . . A present for a friend . . . It helps you meet the debts you owe . . . Or save an extra bit . . . Against that rainy day when you . . . May be in need of it . . . While there are some who borrow cash . . . Till payday comes and then . . . They pay it off and very soon . . . They borrow it again.

UNITED WORLD

There is not room enough on earth . . . For those who want to fight . . . And those who feel that freedom is . . . A basic, human right . . . But somewhere in the days to come . . . There has to be a dawn . . . Where everyone agrees and where . . . The final line is drawn . . . We have to have security . . . And calm for evermore . . . Or else it is a useless goal . . . We have been striving for . . . So let us get together now . . . And plan the years ahead . . . That everyone may live in peace . . . And have his share of bread . . . But also let us keep our watch . . . Throughout each day and night . . . And guard our liberty with all . . . Our military might.

A MOTHER'S DAY

There is no time, there is no sun . . . That tells when mother's day is done . . . From cleaning house and making beds . . . To combing curly little heads . . . Preparing breakfast, dinner, lunch . . . And cookies in between to munch . . . From shopping at the corner store . . . To putting wax upon the floor . . . Arranging things and washing clothes . . . And ironing and mending those . . . She even does the garden work . . . That everybody else will shirk . . . And after they have gone to sleep . . . She has her budget book to keep . . . There is no time, there is no sun . . . That tells when mother's day is done.

A LITTLE OF YOU

When I lift up the telephone . . . Or heed the postman's ring . . . I always want your words to be . . . The message it will bring . . . I always long to hear your voice . . . Inviting me to hope . . . Or recognize your writing on . . . The silent envelope . . . Because it makes my lonely heart . . . As glad as it can be . . . To know that now and then you take . . . The time to think of me . . . I treasure every word you say . . . And every line you write . . . And only when I dream of you . . . Do I enjoy the night . . . I do not ask for all of you . . . Or yet the greater part . . . But I shall be content to have . . . A corner of your heart.

LIVE AND LEARN

My life is crowded with mistakes . . . Of every shape and size . . . And many of them were the ones . . . I made with open eyes . . . I should have had more sense of course . . . And as I went along . . . I should have taken greater care . . . To choose the right from wrong . . . Perhaps my mind was lazy or . . . I thought that I was good . . . Without regard to anything . . . I could have done or should . . . But now I am not sorry for . . . The errors I have made . . . Because at least I took a chance . . . And I was not afraid . . . And now I know a lot of things . . . I did not realize then . . . And maybe I shall never make . . . The same mistakes again.

DECEMBER PRAYER

Be with me in December, God . . . And keep me close to You
. . . That I may be unselfish in . . . Whatever deeds I do . . .
Help me to walk a worthy path . . . And with a conscience clear
. . . To make this month by far the best . . . Of all the months this
year . . . Let me be kind to everyone . . . I meet along the way . . .
Especially in honor of . . . Your name on Christmas Day . . . I
want to think of others and . . . The trials they endure . . . And
share my worldly goods with all . . . The penniless and poor . . .
And when December disappears . . . Before the new year's dawn
. . . Be with me, God, and bless me with . . . The courage to go on.

SHINE-BOY

He polishes the boots and shoes . . . Of black and tan and white
. . . That people wear to work or play . . . Or when they march
and fight . . . He covers all the leather with . . . A wax or liquid
smear . . . And then applies a special cloth . . . To make the shine
appear . . . It takes a lot of energy . . . To brighten up a shoe . . .
And frequently the customer . . . Is in a hurry too . . . But if the
shine-boy knows his job . . . And how to build his trade . . . He
earns a living and in time . . . His fortune will be made . . . Especially if he can add . . . A tip to every fee . . . By giving service
with a smile . . . And personality.

BOY ON A DOORSTEP

He sits and whistles gaily while . . . He whittles with his knife
. . . Unmindful of the morning sun . . . And passing stream of
life . . . Unconscious of his shabby clothes . . . And grimy hands
and face . . . Intent upon his carving and . . . Contented in his
place . . . He knows not any struggle for . . . His daily milk and
bread . . . Nor any thought of darkness and . . . A pillow for his
head . . . He cannot read the papers, with . . . Their headlines
black and bold . . . That shower bombs and screams and sobs . . .
And bodies stark and cold . . . He only sits and whistles while
. . . He whittles with his knife . . . And carves his tiny portion of
. . . The figure that is life.

THE FRIEND IN YOU

My days are bright with happiness . . . My skies are always blue
. . . And life is wonderful because . . . I found a friend in you
. . . The kind of friend whose faithfulness . . . Is everything it
seems . . . Who shares my fondest hopes with me . . . And understands my dreams . . . Who constantly inspires me . . . To put my
fears away . . . And trust in God to help me live . . . A more
courageous day . . . Who seems to read my very thoughts . . .
And knows just how I feel . . . And who is there to serve me
though . . . I utter no appeal . . . The world is gay and colorful
. . . And life itself is new . . . And I am very grateful for . . . The
friend I found in you.

COMMITTEES

Committees are the special groups . . . To which the work is
tossed . . . When there is any problem of . . . Production or of
cost . . . Appointed groups that are composed . . . Of those selected
few . . . Who either know or have to learn . . . Exactly what to
do . . . Invariably the members have . . . A chairman at their
head . . . Who weighs and ponders everything . . . That everyone
has said . . . And then the whole committee votes . . . And recommends a way . . . To solve the situation with . . . The minimum
delay . . . Though now and then the study group . . . Consists of
only one . . . Who either knows or thinks that he . . . Can get the
project done.

LOYALTY

Some citizens maintain that they . . . Are loyal, stanch and true
. . . And yet they hesitate to cheer . . . The great red, white and
blue . . . They show a bashful manner when . . . The stars and
stripes are raised . . . And look devoid of interest when . . . America is praised . . . And while they are not traitors, and . . . Although they wish us well . . . They do not seem to understand . . .
That all their actions tell . . . They do not realize that our foe
. . . Is wishing just for that . . . A simple thing like failing to . . .
Salute or raise a hat . . . It never once occurs to them . . . That
everything they do . . . Is copied by the younger folks . . . And
multiplied by two.

BEGIN AGAIN

Let me put all my past away . . . For what I have to do . . . And let me start another day . . . As though my life were new . . . Let me forget the yesteryears . . . And every little part . . . Of all the smiles and all the tears . . . They offer to my heart . . . I want to know that they are gone . . . And they will not return . . . And then I want to carry on . . . Where I may live and learn . . . Because whatever I recall . . . Was never meant to last . . . And there can be no point at all . . . To living in the past . . . I want to pack and put away . . . The hours that are done . . . And bravely start another day . . . Beneath a brighter sun.

BASEBALL

The game of baseball is the king . . . Of all the games we play . . . And it is one pursuit that is . . . Distinctly U. S. A. . . . The people swarm into the stands . . . To see their favorite teams . . . And munch their hot dogs when their lungs . . . Are not engaged in screams . . . The pitcher hurls the horsehide and . . . The batter gets a hit . . . Or else the ball goes sailing and . . . Some fielder smothers it . . . A clever runner steals a base . . . A player takes a walk . . . Or managers and umpires . . . Decide to have a talk . . . The crowd is gay or gloomy or . . . Completely in suspense . . . But it goes wild when someone knocks . . . The ball beyond the fence.

PAINTED KITCHEN

We had our kitchen painted and . . . Of course I must admit . . . It took away the dirt and grime . . . And really brightened it . . . But all day long I could not go . . . Beyond that kitchen door . . . For fear that it would bring about . . . A real domestic war . . . I could not raid the ice box for . . . A morsel after meals . . . Though that is when the greatest pangs . . . A man in hunger feels . . . I could not get the orange juice . . . Or any other drink . . . Indeed I could not even have . . . Some water from the sink . . . But most annoying was the fact . . . That never did I dare . . . To sample or to sniff the food . . . My wife was cooking there.

46

PRAISE

The modest fellow shuns it, though . . . They leave it at his door . . . The selfish one desires it . . . And looks for more and more . . . It's something that can turn your head . . . And make your mind forget . . . How fortunate you are that you . . . And recognition met . . . It rests upon the shoulders of . . . The hero and the one . . . Who knows the knack of playing up . . . The things that he has done . . . It's printed in the paper or . . . Is spoken once again . . . Inscribed upon a tombstone or . . . The hearts of fellow-men . . . But he whose soul can truly weigh . . . His worth upon this sod . . . Will take it in his humble stride . . . And pass it on to God.

MY EMPTY HOURS

I add my empty hours and . . . The moments that are blue . . . And all they ever total is . . . My loneliness for you . . . I wander in the darkness while . . . I look around for light . . . But there are only shadows in . . . My everlasting night . . . I never see a single star . . . Or any beacon shine . . . To offer me a ray of hope . . . Or other happy sign . . . And yet I know the dawn will come . . . With all its glory gay . . . And there will be a golden sun . . . To take my tears away . . . But nothing else can comfort or . . . Console me until then . . . And I shall not rejoice until . . . You come to me again.

BLESS THEM, O LORD

O Lord, I know that I am just . . . Another human soul . . . Intent on trying to attain . . . That everlasting goal . . . But I am not concerned so much . . . About my final score . . . As bringing happiness to those . . . Whom I am living for . . . I want to gather comfort for . . . My children and my wife . . . And give them everything their hearts . . . Desire in this life . . . And so I come to You today . . . Upon my bended knee . . . Imploring You to turn my dream . . . Into reality . . . That they may have Your blessings of . . . Unlimited amount . . . While I incur the debits on . . . My overcharged account.

CANDY STORE

The candy store is something like . . . A fairyland for youth . . . Where youngsters go to satisfy . . . The sweetness of a tooth . . . Its window is inviting with . . . Its jars and boxes bright . . . Of chocolates, nuts and peppermints . . . That tempt the appetite . . . The candy store is meant for him . . . Who has a special date . . . And for the lady who is not . . . Concerned about her weight . . . It is the place where people send . . . A package on its way . . . To celebrate a birthday or . . . To honor Mother's day . . . Where some good bosses think about . . . The stenos they would please . . . And husbands rush when they recall . . . Their anniversaries.

REPORTER

Whatever his opinion or . . . The course that he would choose . . . The true reporter always sticks . . . To what is strictly news . . . He handles an assignment or . . . He happens to be there . . . When something starts a fire or . . . A bullet cuts the air . . . He covers politicians and . . . The odds that ride a horse . . . And telephones the trial of . . . A prominent divorce . . . He tells about the weather or . . . The progress of the town . . . And how the cost of living now . . . Is going up or down . . . The true reporter is the one . . . With little time for play . . . Who hopes to be an editor . . . Or write a book some day.

AMERICA'S MOTHERS

America's mothers are brave and true . . . America's mothers are strong . . . They are the red, the white, the blue . . . They are the nation's song . . . Red for the blood of America's pride . . . Flowing in tireless veins . . . Working for victory, side by side . . . Turning the wheels and cranes . . . White for the uniform on the field . . . White by the hospital bed . . . Healing the warrior on his shield . . . Whispering prayers for the dead . . . Blue for the stars the banners unfold . . . When sons and daughters are gone . . . Blue for the stars that turn to gold . . . In the mist of a silent dawn . . . They are the women who gave us birth . . . And the women who bear our sons . . . Sharing our destiny over the earth . . . Guiding our souls and our guns . . . They are the song of the liberty bell . . . Answering America's call . . . They are the women we love so well . . . God bless and protect them all!

YOUR FRIENDSHIP

Your friendship is the glowing sun . . . That warms the winding road . . . And lightens every step I take . . . Beneath my daily load . . . It is the soft and silvery note . . . That leaves the convent bell . . . The tender flower that I pick . . . To wear in my lapel . . . It is the murmur of the brook . . . The laughter of a child . . . And all the fragrance and romance . . . Of woods and grasses wild . . . Your friendship is the echo in . . . The hills that hold the dawn . . . And every dream that lingers when . . . The purple dusk is gone . . . It is the quiet gentleness . . . Of winds that walk the sea . . . It is the all-embracing gift . . . My God has given me.

LABOR PROBLEMS

Some jobs are quite important and . . . The salaries they pay . . . Are all that anyone could earn . . . In any working day . . . While other tasks are meager and . . . The compensation low . . . According to what bosses are . . . Expected to bestow . . . But there are occupations where . . . The labor does not fit . . . The wages and the hours that . . . Are figured out for it . . . The efforts may exceed by far . . . The money that is made . . . And then again the worker may . . . Be highly overpaid . . . And that is why we talk about . . . Our losses and our gains . . . And why the country always seems . . . To suffer labor pains.

SELF-EDUCATION

Sometimes self-educated folks . . . Achieve supreme success . . . And in that fact they find a source . . . Of pride and happiness . . . They are entitled to their joy . . . And they deserve the praise . . . They get from all the people for . . . Their persevering ways . . . But they are rare exceptions to . . . The well established rule . . . That basic education is . . . Acquired in the school . . . For it is so much wiser to . . . Be thoroughly prepared . . . Than run the risk of failure for . . . The sake of having dared . . . Self-educated scholars may . . . Succeed in what they do . . . But school is much the safer way . . . To see the struggle through.

49

WE MISS YOU, DADDY

Dear Daddy, you are far away . . . We miss you very much . . .
But I am glad that I can write . . . And we can keep in touch . . .
I know what you are doing there . . . 'Cause Mommy let me know
. . . How you are fighting so that I . . . Can eat and sleep and
grow . . . She said that you are shooting now . . . So I can run
and play . . . And we can have our home and I . . . Can go to
school each day . . . Gee, Daddy dear, I think you're swell . . . To
do all that for me . . . I wish that I could help you now . . . To
keep our country free . . . But anyway I pray for you . . . Each
morning and each night . . . So God will take good care of you
. . . And bring you back all right.

HAVE COURAGE, SON

Dear son, I got your message and . . . I thank you very much
. . . I too am glad that you and I . . . Can always keep in touch
. . . Yes, I am fighting very hard . . . To keep our country free . . .
And I need all the fervent prayers . . . That you can say for
me . . . You are too young to hold a gun . . . But there are other
ways . . . Of being a good soldier in . . . These terrifying days . . .
You have a duty right at home . . . Of doing all you can . . . To
grow in mind and body and . . . Become a worthy man . . . Be
good to Mommy and obey . . . Her every word to you . . . Be always honest and sincere . . . And keep your courage true . . . You
need your sleep, your food and all . . . The sunshine in the sky . . .
So you can carry on some day . . . When we must say good-by.

KINDNESS TO ALL

The poor deserve our charity . . . And we are glad to give . . .
The money, food and clothes that will . . . Enable them to live
. . . But charity is not confined . . . To gifts of earthly things . . .
For it includes the happiness . . . A friendly feeling brings . . .
And charity should never be . . . Restricted to the poor . . . As long
as wealthy people have . . . Their problems to endure . . . Success
and riches offer no . . . Excuse for being rude . . . But in their
way they too deserve . . . A kindly attitude . . . And not infrequently the ones . . . Who have the most to spend . . . Are those
who do their best to be . . . The needy person's friend.

I WOULD GATHER STARS

I wish I had a ladder that . . . Would reach so very high . . .
That I could gather all the stars . . . That decorate the sky . . . And
bring them down upon the earth . . . As small as they appear . . .
To any human being who . . . Is watching them from here
. . . And fashion you a gorgeous gown . . . And slippers for your
feet . . . A carriage great to carry you . . . Along the gayest street
. . . And fashion you a bracelet and . . . A bauble for your ear . . .
A ring for every finger and . . . A brilliant lavaliere . . . And those
remaining over I . . . Would surely set apart . . . And offer to
exchange them for . . . A corner of your heart.

CHILD OF GOD

A little child belongs to God . . . As much as every prayer . . .
And while it is our baby it . . . Is only in our care . . . It really
is His boy or girl . . . By every right we know . . . Not just because He gives it life . . . And helps its body grow . . . But more
importantly because . . . In His beloved heart . . . He wants the
age of innocence . . . To be His counterpart . . . He loves all little
children and . . . While they are young and new . . . He longs to
have them honor Him . . . By being good and true . . . That we
who walk in later years . . . May not forget the day . . . When we
ourselves belonged to God . . . In that immaculate way.

PHOTOGRAPH

A photograph is more than just . . . A gift to bring or send . . .
And more than just the likeness of . . . A relative or friend . . . It
is a kindly greeting and . . . A memory to hold . . . Of happy
times and pleasant things . . . However new or old . . . It is a
mirror that reflects . . . Companionship and cheer . . . And now
and then the wistfulness . . . That turns into a tear . . . A photograph is something to . . . Adorn a desk or wall . . . Or carry in
a pocket and . . . Display to one and all . . . It is a faithful portrait of . . . The smile that friendship shares . . . To add its sunshine and to show . . . That someone really cares.

WIFE AT THE WHEEL

I've taken some chances with jobs and finances . . . And always I've come out alive . . . But now I am nettled, my nerves are unsettled . . . I'm teaching my wife how to drive . . . I've tackled some troubles and blown up some bubbles . . . And suffered the worst with a smile . . . But this occupation of car education . . . Has all of them beat by a mile . . . For she has the notion that autos in motion . . . Are easy to handle and turn . . . And traffic confusion is just an illusion . . . And certainly not her concern . . . She steps on the starter and then she gets smarter . . . By getting the gas to disperse . . . And when you have reckoned she's put it in second . . . It suddenly goes in reverse . . . Oh, husbands and scholars, go squander your dollars . . . But if you would long be alive . . . Invite not the terror that follows the error . . . Of teaching your wife how to drive.

SPARE TIME

Success in life depends of course . . . On what we do each day . . . And whether we apply ourselves . . . Or fritter time away . . . But also there is time beyond . . . The setting of the sun . . . That is invaluable to us . . . In getting something done . . . And while the night is ours to spend . . . In any way we choose . . . It offers opportunities . . . That we may take or lose . . . So why not make the most of all . . . The time we have to spare . . . And lay a real foundation for . . . Our castle in the air? . . . Tomorrow we shall never miss . . . The fun refused tonight . . . If we are that much nearer to . . . The goal we have in sight.

DEAR FRIEND

This letter is to let you know . . . I want to be your friend . . . And that I hope our friendship is . . . The kind that will not end . . . That it will reach through all the years . . . And over every sea . . . And that it will be part of us . . . Wherever we may be . . . I want to serve you always and . . . In every way I know . . . However long may be the rain . . . Or wild the winds that blow . . . And every bit as eagerly . . . I place my faith in you . . . That in your kindness all the skies . . . Will be forever blue . . . And so I send this greeting and . . . Reminder to your heart . . . That we have promised to be friends . . . However far apart.

DONNIE'S SHOES

We always find ourselves beset . . . With budgetary blues . . .
When we discover Donnie needs . . . Another pair of shoes . . .
Each time we take him to the store . . . We buy a sturdy pair
. . . And caution him to treat them with . . . The very best of
care . . . But being just a youngster he . . . Must exercise his feet
. . . And so he kicks and scrapes and slides . . . While playing on
the street . . . He wears the leather out so fast . . . We don't know
what to do . . . It seems that almost every week . . . His toes are
coming through . . . With all our might we strive to win . . . But
in the end we lose . . . I guess we'll have to fit him with . . . A pair
of iron shoes!

FIVE O'CLOCK

The whistle blows and life becomes . . . A steady stream of feet
. . . As silent men and weary maids . . . Pour out upon the street
. . . The sun is slowly going down . . . The shadows cross the
sky . . . The bus and trolley, limousine . . . And cab go racing
by . . . The lights in office windows dim . . . And those in shops
grow bright . . . Cafés and theaters begin . . . To live their day by
night . . . The newsboy hawks the printed page . . . The traffic
signals blink . . . While idle men in empty parks . . . Are left alone
to think . . . And all along the avenues . . . There is a peaceful air
. . . The world is going home again . . . To sleep in comfort there.

HEART TO HEART

My heart is grateful to your heart . . . For everything today . . .
Because your loving heart is part . . . Of everything I say . . . And
it is part of everything . . . I ever try to do . . . In autumn, winter
and in spring . . . And in the summer too . . . To you I owe the
thoughts I think . . . When skies are dark or fair . . . And every
time I sleep a wink . . . My dream is yours to share . . . I am indebted to you, dear . . . For all my life, I guess . . . And most of all
from year to year . . . For endless happiness . . . And so my heart
would tell your heart . . . The gratefulness in me . . . Because you
are the sweetest part . . . Of every memory.

SPENDING SUNDAY

On Sunday we may rest ourselves . . . On our domestic perch
. . . And we are never legally . . . Compelled to go to church . . .
We may enjoy a game of golf . . . Beginning in the dawn . . . Or
read the paper for the news . . . Of what is going on . . . But if
we are at all concerned . . . About our future days . . . We ought
to weigh the value of . . . Our ordinary ways . . . And we should
ask ourselves how much . . . Our deeds are really worth . . . And
what examples they present . . . For other folks on earth . . . Because the things we do or say . . . While we are on this sod . . . Are
those for which eventually . . . We must account to God.

CEILING ON LOANS

I will lend you a book . . . Or a table and chair . . . My garden
utensils . . . Or chinaware . . . You may borrow my car . . . And
my pass to the show . . . And my time is as free . . . As the sun
and the snow . . . You may help yourself . . . To the clothes I
wear . . . And what money I have . . . I will gladly share . . . You
have only to ask . . . For my pencil or pen . . . My typewriter,
phone . . . Or the use of my den . . . Indeed you may borrow . . .
Whatever is mine . . . With never a thought . . . Of a fee or a fine
. . . With one small exception . . . That stands all apart . . . I will
lend you my life . . . But never my heart.

VISIT THE SICK

There is no person lonelier . . . Than he who lies in bed . . .
And must depend on others to . . . Be comfortable and fed . . .
Who never has a visitor . . . To talk to him and smile . . . And
make the life he has to live . . . A little more worth while . . . He
does not ask for magazines . . . For candy, fruit and such . . . But
just a friendly visit and . . . The words that mean so much . . . He
wants to see the sun come out . . . In place of all the rain . . . And
know that someone cares about . . . His trouble and his pain . . .
And surely somewhere out of all . . . The moments made for play
. . . There must be time to call on him . . . And say hello today.

54

ARE YOU AN AMERICAN?

Do you go to church on Sunday? . . . Do you say a little prayer
. . . For the soldier and the sailor . . . Who are fighting over
there? . . . Do you try to do your duty . . . As a citizen should
do . . . Buying bonds and writing letters . . . To the ones who
write to you? . . . Are you really patriotic . . . As you go about
your task? . . . Are you giving all the effort . . . Every service man
could ask? . . . Do you think about the future . . . With a neighborly concern . . . To the hour when the soldier . . . And the
sailor will return? . . . If you honestly can answer . . . Every question with a "yes" . . . You deserve a decoration . . . From the hand
of happiness.

FRIENDLY WIND

The passing wind has always been . . . A kindly friend to me
. . . Because in lonely moments it . . . Has kept me company . . .
Along the street where people stroll . . . Without a sign or word
. . . It has imparted messages . . . That only I have heard . . . The
messages of memory . . . That fill a friendly breeze . . . When it
is whispering among . . . The gently swaying trees . . . The wind
has made me ready for . . . The winter's icy hold . . . By howling
down the chimney-place . . . To warn me of the cold . . . Each
spring it has invited me . . . To leave my work and play . . . And
always it has tried so hard . . . To blow the rain away.

CARPENTER

He makes the wall and window frame . . . The ceiling and the
floor . . . The rafters underneath the roof . . . And every kind of
door . . . He manufactures cabinets . . . The table and the chair
. . . The dresser, desk and vanity . . . And every wooden ware . . .
He hammers and he saws and planes . . . And drills precision holes
. . . And he can make most anything . . . From ships to fishing
poles . . . His trade is almost old as time . . . And it will never die
. . . As long as there is any tree . . . That rises to the sky . . . His
station may be humble but . . . He earns his daily bread . . . And
he is best prepared to hit . . . The nail right on the head.

THE BOSS AND I

When I am sitting at my desk . . . As busy as can be . . . The boss is never there to watch . . . Or be aware of me . . . And if I do a job that should . . . Be given special praise . . . It never seems to reach his ears . . . Or captivate his gaze . . . But if I take a second off . . . To make a side remark . . . He always happens to be there . . . With his tremendous bark . . . He notices my least mistake . . . Or if I slow my pace . . . And every time he calls me I . . . Am at some other place . . . And that explains the sorry part . . . Of all my working days . . . And why I never have the nerve . . . To ask him for a raise.

ARCHERY

In Sherwood Forest lived a man . . . Who glorified the bow . . . According to the story book . . . That all the children know . . . But whether he existed or . . . His deeds were merely dreams . . . The benefit of archery . . . Is everything it seems . . . It is a healthy exercise . . . That strengthens arm and hand . . . And trains the eye and teaches you . . . A sturdy way to stand . . . It is a test of human skill . . . That everyone should try . . . And it provides a lot of fun . . . Wherever arrows fly . . . And after all is said and done . . . It is the mighty dart . . . That wings the way to lasting love . . . When Cupid strikes the heart.

TEACHER

The duties of a teacher are . . . As heavy as can be . . . Regardless of the type of school . . . Or whether "he" or "she" . . . Because the teacher must possess . . . A knowledge that will shine . . . And in addition has to keep . . . The students right in line . . . There are a thousand questions to . . . Be answered every day . . . And papers must be graded when . . . The books are put away . . . The pleasures of an evening out . . . Are seldom to be shared . . . Because the next day's lesson must . . . Be carefully prepared . . . And yet there is a glory in . . . This timeless atmosphere . . . The teacher helps tomorrow's world . . . Prepare for its career.

WIFE AT WORK

My wife is always cleaning house . . . And tidying each room
. . . She almost never goes about . . . Without a mop or broom
. . . She sweeps and dusts, arranges things . . . And chases every
speck . . . Until the toughest admiral . . . Would compliment her
deck . . . She says she might as well keep house . . . For chickens
or a horse . . . And squarely puts the blame on us . . . (The boys
and me, of course) . . . But for the very life of me . . . I cannot
feel that way . . . Because to me this dwelling looks . . . As clean
and bright as day . . . And I can only figure out . . . That if her
time were spent . . . On anything but cleaning house . . . She
would not be content.

BE THANKFUL

Be thankful for your health today . . . Your children and your
wife . . . For all of your possessions and . . . The beauty of this
life . . . Be grateful for the chance to work . . . And buy your
daily bread . . . For liberty and leisure and . . . A place to rest
your head . . . Be mindful of misfortune that . . . Befalls your
fellow-man . . . Consider his adversity . . . And help him, if you
can . . . Appreciate the hour that . . . Is all your own to spend . . .
The wisdom of the weather and . . . The kindness of a friend
. . . Be thoughtful of tomorrow and . . . Remember what is gone
. . . Be thankful unto Heaven for . . . The courage to go on.

HALF-MOON

The moon is only half tonight . . . And that is how I feel . . . Because when you are gone from me . . . My life is never real . . . I
am but half as happy as . . . When you are at my side . . . And I
have only half as much . . . Of courage and of pride . . . I find no
more than half the joy . . . In any smile or laugh . . . And every
time I hear your name . . . My heart is torn in half . . . My memories of yesteryear . . . Divide my dreams in two . . . Because one-
half of all of them . . . Belong so much to you . . . And I am
never more than half . . . Of what I want to be . . . When you are
gone—because you are . . . The other half of me.

57

OUT OF THE NIGHT

In two more days they would have wed . . . And shared the joys
of life . . . This youthful, brave lieutenant and . . . His lovely,
promised wife . . . While now his wings of silvery gray . . . That
glistened in the sun . . . Are markers on the sudden grave . . .
Where flying days are done . . . He fired not a single shot . . . Nor
saw the vanquished fall . . . And yet in his unselfish way . . . He
gave his very all . . . Her hero has departed but . . . His memory
lingers on . . . And she can hear his motor roar . . . To greet the
golden dawn . . . With every wind that rushes by . . . She gazes
into space . . . In every plane that sweeps the sky . . . She sees her
lover's face.

PEDESTRIAN

The humble human being who . . . Depends upon his feet . . . Is
known as a pedestrian when . . . He walks along the street . . . He
has to watch the traffic light . . . Wherever he would cross . . .
Although the time between may mean . . . A most important loss
. . . He is the daily target for . . . The foolish folks who drive . . .
And he is mighty fortunate . . . If he can stay alive . . . He has to
ride the street car or . . . He has to board the bus . . . And many
are the things in life . . . He has a mind to cuss . . . But always he
is fully free . . . To wander or to stay . . . And never does he need
a place . . . To park his car all day.

MY OPEN HEART

To you, my brother, I extend . . . An open heart today . . . I
want to bring you cheer and be . . . Of help in every way . . . I
long to lend you confidence . . . To meet and conquer strife . . .
And render every service that . . . Will further you in life . . . If
you have any trouble or . . . The very smallest care . . . Remember
it is just the thing . . . That I am glad to share . . . And if you find
some happiness . . . I shall be happy too . . . Because I always look
for joy . . . That will encourage you . . . Because wherever I may
go . . . I always want to give . . . That brotherly devotion to . . .
The world in which we live.

DAY AT A TIME

If I could see the future now . . . And everything within it . . .
I wonder if my heart would have . . . The courage to begin it
. . . Of course the brighter part would seem . . . Decidedly inviting
. . . And certain incidents would seem . . . Exceedingly exciting . . .
But what about the darker side? . . . And what if some tomorrow
. . . Presented only promises . . . Of loneliness and sorrow? . . . I
would not feel the future was . . . The way I meant to make it
. . . And probably I would not be . . . Prepared to undertake it . . .
I have enough to do right now . . . To make my life more pleasant
. . . So why not let the future wait . . . Until I live the present?

FOSTER-MOTHER

There is no mother who is more . . . Deserving of our praise . . .
Than she who takes another's child . . . To comfort and to raise
. . . Who has the blessing of the court . . . To keep and call her
own . . . The baby someone selfishly . . . Allowed to live alone
. . . Her name is foster-mother but . . . It should be angel-queen
. . . For she is all the nobleness . . . That motherhood can
mean . . . She is a bit of Heaven on . . . A cold and cruel earth
. . . Where all too often human life . . . Is deemed of little worth
. . . Her child belongs to her not by . . . The grace of nature's
art . . . But by the choice made freely from . . . The goodness of
her heart.

NO JOB TOO BIG

So many times I find I have . . . A duty to fulfill . . . And at the
moment it appears . . . To be impossible . . . I wonder if my mind
can cope . . . With what I have to do . . . And if I undertake the
task . . . I ever will get through . . . But finally I start it and . . .
The hours wander by . . . And gradually I tell myself . . . It must
be worth a try . . . It may require patience from . . . The time it
is begun . . . And yet I go right on with it . . . And always get
it done . . . And then once more I realize that . . . There is no job
too great . . . If I begin it bravely and . . . I give it all my weight.

SO MANY MILES

So many miles divide us now . . . So many fields of green . . . So many roads, so many towns . . . Are scattered in between . . . It seems as though I never could . . . Reach out and touch your hand . . . Although we too are still within . . . The borders of this land . . . So many fences, woods and streams . . . Appear to bar the way . . . And every hour multiplies . . . The slowness of the day . . . And yet each night when I look up . . . And see the starry sky . . . I know that you are waiting, too . . . For time to wander by . . . And to each little silver star . . . I throw a kiss or two . . . And hope that they will hear me pray . . . And drop them down to you.

LAME BOY

He looks about this world of ours . . . And wonders how it feels . . . To get around without the aid . . . Of crutches or of wheels . . . He watches other children walk . . . And sees them jump and run . . . And often wishes he could rise . . . And share their daily fun . . . But he is not so fortunate . . . And all too well he knows . . . He has to have support and help . . . No matter where he goes . . . For him there is no football and . . . No swimming in the lake . . . No track to run, no bike to ride . . . No tree to climb and shake . . . He cannot hurdle fences or . . . Go wading in the stream . . . He has to sit or hobble on . . . And be content to dream.

GOD BLESS YOU

May God be always good to you . . . By answering your prayers . . . And giving you the strength you need . . . To carry all your cares . . . May He console you when your heart . . . Is overwhelmed with tears . . . And bless you with the bravery . . . To overcome your fears . . . If you desire worldly wealth . . . Or wisdom in your schemes . . . I hope He favors you with both . . . Beyond your fondest dreams . . . I hope He gives you everything . . . You ever ask Him for . . . And that His guiding grace will be . . . Forever at your door . . . May God encourage you to play . . . A fair and honest game . . . And may His love inspire you . . . To glorify His name.

MISSING IN ACTION

These are the words of cruelty ... The war must oft convey
... "Your son (or husband) is among ... The missing men today" ... To her these words can only mean ... Uncertainty and
fear ... The anguish of an endless wait ... From week to month
to year ... For her they hold but little hope ... Beyond her faith
in God ... And she would almost rather know ... His cross
adorned the sod ... There is no thought to comfort her ...
Throughout the day or night ... While in her mind she strives
to find ... The picture of his plight ... And yet she has to carry
on ... Across each weary mile ... And hide her broken heart
beneath ... A patriotic smile.

WHAT IS A FRIEND?

What is a friend? A friend is one ... Who takes you by the
hand ... Who listens to your troubles and ... Who tries to
understand ... Who comforts you in sickness and ... Rejoices
in your health ... And who is always at your side ... In poverty
or wealth ... Who does not ask for payment or ... Expect the
slightest share ... And who will keep your secret when ...
Entrusted to his care ... A friend is one who really means ...
The praises he presents ... And criticizes only to ... Promote
your competence ... Who always serves you faithfully ... And
is sincere and true ... And who would merely like to have ...
The same respect from you.

SINGER

The singer is a creature of ... My very special choice ... Especially if he can claim ... A gorgeous, golden voice ... He may
incline to crooning or ... The operatic note ... But if he has the
quality ... He always gets my vote ... Because when he commands the stage ... Or occupies the air ... He liberates my lonely
heart ... From trouble and from care ... He takes away the
shadows and ... He ushers in the sun ... And rests my weary
body when ... The working day is done ... He is the inspiration true ... The courage and the zest ... That help me live a
humble life ... And give my very best.

OUR MONEY

A little cash is handy and . . . A fortune has its way . . . Of adding to the comforts of . . . An ordinary day . . . But money does not mean so much . . . When we define its worth . . . According to the principle . . . Of doing good on earth . . . It merely is a medium . . . Of getting things we need . . . Or something that enables us . . . To do a kindly deed . . . Our money is a blessing if . . . We use it in a way . . . That helps the poor and penniless . . . To live a better day . . . But if we spend it selfishly . . . Our money is a curse . . . And all our schemes and saintly dreams . . . Are locked inside a purse.

JIMMIE'S LESSONS

When Jimmie has to learn a piece . . . To say in school next day . . . His mother has a struggle and . . . I feel my hair get gray . . . He never quite remembers that . . . He has to memorize . . . Until it's time to go to bed . . . And close his little eyes . . . It takes about an hour and . . . The patience of a saint . . . Before he knows it well enough . . . To silence each complaint . . . And when he has it down real pat . . . And tries it just once more . . . He starts again to hesitate . . . And stumble as before . . . But when next evening I come home . . . My fears forever fade . . . For I can tell by his proud smile . . . He made a perfect grade.

SONG OF LIFE

Dreams are made for dreaming . . . Songs are made to sing . . . Rain is part of April . . . Love is part of spring . . . Fragrance comes from flowers . . . Flowers come from seeds . . . Things are judged by money . . . We are judged by deeds . . . Rings adorn the finger . . . Stars adorn the sky . . . Smiles are what we treasure . . . Tears are what we cry . . . Beauty is a virtue . . . Ugliness is sin . . . What must have an ending . . . Also must begin . . . Courage takes a challenge . . . Vigilance takes care . . . Truth defeats deception . . . Faith defeats despair . . . Colors form the rainbow . . . Waters form the sea . . . I belong to you, dear . . . You belong to me.

I NEED THE STARS

I need the stars to comfort me . . . Whenever I am blue . . .
Because wherever you may be . . . I know they shine on you . . .
And in the deepness of the night . . . When loneliness is great
. . . I know you see their silver light . . . And you must also wait
. . . These hours are forever long . . . But life is longer yet . . .
And you and I have heard a song . . . We never will forget . . . No
matter how the tide may flow . . . Or bridges wash away . . .
No matter how the wind may blow . . . The leaves of yesterday
. . . I know the hours must go by . . . But every now and then . . .
I cannot help it if I cry . . . To be with you again . . . And when
the sun goes down, my love . . . And darkness lies ahead . . . I
need the silver stars above . . . To keep me comforted.

PINAFORE PLAYTIME

Kristina likes her home but she . . . Prefers to be outdoors . . .
And most of all she likes to dress . . . In pretty pinafores . . . She
has her sandbox on the porch . . . In which she often plays . . .
And there are many other things . . . To occupy her days . . . She
likes to wheel her buggy with . . . Her dollies tucked inside . . .
And now and then she comes to me . . . To get a buggy ride
. . . She wants her older brothers to . . . Be near as they can be . . .
So they will always talk to her . . . And watch her carefully . . .
She is a little darling whom . . . We naturally adore . . . Especially
when she has on . . . A pretty pinafore.

GIFT

A gift is something that we buy . . . To carry or to send . . . To
someone near and dear to us . . . Or just a business friend . . .
Or maybe it is something we . . . Have fashioned with our hands
. . . To give that personal appeal . . . That friendship understands
. . . It should be chosen carefully . . . Without a sign of haste . . .
And not according to our likes . . . But to the other's taste . . . Because it is a message to . . . Express the way we feel . . . And illus-
trate our sentiment . . . Of kindness that is real . . . And whether
we use pennies or . . . We spend immense amounts . . . The spirit
of our giving it . . . Is all that really counts.

AMERICA IS GOOD TO ME

America is good to me . . . She gives me work and pay . . . A night of peaceful slumber and . . . Some leisure every day . . . She lets me say the things I want . . . And do what I may please . . . If I am wronged, I know I have . . . My legal remedies . . . I have my home and family . . . And clothes and food and drink . . . And when I go inside a church . . . I worship as I think . . . I cast my vote for government . . . And help to build my town . . . Where every person is a king . . . But no one wears a crown . . . America is good to me . . . My children and my wife . . . And unto her in peace and war . . . I will devote my life.

BELIEVE ME, LORD

Believe me, Lord, I want to do . . . The very best I can . . . And be of faithful service to . . . My every fellow-man . . . To be a loving husband and . . . A father kind and good . . . And do my part in building up . . . A better neighborhood . . . I know I do not measure up . . . To all I ought to be . . . But I implore You, Lord, to look . . . With kindliness on me . . . I have my human weaknesses . . . And now and then I fall . . . And there are crowded moments when . . . I do not hear Your call . . . But in my heart I love You, Lord . . . And I am grateful too . . . For every blessing great and small . . . That I receive from You.

TO ALL MY FRIENDS

I have so many friends today . . . I cannot count them all . . . And many are the names I am . . . Unable to recall . . . But still I try to think of them . . . And in my heart I know . . . They helped me find some happiness . . . However long ago . . . They all inspired me to live . . . A better life on earth . . . And they encouraged me to be . . . Of more enduring worth . . . And so I am indebted to . . . A host of friends today . . . Who graciously contributed . . . To help me on my way . . . And they may rest assured that I . . . Am at their beck and call . . . To serve them faithfully today . . . In any way at all.

PASSING PARADE

I walk along the busy street . . . And watch the people pass . . .
And it is just as if the world . . . Were in a looking-glass . . . Not
anybody speaks to me . . . Or ever turns around . . . It seems to
me they might as well . . . Be shadows on the ground . . . I wonder
what their hurry is . . . Or why their pace is slow . . . What idle
things they think about . . . And what they really know . . . I
wonder what they plan to do . . . And what they hope to be . . .
What dreams they dream and if they have . . . A happy memory
. . . I watch them walk along the street . . . All hours of the day
. . . And while I wonder who they are . . . I merely go my way.

RUMMAGING

I like to clean a closet out . . . Or rummage through a trunk
. . . To separate the better things . . . From what is merely junk
. . . Then rearrange the better things . . . To use some later
day . . . And gather up the dusty trash . . . And have it hauled
away . . . But when I start a job like that . . . My wife gets good
and mad . . . Because I find so many things . . . I did not know I
had . . . And when I scrutinize the stuff . . . I am inclined to doubt
. . . That there are any articles . . . That ought to be thrown out
. . . And so although my rummaging . . . Is always lots of fun . . .
It is one job around the house . . . That never quite gets done.

WHY DID YOU GO?

Why did you leave me when the sky . . . Was bright with golden
sun? . . . Why did you leave me when our hearts . . . Were woven
into one? . . . Why did you have to go away . . . And leave my
soul beset . . . With memories of happiness . . . I never can forget?
. . . You told me once you loved me, dear . . . And I believed you
too . . . What made you change your mind, my love? . . . You
know, I trusted you . . . Why did you say good-by to me . . .
When we were happy, dear? . . . Why did you turn your smile away
. . . And leave me with a tear? . . . I gave you all I had to give . . .
But all I asked of you . . . Was just a little of yourself . . . To make
my dreams come true.

WORTHY MAN

He is a man of worthy soul . . . Who does the best he can . . . To give his gratitude to God . . . And serve his fellow-man . . . Who lives his life unselfishly . . . That other men may share . . . His every daily blessing and . . . The power of his prayer . . . He may not gather great renown . . . Upon a worldly plane . . . But his accomplishment becomes . . . His everlasting gain . . . To him belongs the happiness . . . Of being good and kind . . . To everyone of heavy heart . . . Or troubled in his mind . . . For him there is no hopeless task . . . Or fear of any odds . . . While everything he does reflects . . . The glory that is God's.

GREENER GRASS

Chicago is too bleak and damp . . . New York is just as bad . . . In Florida the hurricanes . . . Leave many people sad . . . The California towns can feel . . . The earth begin to quake . . . Along the Mississippi route . . . The waters rise and break . . . Duluth, Cheyenne and Helena . . . Are cold as they can be . . . In Washington and Oregon . . . It rains eternally . . . Throughout the South it gets too hot . . . While Kansas folks despair . . . Of keeping homes and cows and pigs . . . From flying through the air . . . So what's the use of sighing for . . . The places near and far? . . . We might as well be satisfied . . . To stay right where we are.

MILKMAN

He always used to come around . . . Before the crack of dawn . . . In bright or rainy weather he . . . Could be depended on . . . He brought us butter, milk and eggs . . . And packages of cheese . . . And even as to quantity . . . He never failed to please . . . But now it is a different tale . . . And we are glad of course . . . If thrice a week we see his truck . . . Or gaze upon his horse . . . We get our milk but other things . . . For which our stomachs sigh . . . Require points and usually . . . Are very hard to buy . . . We really do appreciate . . . His service during war . . . But after it is over we . . . Will love him so much more.

GOOD COMPANY

I like to have my friends around . . . When nightly shadows fall . . . And hear their laughter echo loud . . . From every nook and wall . . . I like to lift my glass with them . . . And drink a toast to life . . . And listen to the compliments . . . They pay my charming wife . . . And talk about our yesterdays . . . When we were not too old . . . To read about the Rover Boys . . . And search for hidden gold . . . I like to climb the hills again . . . And count them one by one . . . Compare our notes and summarize . . . The battles we have won . . . And through the conversation share . . . Our greatest joys today . . . The little sons and daughters we . . . Are guiding on their way.

FILE CLERK

The clerk who keeps the office files . . . Has quite a job to do . . . In caring for the old as well . . . As correspondence new . . . Each piece of paper has to be . . . Precisely in its place . . . And there must be a folder new . . . For every separate case . . . There has to be a system so . . . The clerk will not forget . . . And he or she quite obviously . . . Must know the alphabet . . . And he or she must be prepared . . . To pull the proper file . . . If he or she would like to see . . . The boss display a smile . . . The summons for a memo is . . . A most important "must" . . . But clerks are not to blame if files . . . Are left to gather dust.

DRUMSTICK DEAL

Whenever we have chicken or . . . Some other bird to eat . . . The children think the drumstick is . . . The most delicious treat . . . Now while a bird has two of them . . . Our offsprings number three . . . And normally that would present . . . A great perplexity . . . But we have found a special way . . . To carve the roasted bird . . . So our two boys each get a leg . . . While sister gets a third . . . Of course some people might describe . . . That third one as a wing . . . But our Kristina darling knows . . . That it is no such thing . . . Her daddy says it is a leg . . . Her brothers both agree . . . And after all she is as smart . . . As any girl of three.

MY DIARY

I keep a little diary . . . Of all the things I do . . . At least the more important and . . . Especially the new . . . Its only purpose is to keep . . . A record of the past . . . Of memories that I would have . . . As long as I shall last . . . It does not show my deepest thoughts . . . And it does not embrace . . . The picture and the story true . . . Of every name and place . . . For there are certain things in life . . . That wear a special crown . . . And are too dear and sacred to . . . Be ever written down . . . There are the dreams that we have shared . . . And those that are to be . . . And there are confidential words . . . That you have said to me.

CHILD IN CHURCH

He is too young to understand . . . The gospel and the prayer . . . But in his own small way he feels . . . God's presence in the air . . . He knows there is a border line . . . Between the right and wrong . . . And when temptation faces him . . . He should be brave and strong . . . He knows his parents smile with joy . . . When he is good all day . . . As surely as their hearts are sad . . . When he does not obey . . . He knows that when he goes to church . . . He should not speak out loud . . . But he should pray in silence with . . . His head in reverence bowed . . . And thus he learns the ways of life . . . However strange or odd . . . And he begins to understand . . . He owes his life to God.

NIGHT WITHOUT END

I wish this night would never end . . . Because I am with you . . . And only in your company . . . Do all my dreams come true . . . The very nearness of yourself . . . Is all I ever need . . . To give me courage and the strength . . . To struggle and succeed . . . I only want to hold you close . . . And look into your eyes . . . To see the beauty of this life . . . Without the least disguise . . . I want to kiss your lips again . . . And hear them say to me . . . That you are mine to have and hold . . . For all eternity . . . And so I wish this night with you . . . Would never know an end . . . Because you are my sweetheart and . . . My everlasting friend.

BIRTHDAY

A birthday is a merry time . . . For little girls and boys . . .
Because it always promises . . . To bring them books and toys
. . . And then there is a special cake . . . With candles all aglow
. . . For little hearts to make a wish . . . And little lips to blow . . .
A birthday is a happy time . . . For husbands and for wives . . .
When they may well appreciate . . . The blessings of their lives
. . . While as for folks of middle age . . . It comes and goes away
. . . In much the mood and manner of . . . An ordinary day . . .
A birthday is the harvest time . . . For those in later years . . .
When they may gather all their dreams . . . Of golden smiles and
tears.

A MOTHER'S PRAYER

No matter where they send you, son . . . Be brave in all you do
. . . Be loyal and devoted to . . . The great red, white and blue . . .
Whatever they may ask of you . . . However high the price . . .
Remember that our liberty . . . Is worth the sacrifice . . . In every
battle do your part . . . With ready heart and hand . . . Be willing
and obedient . . . To every new command . . . Remember that I
love you and . . . My proud heart cannot ache . . . So long as you
fight valiantly . . . To win for freedom's sake . . . And I would
rather bend my knee . . . Beside a hero's grave . . . Than bow
my head before my boy . . . Because he was not brave.

FRIENDLY FLOWERS

I love the little flowers in . . . The garden that I tend . . . Because
to me each one of them . . . Is like a special friend . . . In fact
when I am planting them . . . I name them one and all . . .
According to the titles of . . . The faces I recall . . . I give each
one the best of care . . . To help their petals grow . . . The
same as I would serve the needs . . . Of every friend I know . . .
My little flowers represent . . . The folks who favor me . . . With
kindness and companionship . . . And gentle sympathy . . . They
are the understanding souls . . . Who whisper to my heart . . .
The sentiments in which no friends . . . Could ever grow apart.

STENOGRAPHER

A good stenographer is one . . . Who does her work real well
. . . Who writes her notes and never has . . . To ask you how to
spell . . . Who types your letters neatly and . . . Who keeps the
paper clean . . . And never tells another soul . . . What she has
heard or seen . . . She may enjoy a cigaret . . . And now and then
a rest . . . But she is prompt, efficient and . . . Conservatively
dressed . . . She takes good care of her machine . . . And makes
it fairly hum . . . And does not primp her face all day . . . Or fill
it up with gum . . . She does not tell you what to do . . . Or sit
around and stare . . . But she attends to business and . . . Her kind
is somewhat rare.

TWO SLEEPY HEADS

Each night when I look in upon . . . Two sleepy, childish heads
. . . I'm sure I see two angels there . . . Beside their little beds . . .
I see them standing there as though . . . They were a magic
charm . . . To guide my boys through slumberland . . . And keep
them from all harm . . . And then I go to bed and know . . . There
is no tide to stem . . . That God, Who gives all angels life . . .
Is watching over them . . . Just as He keeps them healthy and . . .
Contented in their play . . . And helps them grow in goodness and
. . . In grace from day to day . . . And just as He will lead them
on . . . Through struggle and through strife . . . To happiness and
glory and . . . The beauty of this life.

CONGRATULATIONS

Sincere congratulations and . . . Good luck to you today . . .
May your diploma help you gain . . . Success in every way . . .
May progress mark your every step . . . Along your rise to fame
. . . And may your deeds endow you with . . . A good and noble
name . . . May you fulfill your high ideals . . . Without a doubt
or guess . . . And may your friendships multiply . . . Your daily
happiness . . . Keep up the courage you have shown . . . And
never shirk or quit . . . You know, you only get from life . . .
What you put into it . . . You well deserve the honor that . . . The
school has given you . . . And so congratulations and . . . May all
your dreams come true.

THE SIMPLE LIFE

I only want the simple life . . . The chance to work each day
. . . And be beside my loving wife . . . When there is time for
play . . . To eat in peace, to read a book . . . Or take a quiet walk
. . . Enjoy the meadow and the brook . . . Or merely sit and talk
. . . I only want to get the mail . . . That comes addressed to
me . . . To have my health and to inhale . . . The air that God
made free . . . I do not ask for pomp or fame . . . Or money in the
bank . . . But I would rather have a name . . . Of ordinary rank
. . . I only want to give my best . . . And sing the simpler songs
. . . To do my job and leave the rest . . . Wherever it belongs.

VISION

Stars were in the sky tonight . . . When I went down the street
. . . And as I walked, I thought I heard . . . The sound of dancing
feet . . . I thought I saw you near me while . . . The shadows
glided by . . . But you were gone as quickly as . . . A vision mocks
the eye . . . And though I searched for blocks and blocks . . . And
looked in every place . . . I could not find your wistful eyes . . .
Or yet your winsome face . . . I could not touch a hand so soft
. . . Or lips so young and gay . . . As those you shyly offered
me . . . One breathless yesterday . . . And so I wandered home
again . . . To mingle silent tears . . . With vagaries that oft disturb
. . . The dust of bygone years.

A PRAYER

A prayer is just a simple way . . . Of asking God to hear . . .
Whatever words we want to say . . . Of sentiment sincere . . . The
words that spell our problems out . . . And ask His timely aid
. . . Whenever we are filled with doubt . . . Or we are too afraid
. . . When tragedy is near at hand . . . Or it has struck a blow . . .
And only God will understand . . . The suffering we know . . .
But also in a prayer we give . . . The gratitude we feel . . . Because
we are allowed to live . . . And share the commonweal . . . A
prayer is like a letter or . . . A telegram we send . . . When we
would penetrate the door . . . Of our beloved Friend.

TO HAVE AND TO HOLD

It used to be a simple thing . . . For people to get rich . . . If they had brains and fortitude . . . But now there is a hitch . . . Because the more we earn today . . . The more we pay in tax . . . And Uncle Sam is never slow . . . In bringing down the ax . . . We have to make three times as much . . . And sometimes even more . . . In order to retain the sum . . . That we are striving for . . . Of course we know it has to be . . . Because we have to fight . . . And for the sake of future peace . . . We know that it is right . . . But it will sure be wonderful . . . When better days return . . . And we can keep the greater part . . . Of all the cash we earn.

USHERETTE

I like the lovely little Miss . . . Who greets me at the door . . . When I go in to see a show . . . I have not seen before . . . It may be just to pass the time . . . Or beat a thunderstorm . . . But when I go there I adore . . . Her nifty uniform . . . And I am always happy and . . . I think it is just fine . . . If there is quite a crowd ahead . . . And I must stand in line . . . Because I watch her manner as . . . She fills each empty seat . . . And every movement that she makes . . . Is beautiful and neat . . . And while the movie may be dull . . . I cannot once forget . . . The genuine attraction of . . . The lovely usherette.

⌄ TRUE FRIEND

I know of nothing quite so grand . . . As just to have a friend . . . A person who can understand . . . Whatever thoughts I send . . . An individual who tries . . . To help in every way . . . Who has the heart to sympathize . . . Whenever clouds are gray . . . The one who criticizes me . . . When I am really wrong . . . And somehow makes it seem to be . . . As pleasant as a song . . . The kind of person who will come . . . In answer to my call . . . Without expecting any sum . . . Or compliment at all . . . The one who means his word of praise . . . For some good deed I do . . . And in so many other ways . . . Confirms a friendship true.

72

NO NEED TO ENVY

Why should I envy any man . . . For what he may possess . . .
When life is filled with many forms . . . Of wealth and happiness?
. . . I have my opportunities . . . The same as anyone . . . To
climb the hills and reach a place . . . Of glory in the sun . . . It may
not be a palace with . . . The jewels of a king . . . And there may
be no great acclaim . . . By any following . . . But if I keep my
honor and . . . Maintain my self-respect . . . And if I let the good
in me . . . Produce its best effect . . . I shall be richer in my way
. . . Than they who gather gold . . . And I shall have as many
joys . . . As ever I can hold.

OUR TWO BOYS

While Jimmie dear gets dressed for school . . . And scrubs his
dirt away . . . Our Donnie sets the table for . . . The first meal of
the day . . . We all sit down to eat and then . . . I hurry to the
door . . . To catch the street car and to read . . . The news about
the war . . . Our Jimmie rides his bike to school . . . And Mother
starts her tasks . . . As Donnie meditates upon . . . The thousand
things he asks . . . And when I get back home I find . . . My
sweetheart waiting there . . . But our two boys are playing out
. . . And may be anywhere . . . Eventually we round them up . . .
And after they are fed . . . They have a lot of fun before . . . They
tumble into bed . . . And then my wife and I sit down . . . To rest
and talk and read . . . And thank our God for giving us . . . Two
boys to dress and feed.

TO BE WITH YOU

I want to be with you tonight . . . And hold you in my arms . . .
And gently gather to myself . . . Your many wondrous charms
. . . I want to walk beside you in . . . The garden of my dreams
. . . And tell you all my hopes and my . . . Ambitions and my
schemes . . . For they can matter only when . . . I know you love
me, dear . . . And life is precious only when . . . Your helping
hand is near . . . You are my calendar of days . . . And all the
countless nights . . . Where I would wander in my search . . .
For heavenly delights . . . And just because you mean so much
. . . And for the joy you give . . . I want to be with you tonight
. . . And every night I live.

TONIGHT ON DECK

Tonight on deck we kneel and pray . . . Tomorrow we shall land . . . O Lord, we place our destiny . . . In your protecting hand . . . Guide our invasion fleet at dawn . . . And calm the winds that blow . . . That we may safely reach the shore . . . And overcome the foe . . . We know that some of us must fall . . . And some of us must die . . . But hold our losses down, O Lord . . . And keep our courage high . . . Give us this night a peaceful sleep . . . And let us dream once more . . . That we are home with those we love . . . Away from all this war . . . Give us this dream and grant that soon . . . It will be coming true . . . And in the meantime, Lord, we leave . . . Our destiny to You.

WEALTHY PAUPER

I met a man upon the street . . . Whose face was lean and drawn . . . He was, I thought, the poorest man . . . I ever gazed upon . . . And truly he was poor in clothes . . . And poorer yet in health . . . But I discovered that he had . . . Another kind of wealth . . . For he was rich in kindliness . . . And goodness of the heart . . . There was not anything he had . . . With which he would not part . . . To everyone who passed his way . . . He gave a word sincere . . . And for each tale of troubled times . . . He had a patient ear . . . And knowing him like this, I think . . . That I would rather be . . . As poor in worldly things if I . . . Could be as heavenly.

BAKER

The baker is the busy man . . . Who bakes our daily bread . . . The staff of life that does so much . . . To keep our bodies fed . . . He gives us white, whole wheat and rye . . . And pumpernickel too . . . As well as raisin and the kind . . . That Frenchmen like to chew . . . He fashions fancy pastries and . . . The plain and sweetened rolls . . . And those delicious doughnuts with . . . Their customary holes . . . But principally his cakes extend . . . His fame throughout the land . . . Particularly on the day . . . A wedding is at hand . . . Indeed he is a busy man . . . For whom it should be said . . . His only loafing is the kind . . . That makes a loaf of bread.

YOU URGE ME ON

I want to thank you for the things . . . That you have done for me . . . To bring me joy and help me build . . . A brighter memory . . . For all your friendship in the past . . . As well as for today . . . And every time you add a smile . . . To help me on my way . . . Perhaps you do not know it but . . . The very thought of you . . . Is helping me in everything . . . I undertake to do . . . I keep your kindness in my mind . . . And when the road is long . . . I follow your encouragement . . . And life is like a song . . . And every time I mark a mile . . . Or gain another grade . . . I think of you and thank you for . . . The progress I have made.

CHIMNEY SMOKE

On every roof a chimney smokes . . . And that's a likely sign . . . The families are gathered there . . . To rest and drink and dine . . . It signifies that unity . . . And love prevail within . . . And only those who feel the same . . . Are ever welcomed in . . . It means that true Americans . . . Are living as they should . . . Contributing to make this land . . . More powerful and good . . . It shows they have a purpose and . . . A great and common goal . . . And each of them is guided by . . . A conscience and a soul . . . There is no better way on earth . . . To live and grow in grace . . . And to that end the happy home . . . Is quite the perfect place.

ANNAPOLIS MIDDIE

In uniform of navy blue . . . He practices his stride . . . To gain the great diploma that . . . Will be his joy and pride . . . He studies everything that floats . . . From raft to battleship . . . And how to guide it through the waves . . . Without the slightest slip . . . He masters mathematics and . . . The way the stars are set . . . And he is taught the perfect poise . . . Of social etiquette . . . His inspirations are the men . . . Who won our naval wars . . . And who with their courageous strength . . . Protected all our shores . . . His creed is to be honest and . . . Forever to obey . . . And in his heart he hopes to be . . . An admiral some day.

WONDERS OF LIFE

I see the sky, the earth, the tree . . . I watch the changing weather
. . . I marvel at the mystery . . . Of how they came together . . .
I wander through the fields of grain . . . The meadow sweet with
clover . . . And in the smallness of my brain . . . I try to think it
over . . . Why does a softness stir the soil . . . When spring comes
stepping lightly? . . . Why does a pot of water boil . . . When
fire holds it tightly? . . . What keeps the golden sun alive? . . .
Who knows the planets' story? . . . Whence do the moon and
stars derive . . . Their everlasting glory? . . . Each part is like a
perfect gem . . . Precisely hewn and mated . . . I only know that
all of them . . . Are things The Lord created.

WIFE IN THE KITCHEN

It seems that she is always there . . . With busy hands and eyes
. . . To please the people of the house . . . With chicken, cake and
pies . . . She has the knack of knowing when . . . The water boils
too much . . . And when the peas and carrots have . . . That soft,
inviting touch . . . She boils the eggs for breakfast and . . . She
fries the meat at night . . . For lunch she makes the sandwiches . . .
That taste exactly right . . . And in between she's occupied . . .
With cookies and the like . . . So no one in the family . . . May
start a hunger strike . . . And none would dare disturb her work
. . . Or try to change her ways . . . For in the kitchen she is lord
. . . Of all that she surveys.

MY SONG FOR YOU

If I could really write a song . . . With music soft and sweet . . .
I would compose a masterpiece . . . And lay it at your feet . . . The
melody would be divine . . . The words would be supreme . . .
And when you heard it you would think . . . That you were in a
dream . . . Of course you know I cannot write . . . And I cannot
compose . . . I am not schooled in music or . . . In poetry or prose
. . . But this is just to tell you, dear . . . I think so much of you . . .
That I would give you everything . . . That I could ever do . . .
That I adore you, darling, and . . . You mean so much to me
. . . That I am yours in all the ways . . . That I could ever be.

76

PRAYER FOR PROTECTION

O Lord, protect us from the foe . . . On every battlefield . . .
That we may never once retreat . . . Or be compelled to yield
. . . Protect our towns and homes against . . . The ravages of war
. . . And let no flood or fire find . . . A pathway to our door . . .
Watch over all our children, Lord . . . In school and on the street
. . . Protect their health in rain and snow . . . And when they
drink or eat . . . And Lord, protect us from ourselves . . . Our
greed and selfish pride . . . From anger, jealousy and hate . . .
And all our weaker side . . . Guard us against the foolish things
. . . We are inclined to do . . . That we may live a better life . . .
Of gratitude to You.

ONLY A SMILE

A friend of mine came over and . . . We talked about this life
. . . The happiness of laughter and . . . The foolishness of strife
. . . How much it means to face the world . . . With faith and
courage true . . . To undertake a certain task . . . And really see it
through . . . And how unfortunate it is . . . To sorrow and despair
. . . And not to have the confidence . . . To conquer everywhere
. . . We said some people do not see . . . The comfort they could
find . . . If they would only try to smile . . . And leave their tears
behind . . . And then we wished with all our hearts . . . That we
could find a way . . . To show the world the wisdom of . . .
A smile for every day.

GIRL IN A GARDEN

She stoops to smell the flowers and . . . To touch the petals frail
. . . She turns a longing, girlish gaze . . . Upon the moonbeams
pale . . . She dances lightly on the lawn . . . Inhales the cool, night
air . . . And glances in her mirror to . . . Adjust her flowing hair
. . . Her white and dainty fingers smooth . . . The folds about her
frock . . . And now and then she listens for . . . The chiming of
a clock . . . That little bench must be in place . . . Beneath the
darkest tree . . . And at that certain angle where . . . The people
cannot see . . . She hears the creaking of the gate . . . And footsteps drawing nigh . . . And, peering through the shadows long
. . . She breathes a gentle sigh.

WHEN YOU ARE LONELY

When you are lonely and it seems . . . The shadows never end
. . . And when you walk with empty dreams . . . Remember God,
my friend . . . Let not your eyes be filled with tears . . . That tell
your sufferings . . . But look back over all the years . . . And mark
the better things . . . Behold the beauties of the past . . . However small or few . . . That maybe were not meant to last . . .
But they were made for you . . . Hold high the courage in your
heart . . . And though you see no sign . . . Remember that your
life is part . . . Of God's supreme design . . . Remember, friend,
that God is there . . . Wherever you may be . . . And that with all
His loving care . . . He keeps you company.

YOUR CARRIER

Your carrier is just a boy . . . Who hopes someday to be . . . A
good and useful citizen . . . In his community . . . He brings the
paper to your door . . . In sunshine and in rain . . . And tries his
best to show no sign . . . Of weariness or strain . . . He makes
collections faithfully . . . And keeps his own accounts . . . And
as his savings slowly rise . . . His self-assurance mounts . . . In
school he pays attention to . . . The lesson of the day . . . And
when he has some time to spare . . . He turns to healthy play
. . . Your carrier is just a boy . . . Who does the best he can . . .
To grow in strength and character . . . And serve his fellow-man.

GOD REST YOU, MR. PRESIDENT

God rest you, Mr. President . . . Who gave your very all . . .
That men might live in liberty . . . Where tyranny must fall . . .
You shaped the strategy beyond . . . The diplomatic door . . . You
aimed our weapons and you planned . . . The peace to follow war
. . . You fought our economic ills . . . And every form of strife . . .
You struggled to provide for us . . . The more abundant life . . .
You strove for harmony at home . . . And calm across the seas
. . . You led the spearhead of attack . . . On childhood's dread
disease . . . We called you Chief and F.D.R. . . . To show our
love for you . . . And four times sought your leadership . . . To
see us safely through . . . You will be praised and honored by . . .
The world you helped make free . . . Your faith and courage will
be told . . . To all posterity . . . On marble walls and monuments
. . . Your name will stand apart . . . And it will live forever in . . .
Your country's grateful heart.

RECOMMENDATION

I like to recommend a friend . . . To people I have met . . . For credit reasons or a job . . . That he would like to get . . . And I will spend an hour on . . . The letter that I write . . . And do whatever else I can . . . To help him in his plight . . . But I must feel assured that he . . . Is worthy of that aid . . . And I must figure he is quite . . . Prepared to make the grade . . . Because as much as I would like . . . To see a guy get set . . . I would not knowingly deceive . . . The people I have met . . . And it would be unjust to him . . . To dramatize his past . . . If I had reason to believe . . . That he would never last.

THE FOLKS AT HOME

It's certainly convenient and . . . Indeed we know it pays . . . To call upon the folks at home . . . Throughout the holidays . . . But pity ma and pity pa . . . For all the work that's done . . . To make it certain that our stay . . . Will be a pleasant one . . . They have to decorate the house . . . And trim the Christmas tree . . . And set as many places as . . . They would for company . . . And entertain our youngsters while . . . We take in every sight . . . And sleep on cots while we enjoy . . . Their bedroom every night . . . And most of all, I think they do . . . Deserve a blessing when . . . They help us pack and say they hope . . . We'll visit them again.

LIFE IS A CHANCE

The world is mine to wander in . . . And dreams are mine to choose . . . But life is just a game of chance . . . And I may win or lose . . . For I may play the hand I hold . . . Or toss the cards away . . . And still there is no certainty . . . The sun will shine today . . . I may be bold or hesitant . . . And either path I take . . . May be the more successful one . . . For my peculiar sake . . . Yet somewhere as I go along . . . I surely must decide . . . And well I know I ought to let . . . My conscience be my guide . . . But whether I am satisfied . . . To linger or advance . . . The wheel of fortune goes around . . . And I must take a chance.

LET US REJOICE

Let us rejoice that Christ, our Lord . . . Has risen from the dead . . . And in the glory of His name . . . Let us be comforted . . . At Calvary upon a cross . . . He gave His life that we . . . Might someday earn the right to share . . . In His eternity . . . He saved the world from all the sins . . . We would possess today . . . If we did not repent and try . . . To live a better way . . . So let us show our gratitude . . . In everything we do . . . By being kindly neighbors all . . . And Christians good and true . . . Let us give thanks to Christ, our Lord . . . And honor Him today . . . For helping us to understand . . . And showing us the way.

LADY'S PURSE

A lady's purse is something that . . . Deserves a sort of prize . . . Especially for all it holds . . . Despite its modest size . . . It usually contains the things . . . That help her face to pass . . . Including lipstick, powder, rouge . . . And her own looking-glass . . . But also there are bobby pins . . . A handkerchief or two . . . Some cigarets and matches and . . . A bit of gum to chew . . . A list of groceries to buy . . . A letter from a friend . . . A pair of gloves, some ribbon and . . . A little cash to spend . . . And that is why the other sex . . . Is given to despair . . . When ladies board a trolley car . . . And fumble for their fare.

UNLESS I HAVE YOU

There is nothing for me if I cannot have you . . . To love and to hold in my heart . . . But if I can see that your promise is true . . . Then nothing can keep us apart . . . For a kiss and a song and the pleasure they give . . . Are only a passing delight . . . If I do not belong in the world where you live . . . From the sun to the stars in the night . . . I can carry my schemes to the top of the moon . . . I can gather a thousand charms . . . But I know that my dreams will be vanishing soon . . . If you wander away from my arms . . . I shall welcome the rain and the desert of heat . . . And forever forget every fear . . . I shall smile over pain, I shall laugh at defeat . . . If I know that your lips are sincere . . . Oh, whatever you do, let your conscience be free . . . In the promise you choose to impart . . . But unless I have you, there is nothing for me . . . And nothing to comfort my heart.

HELP YOURSELF

Help yourself to happiness . . . There's plenty to be had . . .
What's the use of crying when . . . It's easy to be glad? . . . Hold
your head up high and see . . . The sunshine all around . . . Shadows,
dust and feet are all . . . You'll see upon the ground . . .
Shake the hands of others and . . . Exchange a kindly word . . .
Let your voice be friendly and . . . Your speeches will be heard
. . . Keep on trying, even though . . . The odds against you
mount . . . Faith and perseverance are . . . The things that really
count . . . Keep your chin up all the time . . . And let them see
that smile . . . And soon you'll be acknowledging . . . That life
is worth the while.

GIVE ME YOUR CARES

When you have any tears to hide . . . Or doubts to put away . . .
Please give them all to me, my dear . . . As part of my today . . .
Let me assume whatever thoughts . . . Are heavy on your heart
. . . And let my love encourage you . . . To carry on your art . . .
Give me your weary eyes to close . . . While I endure the
night . . . And dip your dreams in silver stars . . . To make them
extra bright . . . Let me have all the little cares . . . That ever
bother you . . . That you may never have to have . . . The smallest
thing to do . . . And let me promise you, my dear . . . That when
my life is old . . . Whatever love remains in me . . . Will still be
yours to hold.

SATURDAY SHOPPING

On Saturday we shop around . . . For vegetables and meat . . .
And we particularly plan . . . To have a Sunday treat . . . We like
a roast of beef or lamb . . . With gravy thick and brown . . . And
whipped potatoes, peas and pie . . . And milk to wash it down . . .
And so we gather all we need . . . For our delicious spread . . . Including
olives, celery . . . And different kinds of bread . . . We always
buy sufficient to . . . Be sure we get our fill . . . And everything
is wonderful . . . Until we pay our bill . . . When suddenly
we stop and think . . . About our present plight . . . We have
enough for Sunday but . . . What shall we eat tonight?

I LOVE YOU, GOD

I love You, God, not just because . . . You let me have a life . . .
Or just because You blessed me with . . . My children and my wife
. . . But also, God, because Your grace . . . Is guiding me each
day . . . And You are helping me to reach . . . The goal for which
I pray . . . Because You sort of overlook . . . The faults there are
in me . . . And give me one more chance to gain . . . Your great
eternity . . . Because You understand me, God . . . . No matter
what I do . . . As long as I am constant in . . . My loyalty to You
. . . And that is why I try to live . . . In humbleness or fame . . .
According to the glory of . . . Your everlasting name.

SALVATION ARMY

They are the soldiers of The Lord . . . Whose hearts are brave
and stout . . . They are the angels of the street . . . Who help the
down and out . . . They do not look for glory and . . . They do not
ask for praise . . . They do not seek the profit of . . . Our cold and
selfish ways . . . They only want to serve the poor . . . And those
in deep despair . . . And teach a pleasure-seeking world . . . The
value of a prayer . . . They strive to soften sorrow with . . . A
bright and sunny smile . . . And show the more unfortunate . . .
That life is worth the while . . . And this is why they ask of us . . .
The little help we give . . . That faith and hope and charity
. . . And love may always live.

I HAVE MY FRIENDS

If I had nothing else in life . . . To make me glad today . . . I
would remember all the friends . . . Who ever came my way . . .
The ones who took me by the hand . . . And gave their smiles to
me . . . Who helped me on and did so much . . . To brighten
memory . . . I would remember those who spoke . . . A kindly
word or two . . . Especially at a time when I . . . Was feeling sort
of blue . . . Yes, they would all return to me . . . And linger in
my mind . . . And I would have the joys again . . . I had to leave
behind . . . But I am really not in need . . . Of happiness today
. . . Because I still have all the friends . . . Who ever came my way.

BUYING A SUIT (OR TWO)

It's hard enough to buy a shirt . . . Pajamas or a hat . . . An
overcoat, a pair of shoes . . . Or even a cravat . . . But when it
comes to purchasing . . . The suit you need so much . . . Your
whole design of life assumes . . . A sad and sorry touch . . . You
try the double-breasted type . . . And then the single kind . . . A
color that's conventional . . . And that which knocks you blind . . .
The salesman likes each one the best . . . But there's your wife, and
she . . . Appraises every coat and vest . . . With grave uncertainty
. . . You want the dark, she wants the light . . . You know not
what to do . . . Until at last in deep despair . . . You go and order
two.

SERVE OTHERS

If you would be successful in . . . Whatever things you do . . .
Give your community and church . . . At least a part of you . . .
Contribute something to the folks . . . Who live along your street
. . . If nothing more than solace when . . . They have to face
defeat . . . And when you find yourself in church . . . Remember
God is there . . . And try to ease the burden that . . . Your fellow-
man must bear . . . Be mindful of the blessings great . . . You
have received yourself . . . And slip a little share of them . . . On
someone else's shelf . . . Whatever money, work or words . . .
Your heart decides to give . . . God will be grateful for your help
. . . That someone else may live.

FURLOUGH'S END

Your time is up and you must go . . . And what is there to say?
. . . The hours are but 24 . . . In every night and day . . . It was
so good to have you here . . . If only for a while . . . To hear your
voice, to touch your hand . . . And see your loving smile . . . I
knew this moment had to come . . . And I must not complain . . .
When I return to loneliness . . . And listen to the rain . . . But
oh, my heart will call to you . . . With love and longing deep . . .
And every night I know that I . . . Shall cry myself to sleep . . .
And in the weeks that wander by . . . And vanish into space
. . . Our little world of fragile dreams . . . Will be an empty place
. . . Until the magic colors of . . . A brighter rainbow blend . . .
And you begin a furlough that . . . Will never have an end.

LET US GO TO CHURCH

On this good Sunday we are free . . . To rest, relax and play . . .
But let us not forget that we . . . Should go to church today . . .
One hour more or less we all . . . Can very well afford . . . And
there are blessings great and small . . . For which to thank The
Lord . . . There is the precious gift of health . . . And in the week
just past . . . We may have added to our wealth . . . Or gained
some goal at last . . . We may have learned a lesson taught . . . Or
made another friend . . . Or happily we may have brought . . .
Some trouble to an end . . . And we need strength along the way
. . . To keep the steady pace . . . So let us go to church today . . .
And ask His guiding grace.

APPLE POLISHER

I have no love for anyone . . . Who plays up to his boss . . .
With personal ambition that . . . He wants to get across . . . Who
constantly applauds what his . . . Superior may say . . . And
praises him for everything . . . He does from day to day . . . Who
never disagrees but who . . . Forever answers yes . . . To every
thought or notion his . . . Employer may express . . . I do dislike
the person who . . . Is ready to report . . . The least infraction
of a rule . . . Or impudent retort . . . Who undermines associates
. . . To overcome the dread . . . Of not possessing courage and . . .
The brains to get ahead.

CONVERSATION

A conversation is our way . . . Of interchanging views . . . And
weighing the significance . . . Of more important news . . . It is
the method we pursue . . . In diplomatic lanes . . . Before we strive
in earnest to . . . Consolidate our gains . . . In daily business it
precedes . . . The closing of a deal . . . And on the street it briefly
tells . . . How good or bad we feel . . . A conversation takes our
thoughts . . . And gives them to the air . . . Including all the
gossip of . . . Our women everywhere . . . It seems so indispensable
. . . Wherever humans walk . . . And yet on most occasions it . . .
Is just a lot of talk.

LOSING A FRIEND

What sadder song is there in life . . . Than bringing to an end
. . . Our fond association with . . . A really faithful friend? . . .
We share our deep desires and . . . Divide our smiles and tears . . .
And we are bound by memories . . . Of all the yesteryears . . . We
know each other's feelings and . . . We help each other out . . .
Whenever there is trouble or . . . We entertain a doubt . . . And
then we disagree and then . . . Some jealousy creeps in . . . And
each one keeps the other one . . . From managing to win . . . And
when the wind has cleared away . . . Whatever we pretend . . .
The fact remains that each of us . . . Has lost a faithful friend.

VACATIONING

I like to be vacationing . . . About this time of year . . . When
usually the sun is warm . . . And all the skies are clear . . . To
load the car with what we need . . . And pile the children in . . .
And head for some inviting spot . . . Beyond the city's din . . .
Along a new though friendly road . . . That never seems to
end . . . And where the only message is . . . The postal card I send
. . . I like to swim and fish and live . . . The easy side of life . . .
And listen to the laughter of . . . The youngsters and my wife
. . . But when the holiday is done . . . I gather up my freight . . .
And all I want is just to rest . . . And to recuperate.

THIS DAY IS MINE

This is today—and this one day . . . Is all my own to spend . . .
In wisdom or in foolishness . . . Until its very end . . . I know that
I can use it to . . . Approach a worthy goal . . . And by the way
I serve my God . . . To sanctify my soul . . . Or I can choose to
let it pass . . . As just another day . . . With nothing much accomplished by . . . What I may do or say . . . Yes, I can feed my
appetite . . . And lean against the fence . . . Or I can make another
friend . . . With true benevolence . . . This day is all my own to
use . . . My own to take or give . . . But it is only mine I know
. . . Because God lets me live.

LETTER TO YOUR HEART

I sent a letter to your heart . . . With my return address . . . And pasted on the envelope . . . My stamp of happiness . . . I dated it for every day . . . Of all the years in store . . . And started out by calling you . . . The darling I adore . . . In every line I let you know . . . How much you meant to me . . . And then I wrote my signature . . . With love eternally . . . I dropped it in the mail box where . . . The rainbow seemed to start . . . And asked the angel-carriers . . . To fly it to your heart . . . I hope they took it safely to . . . Your corner of the sky . . . And some day soon your heart will send . . . A favorable reply.

PRAYER FOR THE POOR

O gracious God, consider now . . . The poor throughout the land . . . Bestow on them a blessing with . . . Your kind and gentle hand . . . Give them the courage to endure . . . The trials they must face . . . And ease the burden they must bear . . . In their forgotten place . . . Relieve their hunger and their thirst . . . And keep their bodies warm . . . Protect them from the ravages . . . Of sickness and of storm . . . O gracious God, we ask Your help . . . For all the poor today . . . Not with a miracle but through . . . The simple, earthly way . . . By teaching and inspiring . . . The rest of us to be . . . More conscious of our duty now . . . To practice charity.

STANDING IN LINE

I do not like to stand in line . . . To eat at some café . . . While those who have consumed their meals . . . Appear to stretch their stay . . . It is amazing to behold . . . The sight of empty plates . . . And listen to the idle words . . . Of gossip or debates . . . To see them smoke and finger some . . . Imaginary speck . . . And hear them laugh out loud before . . . They fumble for the check . . . There ought to be some means by which . . . To get them out of there . . . And let the other customers . . . Peruse the bill of fare . . . The line should move much faster in . . . The popular café . . . Except when I am seated and . . . My meal is put away.

LINCOLN

His steps pursued the wiser course . . . Of work and common sense . . . That led him from his humble home . . . To public prominence . . . Familiar for his humor and . . . His slow and easy ways . . . Admired for his judgment in . . . The midst of trying days . . . He won the love and deep esteem . . . Of men by land and sea . . . For human understanding and . . . A heart of sympathy . . . There never was a duty that . . . He shirked upon this earth . . . Nor ever any beauty that . . . He did not know its worth . . . He struggled for united peace . . . And put an end to strife . . . He had to die a martyr's death . . . But saved his country's life.

FRIENDS MEAN MORE

I like to save my money and . . . To know that I am free . . . From ugly threats and challenges . . . To my security . . . I like to know I have enough . . . To meet a rainy day . . . And never have to borrow cash . . . To supplement my pay . . . But more important than success . . . Or how I make amends . . . Is just the simple knowledge that . . . I have a host of friends . . . The thought that if the days ahead . . . Should ever be in doubt . . . There are so many folks who would . . . Be glad to help me out . . . I like to have some cash reserve . . . No matter what amount . . . But far more comforting are all . . . The friends who really count.

POLICEMAN

He wears a uniform of blue . . . And sports a silver star . . . He does the way pedestrians do . . . Or travels in a car . . . He has a whistle and a club . . . His trusty .38 . . . Some tickets and a pencil stub . . . And brains to operate . . . He tells the traffic when to go . . . Helps people cross the street . . . He has a thousand rules to know . . . And he must be discreet . . . He has to practice with his gun . . . And keep himself in trim . . . To shoot the robber on the run . . . Or chase and capture him . . . He has the power to arrest . . . But all along the way . . . He has a thankless job at best . . . And more than earns his pay.

MY FAMILY

I have a wife, a daughter and . . . A pair of handsome boys . . .
What more could I expect to own . . . Of everlasting joys? . . . My
charming sweetheart keeps our house . . . And with her loving care
. . . She raises all the children and . . . She helps me everywhere
. . . Our baby girl is beautiful . . . And quite the little queen . . .
Whose winning smile completely rules . . . Our bright domestic
scene . . . While both her brothers go to school . . . To learn the
right from wrong . . . And by their love and laughter help . . . To
make our life a song . . . Yes, each of them is wonderful . . . And
each one plays a part . . . In gathering the happiness . . . That
fills my grateful heart.

NO DIFFERENT

When I was so much younger I . . . Was silently impressed . . .
With being very different and . . . Apart from all the rest . . . I
used to whisper to myself . . . That there could never be . . . Another individual . . . To quite compare with me . . . I never
thought my problems and . . . Opinions as a lad . . . Could be
considered similar . . . To those that others had . . . But as the
years went by I found . . . That I was much the same . . . As
other folks, except I had . . . My own peculiar name . . . And now
I do not mind it but . . . My heart is filled with song . . . Because
I like their kind and I . . . Am glad that I belong.

AS LONG AS YOU ARE MINE

I do not look for luxury . . . For pleasures old or new . . . I do
not ask for anything . . . As long as I have you . . . I do not keep
a calendar . . . To mark the day or year . . . I do not follow time
or tide . . . As long as you are here . . . You satisfy my every need
. . . Wherever I may be . . . As long as you are at my side . . . To
love and comfort me . . . I do not follow winding trails . . . Or
search for hidden gold . . . As long as you are in my arms . . . To
have and always hold . . . I do not want the moon or stars . . . Or
any dream divine . . . As long as you are true to me . . . As long
as you are mine.

FOR YOU THIS CHRISTMAS

May this of all your Christmas days . . . Turn out to be the best
. . . May each new hour of the clock . . . Become the happiest . . .
May all your friends remember you . . . With cards and gifts
today . . . And may you have a lot of things . . . To share and
give away . . . May all your loved ones near and far . . . Enjoy
this Christmas too . . . Because the knowledge of their joy . . .
Will mean so much to you . . . And when the New Year rolls
around . . . With 12 more months to spend . . . May health and
fortune call on you . . . And stay from start to end . . . May life
be bright and prosperous . . . And full of things that please . . .
And may it add the richest touch . . . To all your memories.

PRAYER FOR PERSEVERANCE

Lord, let Thy wisdom melt into my heart . . . And give me
courage to be always true . . . Teach me to be sincere in what I
do . . . And keep the honor of my daily art . . . Show me the way
to make another start . . . Where life is young and melodies are
new . . . Where goodness grows and jealousies are few . . . And
perseverance plays a noble part . . . For that is all that I would have
today . . . To take the proper path and persevere . . . And be un-
noticed all along the way . . . Until the end of everything is near
. . . And then, before I go, to hear them say . . . His life was like a
prayer from year to year.

TAILOR

The tailor is the gentleman . . . Who cuts and trims and sews
. . . To satisfy his customers . . . According to their clothes . . .
He takes their special measurements . . . And very skilfully . . .
He makes the suit or dress or coat . . . That fits them to a T . . . He
knows the latest styles that come . . . From Paris and New York
. . . And he can fit the barest bone . . . Or many pounds of pork
. . . With needle and with scissors and . . . A spool of thread or
two . . . He turns the pauper to a prince . . . And makes his
dreams come true . . . And while he is admired for . . . His
fashionable line . . . He also is the character . . . Whose stitch in
time saves nine.

DEPEND ON ME

My brother, if you need a hat . . . A garment or a shoe . . . I
will be glad to take it off . . . And offer it to you . . . If you need
food or lodging with . . . A place to rest your head . . . You may
partake of what I have . . . And sleep upon my bed . . . You may
have anything I own . . . Within my strength to give . . . According to the world wherein . . . The best of brothers live . . . For
that is God's design on earth . . . That we should strive to be . . .
As strong as faith, as fond as hope . . . And great as charity . . .
If you will merely call on me . . . And take me by the hand
. . . You may be sure of all the love . . . And wealth at my
command.

KRISTINA'S LUNCH

Kristina has her breakfast in . . . The high chair at our side . . .
And she consumes her cereal . . . With pleasure and with pride
. . . And when the morning meal is done . . . She leaves her lofty
stool . . . While Mommy packs the lunches for . . . The boys to
take to school . . . She runs to Mommy and insists . . . That she
should have one too . . . So she can carry it to class . . . The way
her brothers do . . . And so the package is prepared . . . And tied
with tender care . . . Although of course there really are . . . No
edibles in there . . . And while this plan produces joy . . . For our
young daughter's sake . . . We fear some day the boys will grab
. . . Her bundle by mistake.

CHARGE ACCOUNT

Some people say a charge account . . . Is not the thing to get . . .
Because it merely is a way . . . Of going into debt . . . And that
may well apply to those . . . Who do not care to pay . . . Whatever
obligations they . . . Incur from day to day . . . But charge accounts are handy for . . . The honest folks who buy . . . Especially
when cash on hand . . . Is not exactly high . . . And in addition
they support . . . The credit rating good . . . That speaks respectability . . . Throughout the neighborhood . . . The value of a
charge account . . . Depends upon its use . . . It thrives on proper
handling and . . . It withers with abuse.

DOING THE BEST

No man should ever be ashamed . . . Of how he earns his bread
. . . Or of how little he is paid . . . To keep him clothed and fed
. . . As long as what he does each day . . . Is honorable and
good . . . And he was careful to select . . . The highest job he
could . . . He should not have the least regret . . . Or envy anyone . . . While he is faithful to his task . . . And tries to get it
done . . . Because a man's success in life . . . Is measured not by
fame . . . And not by any sign of wealth . . . But how he plays
the game . . . And kings may rise and stars may fall . . . And glory
come and go . . . But God rewards the humble men . . . Who do
the best they know.

WHAT STARS ARE FOR

I used to think that stars were made . . . To light the way at night
. . . But I am so much older now . . . I know that is not right . . .
I know that God designed them and . . . He set them in the sky . . .
To make the world remember love . . . When night is passing
by . . . To charm the eyes of lovers and . . . To draw their hearts
away . . . From all the hard and certain facts . . . That crowd
the working day . . . He dipped them into silver as . . . A special
sort of mark . . . And gave them each a polish that . . . Would
twinkle in the dark . . . And filled them with a magic dust . . .
That lightly sprinkles down . . . To touch the dreams that lovers
dream . . . In every sleeping town.

WHAT GOD WANTS

God made the world for all of us . . . Not just to please a few
. . . And there are certain little things . . . He wants us all to do
. . . He wants us to be honest and . . . To do the best we can . . .
To set a good example for . . . Our friendly fellow-man . . . He
does not ask us to become . . . Great giants of success . . . To give
our lives or sacrifice . . . Our right to happiness . . . He only
wants us to be kind . . . And share the earth He made . . . To
love and help each other out . . . And not to be afraid . . . He
asks us to obey His laws . . . And keep away from crime . . . And
last and least He asks us all . . . To think of Him some time.

WINTER'S WEALTH

The day is weary on its feet . . . The sunset seems to sigh . . .
While lazy smoke from chimney tops . . . Ties ribbons to the sky
. . . The lights go on in houses and . . . The shadows move about
. . . The moon looks down and one by one . . . The silver stars
come out . . . The wind is whispering a song . . . Among the
empty trees . . . And footsteps winding through the snow . . .
Leave silent memories . . . It is the way of winter time . . . When
day has gone to bed . . . And there are cozy dreams to fill . . .
A little curly head . . . It is the richness of this life . . . To treasure
and to keep . . . It is the wealth of home and hearth . . . And
children sound asleep.

HEROES ALL

Each day we read the articles . . . Of men by east and west . . .
Our soldiers and our sailors and . . . Our fliers and the rest . . .
And there is special glory for . . . A certain name or two . . . For
deeds of extra bravery . . . They did or tried to do . . . We know
they well deserve it and . . . Their gallantry is fine . . . Because
they went beyond the point . . . Where duty draws its line . . .
But let us not forget that war . . . Is not a game of guess . . . That
teamwork is essential to . . . The smallest of success . . . That
everybody does his part . . . When buglers sound their call . .
And everything considered, they . . . Are heroes one and all.

CHOICE OF FRIENDS

I choose my friends for what they are . . . And what they mean to
me . . . And not because some lucky star . . . Has kept them company . . . I choose them not for wealth or fame . . . Or favors
they may do . . . But just because they are the same . . . When
skies are gray or blue . . . Because they mean the words they say
. . . And everything they write . . . And they would never run
away . . . And leave me to my plight . . . They share my fondest
hopes and dreams . . . And help me carry on . . . However dark
the hour seems . . . When happiness is gone . . . They are the
ones with time to spare . . . When I am looking for . . . The kind
of friends who really care . . . And last for evermore.

GIRL REPORTER

She strives to show she is composed . . . Though eager and alert
. . . And does her best to make the boss . . . Forget she wears a
skirt . . . She may not click at first but she . . . Will always try
again . . . Believing that a woman must . . . Compete with all the
men . . . She says she does not really mind . . . To have to work
at night . . . And thrills at flood and fire or . . . A homicide or
fight . . . She thinks her stories ought to have . . . A somewhat
manly touch . . . If ever she is going to . . . Amount to very much
. . . And all the while she works so hard . . . She does not know or
see . . . That she was hired to provide . . . Some femininity.

CITY

The city is a living thing . . . Composed of all our lives . . . And
taxes and the ballot are . . . The things on which it thrives . . . It
has to have its gas mains and . . . The lamps to light the way . . .
The public schools and telephones . . . For which we have to pay
. . . There must be water in the sinks . . . And hydrants on the
streets . . . Good firemen and capable . . . Policemen on their beats
. . . The garbage has to be removed . . . And sewers must be there
. . . While each improvement now and then . . . Requires some
repair . . . The city asks for many things . . . But most of all it
needs . . . The contributions great and small . . . Of our unselfish
deeds.

OFFICE OF MY OWN

I wish I had an office now . . . That I could call my own . . .
Where I could do my work each day . . . And really be alone . . .
Except of course I ought to have . . . A secretary fair . . . To tell
my many visitors . . . That I am never there . . . Except the more
important ones . . . I think I ought to meet . . . Including those
who call on me . . . To take me out to eat . . . And naturally ex-
cepting him . . . Who brings the daily mail . . . And him who
cleans the premises . . . With broom and mop and pail . . . But
otherwise I wish the world . . . Would let me be alone . . . And let
me have some office space . . . To call my very own.

THE GOLF CURSE

The would-be golfer doubts that he . . . Can play with much success . . . But he decides to try his hand . . . And hopes for happiness . . . He buys some inexpensive sticks . . . And swings them in the air . . . He only kicks some divots up . . . But then he does not care . . . He finds it fun and keeps right on . . . From country club to park . . . Until one day he manages . . . To break the hundred mark . . . And then he nearly goes insane . . . His progress seems too slow . . . He buys a set of balanced clubs . . . And studies with a pro . . . His score drops down to 80 and . . . He even passes that . . . And everyone can see his head . . . Is bigger than his hat . . . But now his life is ruined as . . . He reaches for a star . . . Because he actually believes . . . That he can better par!

COLLEGE

Among the proudest moments of . . . Our life from day to day . . . Is when we start our college work . . . At home or far away . . . We feel so very grown in years . . . And not a little wise . . . And everything we say or do . . . We sort of emphasize . . . We study law or medicine . . . Philosophy or art . . . And usually athletics play . . . A most important part . . . Fraternities, sororities . . . And clubs of every kind . . . Contribute happy hours while . . . We educate our mind . . . And then one day our hands receive . . . The coveted degree .   And we go out into the world . . . To shape its history.

TELEPHONE

The telephone appears to be . . . An instrument we use . . . To call the different numbers that . . . We are inclined to choose . . . But it is more than that because . . . It keeps our hearts in touch . . . With all the friends and relatives . . . Who mean so very much . . . It is a business calling card . . . To help us sell and buy . . . Or get a reservation when . . . We want to ride or fly . . . The telephone enables youth . . . To make or break a date . . . And it is indispensable . . . To our affairs of state . . . And so we ought to keep in mind . . . That when we are alone . . . The world is just as close to us . . . As any telephone.

A LITTLE CHANGE

When I was young I used to say . . . I would not really care . . .
To have the riches of a man . . . Who is a millionaire . . . I said
I would be satisfied . . . To have a charming wife . . . Some children and the comforts of . . . An ordinary life . . . And now I
have my family . . . And comforts by the score . . . But somehow
I keep struggling on . . . In search of more and more . . . There
are a hundred things I want . . . To please my wife and boys . . .
Including a piano and . . . A barrel full of toys . . . And judging
from our daily pace . . . I think I shall despair . . . Unless eventually I do . . . Become a millionaire.

BROKEN DATES

Some people make appointments and . . . They never seem to
care . . . If they fulfill their promises . . . Or fail to meet you
there . . . More often they will tell you that . . . They could not
be with you . . . And then they offer an excuse . . . That they are
sure will do . . . They always say how hard they tried . . . To
reach a certain spot . . . Or else they were so occupied . . . They
honestly forgot . . . Sometimes they tell you in advance . . . They
cannot keep the date . . . Because important conferences . . . Will
make the time too late . . . And while I know that there are
times . . . When all these things are true . . . More dates should
be accorded the . . . Attention they are due.

ALL THAT I KNOW

Some day when you are old enough . . . To look at wedding rings
. . . I shall be glad to counsel you . . . And tell you many things . . .
I shall endeavor to describe . . . The beauty that is love . . . And
why you will be singing songs . . . To silver stars above . . . What
makes the sun seem warmer and . . . The moon more bright and
clear . . . And why you will be happier . . . When someone else is
near . . . I shall be prompt to warn you of . . . The thorns around
the rose . . . And of the uninvited wind . . . Of loneliness that
blows . . . But if the sky should fall and if . . . Your heart should
break in two . . . I would not know what words to say . . . To
calm or comfort you.

LORD, LET ME KNOW

O Lord, if there is anything . . . That You would have me do
. . . Please let me know, that I may give . . . My gratitude to You
. . . That I may play my humble part . . . In all Your plans today . . . With every action, every thought . . . And everything I
say . . . For You have been so good to me . . . Throughout the
passing years . . . By comforting my lonely heart . . . And lessen-
ing my tears . . . You have revealed the empty frame . . . Of bitterness and strife . . . And You have shown me how to live . . . A
more enduring life . . . My happy heart is grateful for . . . The
sunshine You bestow . . . And so if I can be of help . . . O Lord,
please let me know.

LET US REMEMBER

Let us remember once again . . . Our men of World War I . . .
Who fought so bravely at the Marne . . . At Soissons and Verdun
. . . Their deeds are deep in history . . . And in our hearts today
. . . And they are worthy of more praise . . . Than we can ever
say . . . Some came back home with empty sleeves . . . On crutches
or in bed . . . And many joined the sacred ranks . . . Of our immortal dead . . . Unselfishly they sacrificed . . . To keep our country free . . . And make the world forever safe . . . For true democracy . . . In reverence let us bow our heads . . . And by our silent
gun . . . Let us remember and salute . . . Our men of World
War I.

POACHED EGGS

If I am staying overnight . . . I always tell my host . . . I want
two eggs for breakfast and . . . I like them poached on toast . . . I
have my morning eggs at home . . . But frequently my wife . . .
Has her ideas concerning how . . . I ought to go through life
. . . She says the eggs are just as good . . . When heated up to
boil . . . And surely they require less . . . Of trouble and of toil
. . . Sometimes the children want them fried . . . Or scrambled
in a mess . . . And she reminds me that I should . . . Promote their
happiness . . . And so I naturally enjoy . . . My breakfast with a
host . . . Who knows I want a pair of eggs . . . And like them
poached on toast.

BANKER

The banker keeps your money but . . . He lets you spend it too
. . . And when you need more ready cash . . . He makes a loan to
you . . . Of course he takes a mortgage on . . . Your auto, house
or lot . . . And he expects your payments to . . . Be met right on
the dot . . . Although if you have rotten luck . . . The chance is
not remote . . . That he will talk it over and . . . Perhaps renew
your note . . . He gives you checks and calendars . . . And for your
bonds and stocks . . . He offers you the rental of . . . A safe de-
posit box . . . His banking hours seem to end . . . With time to
stretch and yawn . . . But actually his work begins . . . When all
the shades are drawn.

GREETING

A greeting is a little thing . . . That means so very much . . .
Especially the kind that has . . . The warm, congenial touch . . . It
brings a friendship closer and . . . Reminds you of it too . . . And
sometimes is the reason why . . . You win a friendship new . . . It
makes the worst of enemies . . . Feel rather mean and small . . .
And makes them wonder why they were . . . Your enemies at all
. . . It gives a ray of sunshine to . . . The beggar on the street . . .
And gladdens him who is too ill . . . To be upon his feet . . . And
whether it is spoken or . . . Conveyed in written style . . . It never
fails to melt a frown . . . And substitute a smile.

WASTE-BASKET

The basket on the office floor . . . Is meant to gather waste . . .
But many are the papers that . . . Are tossed in there in haste . . .
And sometimes quite important ones . . . Are idly thrown away . . .
And then there is a hurried search . . . To save the business day
. . . At other times the items are . . . Not needed any more . . .
And they are promptly put in there . . . To keep them off the floor
. . . In such a basket there are things . . . That are considered
trash . . . Though oftentimes they play a part . . . In multiplying
cash . . . But they have little value when . . . The janitor comes in
. . . To dump the basket's gatherings . . . In some forgotten bin.

WHEN YOU BECAME A MOTHER

When you became a mother, you . . . Began another life . . . And gave me twice the pride and joy . . . To call you spouse and wife . . . You took the stars from all the skies . . . And laid them at my feet . . . Fulfilled the dearest dream I had . . . And made my world complete . . . You gathered up the fragrance rich . . . Of every flower fair . . . And scattered it along my path . . . Of duty and of care . . . When you became a mother, you . . . Were brave as brave can be . . . To suffer and to sacrifice . . . For mankind and for me . . . And that is why I love you so . . . And that is why I say . . . I cannot thank you half enough . . . Today and every day.

MY WAY OF LIVING

I know it is advisable . . . To plan the years ahead . . . And have enough to eat and have . . . A roof above my head . . . I know how good it is to save . . . Against that rainy day . . . When all my plans may suddenly . . . Decide to go astray . . . But also I remind myself . . . That this one day must count . . . And that each passing moment is . . . A valuable amount . . . And so I give my deepest thought . . . To every hour new . . . And make the most of minutes that . . . Are all too brief and few . . . In other words, I live today . . . The best that I know how . . . And let tomorrow wait until . . . Tomorrow's time is now.

THE CHANGING STARS

The stars are not so different now . . . From those that sparkled yesteryear . . . And yet they cannot be the same . . . I saw the others disappear . . . I saw them growing pale and dim . . . I watched them vanish from the sky . . . And it was like the moment when . . . I kissed your lips and said good-by . . . And then the darkness drew away . . . And there were streaks to mark the dawn . . . The bright red sun came slowly up . . . And you and all the stars were gone . . . No, they are not the same tonight . . . These stars that show their light to me . . . But they resemble those I saw . . . Before you were a memory . . . And so I like to look at them . . . And wonder why they must be new . . . Because I wish they were the same . . . And I could see them shine on you.

COBWEB

A cobweb is a dainty thing . . . Suspended from the ceilir
It is a work of art but it . . . Conveys a creepy feeling . . . It
fingers reach through space . . . In every known direction . . . It
hides its face in corners dim . . . And oft escapes detection . . . It
is a flimsy looking thing . . . And yet it holds together . . . Ignoring
time and being all . . . Unmindful of the weather . . . Preferring
peaceful solitude . . . It shies from light and luster . . . And it
is plainly fearful of . . . The searching broom and duster . . . It
is a sign of things once new . . . To older things converted . . . It
marks the place by life and love . . . And laughter long deserted.

POST-WAR PRAYER

Almighty God, not long ago . . . When we were in a war . . .
We called on You to help us win . . . What we were fighting for
. . . And though today we all enjoy . . . The peace we prayed for
then . . . We come to You on bended knee . . . To ask Your help
again . . . We should be grateful for the chance . . . To live a better
life . . . But now we find ourselves embroiled . . . In many forms
of strife . . . Our old domestic problems seem . . . To grow in size
each day . . . Where greed is trying hard to take . . . Our reasoning
away . . . We need Your help, Almighty God . . . To bring
us down to earth . . . That we may all appreciate . . . What peace
is really worth.

LOVE

The element of love is that . . . Which no one can describe . . .
We know we cannot purchase it . . . Or gain it with a bribe
. . . We cannot manufacture it . . . Or ever change its course . . .
Not even when the highest judge . . . Pronounces a divorce . . . It
is a certain sentiment . . . That fills the human heart . . . And
forces all our selfishness . . . And reason to depart . . . It may fly
out the window or . . . Remain upon the sill . . . But we can never
summon or . . . Dispose of it at will . . . It is a certain something
that . . . Is neither old nor new . . . And that will last as long as
life . . . If it is really true.

WINDY CITY ROUNDUP

The wind from blue Lake Michigan . . . Is riding herd again
. . . Straight through Chicago's busy streets . . . Its women and its
men . . . It kicks up all the dust and dirt . . . Stampedes across
the Loop . . . It tramples parks and playgrounds and . . . It scat-
ters every group . . . It lassoes unprotected legs . . . With lariats
of cold . . . It brands the noses, cheeks and ears . . . Of all the
young and old . . . It gallops into buildings where . . . The doors
are left ajar . . . And hurls its roaring strength against . . . The rolling truck and car . . . The wind from blue Lake Michigan . . . Is
wild and young and rough . . . It rides without a saddle and . . .
It never gets enough.

NORWAY'S DAY

Each year this day is Norway's day . . . To celebrate its life . . .
And it is also mine because . . . Of my beloved wife . . . She came
from Norway where the sun . . . Looks down upon the fjords . . .
And where the vikings blazed their trail . . . With unrelenting
swords . . . The land where shining bravery . . . Has always kept
its name . . . And one that through the centuries . . . Has gained
immortal fame . . . It is a valiant country where . . . The breath of
life is free . . . And men will fight to keep their right . . . To peace
and liberty . . . Today belongs to Norway but . . . We all should
celebrate . . . The freedom of its citizens . . . So friendly and so
great.

CABBY

The taxi driver rolls along . . . From morning until night . . . Or
else he undertakes his rounds . . . When there are stars in sight . . .
He gets a call to go somewhere . . . Or merely drives away . . . In
search of some good pick-up that . . . Will multiply his pay . . .
His destination is the bus . . . Or train he has to meet . . . The
ball park, hospital or just . . . A number on a street . . . The famous or forgotten man . . . His company may share . . . But everyone who rides with him . . . Is just another fare . . . His passengers
consider him . . . A hero when it rains . . . And if each trip includes a tip . . . He never once complains.

FRIENDLY STRANGERS

I like the simple friendliness . . . Of strangers on the street . . .
Who have the grace to say hello . . . To anyone they meet . . .
Who never hesitate to smile . . . And lend a helping hand . . . Or
listen to a tale of woe . . . And try to understand . . . Who give
directions if they can . . . And when the rain comes down . . . Will
share their own umbrella with . . . The other folks in town . . . I
always like the strangers who . . . Display their pleasant smiles . . .
To ease the burden of this life . . . And lighten weary miles . . . I
like their simple friendliness . . . Wherever they may go . . . Because they are polite and kind . . . To those they do not know.

NOTE FROM TEACHER

My Jimmie brought a note from school . . . Relating certain facts
. . . About the time the teacher had . . . With Jimmie and his
tacks . . . It seems the youngster had a way . . . Of putting them
around . . . So there would be a sudden shout . . . Whenever they
were found . . . Well, I informed him I was grieved . . . To have a
wayward son . . . Who sacrificed his studies for . . . A bit of foolish fun . . . I frowned as sternly as I could . . . And told him he
should be . . . A better boy if he would make . . . His mark in
history . . . But when I signed the little note . . . That he was told
to bring . . . I smiled as I remembered how . . . I did that very
thing.

LET OTHERS LIVE

Let us be truly tolerant . . . And let us always give . . . Consid-
eration to the way . . . Our neighbors want to live . . . Let us respect their views on life . . . Though we may not agree . . . For
after all they have the right . . . To their philosophy . . . There is
no good to be attained . . . By prejudice or wrath . . . And bigotry
can only bring . . . A harmful aftermath . . . Let us not judge another now . . . Lest we be criticized . . . Let us not walk with scorn
and hate . . . Or we may be despised . . . But let us practice
tolerance . . . And we will surely find . . . That it is worth our
while to be . . . Considerate and kind.

COTTON COMING

The cotton fields are flowering . . . The bolls are fluffy white . . .
And soon we shall be taking in . . . The old familiar sight . . . The
picture of a pair of hands . . . That labor all the day . . . To gather
up the cotton for . . . The mules to haul away . . . The busy place
where it is ginned . . . And seeds are taken out . . . To make another crop next year . . . For folks to talk about . . . The bales that
fill the warehouse and . . . The samples that are sent . . . To get
the grade and staple from . . . The U. S. Government . . . King
Cotton is the one on whom . . . The clothing mills depend . . .
And who reminds us yearly that . . . The farmer is our friend.

O FATHER OF MEN

O God, The Father of all men . . . Hear now our humble plea
. . . Enable us to do our best . . . For our community . . . Help us
to be deserving dads . . . And raise our children right . . . That
they may be good citizens . . . And worthy in Your sight . . . We
want to teach them all we know . . . And guide them on their way
. . . To honesty in every task . . . And fairness in their play . . .
Encourage us to be the kind . . . Of men we ought to be . . . That
our example may endure . . . For all posterity . . . O God, The
Father of all men . . . Inspire us today . . . To show our children
how to live . . . According to Your way.

FORGOTTEN?

Do you remember when we met . . . And what I said to you . . .
And how you turned your head and smiled . . . And said you loved
me too? . . . Do you remember now, my love . . . The promises
we shared . . . Or have these many days disturbed . . . The way
you always cared? . . . Why do you never write me when . . . You
know I am alone? . . . Why is it not your voice when I . . . Pick
up the telephone? . . . You told me I would never be . . . Forgotten in your heart . . . No matter where, no matter how . . . We
had to be apart . . . But now I wonder if you meant . . . Your
promise to be true . . . Because I never see you and . . . I never
hear from you.

WHEN YOU COME BACK

Some day in autumn or in spring . . . When you are done with war . . . Your heart will look for everything . . . The way it was before . . . The house you left will be the same . . . Albeit worse for wear . . . The town will have its honored name . . . Your neighbors will be there . . . Perhaps not all of them because . . . Some went away with you . . . While others will have had to pause . . . As old folks have to do . . . Yes, life must move its restless feet . . . The clock must turn its hands . . . The wings of progress oft are fleet . . . Ambition never stands . . . But all that freedom meant to you . . . When you went into war . . . Will be magnificent and true . . . The way it was before.

JEWELER

He operates a store in which . . . The windows always shine . . . With many different articles . . . Of delicate design . . . He deals in gold and silver and . . . In platinum and such . . . As well as certain diamonds . . . That seem to cost too much . . . He carries brooches, lavalieres . . . And jewels fit for kings . . . And all those sacred wedding bands . . . And bright engagement rings . . . His trade includes engraving work . . . Of any kind you choose . . . And how to make you happy by . . . Preserving baby shoes . . . He handles handsome watches and . . . The clocks with bells that chime . . . And gladly does the best he can . . . To keep the world on time.

COMPANIONSHIP

Companionship means more to me . . . Than many other things . . . Because of all the pleasure and . . . The happiness it brings . . . It means that someone else is there . . . To hear what I would say . . . And in a dozen different ways . . . To pass the time of day . . . To give me courage and advice . . . And lend a helping hand . . . And talk in simple terms about . . . The things we understand . . . Companionship is friendship in . . . The truest sense of all . . . And it designs the fondest dreams . . . Our memories recall . . . It is the bridge that spans the stream . . . Where icy waters flow . . . And it unites us heart and soul . . . With someone nice to know.

103

MY WORRIED WIFE

She worries over little things . . . Like shoes that need repair . . .
A broken cup or saucer or . . . A single graying hair . . . She frets
if Jimmie has a cold . . . Or wheezes in the night . . . Or if his
brother, Donnie, is . . . Not feeling quite all right . . . A muddy
track upon the floor . . . A bed that is not made . . . And any
dozen things like that . . . Will make her look dismayed . . . But
if a great catastrophe . . . Or problem comes along . . . She takes
it right in stride, as though . . . Not anything were wrong . . . She
clears the hurdles high and wide . . . As if equipped with wings
. . . But always she is worrying . . . About the little things.

BURNED FINGERS

When children get their fingers burned . . . Their minds become
aware . . . And usually it teaches them . . . To exercise more care
. . . But we who shape the world today . . . Forget the deepest
burn . . . And though we ought to benefit . . . We never seem to
learn . . . We blunder into something and . . . We pay the price
and then . . . In just a little while we make . . . The same mistake
again . . . Sometimes in life the flame is one . . . We cannot help
but touch . . . But frequently it seems that we . . . Are not concerned too much . . . It matters not how old we are . . . Or what
we may have learned . . . We fool around again until . . . We get
our fingers burned.

GOVERNMENT EMPLOYE

The government employe is . . . A person who is paid . . . According to the duties of . . . A salary and grade . . . Who twice a
month receives a check . . . That very soon is spent . . . To cover
I.O.U.'s and pay . . . For groceries and rent . . . While something
is deducted to . . . Provide for later years . . . When energy grows
less and less . . . And all but disappears . . . The government employe is . . . A creature much decried . . . By those whose party
politics . . . Are on the other side . . . A public servant who must
know . . . A thousand rules or more . . . And faithfully perform
the best . . . In peace as well as war.

MY PHILOSOPHY

When I was young and life was still . . . A little strange to me
. . . I started in to formulate . . . My own philosophy . . . And yet
it was not all my own . . . For much of it was part . . . Of all the
songs and happy dreams . . . That fill the human heart . . . I
wanted to be kind and good . . . And faithful to each vow . . . And
do as much for others as . . . The hours would allow . . . To serve
my God and country and . . . Be worthy of my wife . . . And educate our children to . . . The finer things in life . . . And if today
I have some cause . . . For happiness and pride . . . It is because
by God's good grace . . . I know that I have tried.

PRAYER FOR DADDY

Dear God, be good to Daddy dear . . . On this his special day
. . . And grant that everything he wants . . . Will always come his
way . . . For he has done so much for us . . . And tried so hard to
be . . . A kind provider of the best . . . For all the family . . . He
strives to make our life at home . . . As happy as a song . . . And
never voices one complaint . . . When anything goes wrong . . .
We know that when he is alone . . . He worries quite a bit . . . But
when he sees us he just smiles . . . And never mentions it . . . He
is so good to all of us . . . So loyal and sincere . . . Please listen to
our prayer, O God . . . And bless our Daddy dear.

PRAYER FOR MOTHER

Dear God, be good to Mother dear . . . And bless her heart today . . . For she has been so good to me . . . And kind in every
way . . . Remove the wrinkles from her brow . . . Dispel her every
care . . . And let the stardust mingle with . . . The silver in her
hair . . . Give her the comfort she deserves . . . And make her
dream come true . . . By helping me to give the best . . . That I
could offer You . . . Be good to Mother dear, O God . . . Reward
her wondrous worth . . . And multiply by many years . . . The time
she has on earth . . . For she has done so much for You . . . If only
by the way . . . She has inspired me to live . . . A better life today.

WINDOW WASHER

The window washer's job is one . . . That I would never seek
. . . Especially when he goes up . . . To reach a certain peak . . .
He puts a belt around him and . . . He hooks it to the wall . . .
And I am sure he says a prayer . . . That he will never fall . . . But
on the other hand he has . . . A perfect chance to see . . . What
things are going on inside . . . Some busy company . . . And I
imagine now and then . . . His eyes behold a scene . . . That was
not meant to be a part . . . Of making windows clean . . . And yet
wherever he may go . . . In sunshine or in rain . . . It seems to me
he always is . . . Confronted with a pane.

IT MEANS SO MUCH

Your friendship means so much to me . . . Because with every
dawn . . . It brings me new encouragement . . . And faith to carry
on . . . It helps my struggling mind to solve . . . The problems of
the day . . . And when the shadows show themselves . . . It
brushes them away . . . It gives a deeper meaning to . . . The
nobler things there are . . . And adds to every joy I find . . . However near or far . . . Your friendship is a comfort when . . . The
sun is going down . . . And when the gentle night appears . . . In
gold and silver gown . . . It guides me through the darkness and
. . . It keeps my spirit free . . . And in a thousand other ways . . .
It means so much to me.

WELCOME, WOUNDED

We welcome you with open arms . . . Who gave your very best
. . . To conquer tyranny and win . . . The wars of East and West
. . . Who come on crutches, in your beds . . . Or with your empty
sleeves . . . In token of the things in which . . . Each countryman
believes . . . We honor you for loyalty . . . And courage to the last
. . . And hope your suffering will soon . . . Be hidden in the past
. . . You may be sure that all of us . . . Are more than glad to do
. . . However much is possible . . . To brighten life for you . . .
Because you gave a part of you . . . To hold our fighting ranks . . .
And by your sacrifice you earned . . . Our everlasting thanks.

CHECK

A check is just an instrument . . . In lieu of cash on hand . . .
That tells our bank to pay a sum . . . Of money on demand . . . It
is a piece of paper that . . . We sign a certain way . . . To get some
goods or services . . . For which we have to pay . . . But also it
affords a means . . . To demonstrate that we . . . Are good and
honest and possess . . . Respectability . . . It is a sort of calling card
. . . That really tells our name . . . And whether we are truthful
or . . . We ought to walk in shame . . . Because we know or ought
to know . . . How much we have or lack . . . And if our check
will clear or if . . . It will be coming back.

NOSEY NEIGHBOR

She pries into your private life . . . (It always is a "she") . . .
Intent upon discovering . . . What secrets there may be . . . She
watches from her window when . . . You're sitting home alone
. . . She never fails to listen in . . . Each time you telephone . . .
She notices the clothes you wear . . . She hears the things you say
. . . She knows exactly how you spend . . . Your time from day
to day . . . If Tommy has the measles she . . . Can tell you what to
do . . . And if your husband's working late . . . She adds up two
and two . . . She always publicly proclaims . . . Her motives are
the best . . . While everybody else agrees . . . She is an awful pest.

SO MUCH TO DO

I have so many things to do . . . Before I call it quits . . . That
there are times when life becomes . . . A challenge to my wits . . .
I want to finish every task . . . I ever have begun . . . Because I do
not want to leave . . . The smallest thing undone . . . There are
the friends who need my help . . . Although they may not ask . . .
And there are other folks for whom . . . I could perform a task . . .
And then there is my family . . . That means so much to me
. . . And must be given love and care . . . And helped financially . . . And so my hands are really filled . . . With things I
have to do . . . And I just hope I have the time . . . And strength
to see them through.

RED CROSS NURSES

They are the women who heed the call . . . Of duty by day or
night . . . They are the women who give their all . . . For the
wounded in every fight . . . They are the angels of mercy true . . .
Whether for friend or foe . . . They are the ones who follow
through . . . Wherever the fires glow . . . Theirs are the hands
that heal the hurt . . . Theirs are the hearts that pray . . . Theirs
are the tongues that are never curt . . . At the end of a gruelling
day . . . They are the ones who deserve the aid . . . That all of us
can bestow . . . The kind of aid that will never fade . . . But will
always grow and grow . . . So let us give to the final cent . . . That
honestly we can spare . . . Because we know it will all be spent . . .
For the wounded over there.

WE ARE IN LOVE

I know you will be true to me . . . As I am true to you . . . And
in our joy the gentle sky . . . Will be forever blue . . . I know the
moon will glow and all . . . The stars will seem more bright . . .
Because together we will hold . . . The beauty of the night . . .
And every time the dawn appears . . . The purple hills will fade
. . . And in the golden sun our hearts . . . Will never be afraid . . .
Because we are so much in love . . . That we are bound to be . . .
Together in our every thought . . . And every memory . . . And
that is why I tell myself . . . My dream is coming true . . . As I
begin the happiness . . . Of sharing life with you.

LET ME SERVE YOU

If there is any little thing . . . That you would have me do . . .
I shall be more than glad to be . . . Of service unto you . . . If you
are needing comfort or . . . The counsel of a friend . . . Whatever
I can give will be . . . A privilege to extend . . . And though you
may consider it . . . Enormous in its weight . . . I hope you will
not fear to ask . . . Or even hesitate . . . For that is what a faithful
friend . . . Is really meant to be . . . The kindly voice, the helping
hand . . . The soul of sympathy . . . And just by asking me you
will . . . Be doing kindness too . . . Because you will be giving me
. . . The joy of serving you.

PRAYER BEFORE VICTORY

Almighty God, we need Your help . . . On battlefronts today . . .
To conquer with our weapons and . . . To put the foe away
. . . This is the hour of our need . . . Far greater than before . . .
As here we stand upon the verge . . . Of victory in war . . . Be-
cause we cannot now afford . . . To lose what we have gained . . .
And we must move in wisdom when . . . The freedom is attained
. . . Give us, O God, the strength we need . . . To deal the final
blow . . . That peace may light the sky again . . . And fertile fields
may grow . . . Give us the rest we need so much . . . That we may
build anew . . . And ultimately dedicate . . . A better world to
You.

CURE FOR A COLD

Whenever I contract a cold . . . Whatever time of year . . . My
friends and neighbors offer me . . . Their sympathy and cheer . . .
And each one has a remedy . . . That is by far the best . . . According to experience . . . And undisputed test . . . They tell me they
have tried them all . . . And that they know for sure . . . Their
method is the only one . . . That guarantees a cure . . . Indeed I
do appreciate . . . What they would do for me . . . But I would
never have the time . . . To try each remedy . . . And I am somewhat doubtful I . . . Would live another day . . . If I used everyone's advice . . . To take my cold away.

HITCH-HIKER

He stands along the highway or . . . Upon the city street . . .
And signals to the passing cars . . . To offer him a seat . . . He
wants to keep from paying out . . . The customary fare . . . Be-
cause he knows he does not have . . . The cash to get him there . . .
And so he tries to thumb a ride . . . And when he does succeed
. . . It is because some driver likes . . . To do a kindly deed . . .
But now and then the friendliness . . . Of transportation free . . .
Invites a desperado and . . . Results in tragedy . . . And so the one
who needs a ride . . . Ought never to complain . . . When drivers
leave him standing in . . . The middle of a rain.

REAL FOLKS

The kind of folks I like to meet . . . Are those whose hearts are gay . . . And who become your friends before . . . The passing of a day . . . You get together and you talk . . . And after while it seems . . . That you have known them all your life . . . If only in your dreams . . . Perhaps you dine with them or have . . . A cup of tea or two . . . Or maybe you just sit around . . . And see the evening through . . . But all of you have put away . . . The cloak that strangers wear . . . And there are pleasant moments of . . . Companionship to share . . . Your hearts are drawn together in . . . The meaning of a smile . . . And you have found the friendliness . . . That makes this life worth while.

BOUND TO WIN

I often wonder if our boys . . . Eventually will be . . . A most substantial credit to . . . Their mother and to me . . . I know they are intelligent . . . And eager to succeed . . . And they are conscientious in . . . Performing every deed . . . But life has many twists and turns . . . And people talk of fate . . . And sometimes when mistakes are made . . . Tomorrow is too late . . . And yet I always tell myself . . . That they will be all right . . . Because they are sincere of heart . . . And brave enough to fight . . . They may not be the proteges . . . That constantly astound . . . But they are honest and they keep . . . Their feet upon the ground.

OUT OF THE PAST

I can remember years ago . . . Upon a winter's night . . . When all the paths were paved with snow . . . And all the stars were bright . . . I lingered on the quiet shore . . . Of old St. Mary's Lake . . . And said if I were there no more . . . My heart would surely break . . . I told myself that all my dreams . . . Were woven into one . . . While now it definitely seems . . . They are forever done . . . I cannot ever find again . . . The joys that used to be . . . And now the gold that glittered then . . . Is just a memory . . . But that is life and that is why . . . Some things can never last . . . Although a part of every sky . . . Is taken from the past.

MY ALPHABET

If I composed an alphabet . . . It would not be so long . . . In
fact, eight letters would suffice . . . For any speech or song . . . The
first would be the letter "I" . . . And then the letter "L" . . . With
"O" and "V" and "E" in turn . . . To fit the pattern well . . . The
next would be a "Y" and then . . . Another "O" would do . . . And
for the last, though not the least . . . I'd have the letter "U" . . .
They'd come right in the order named . . . And capitals they'd be
. . . To emphasize the line of words . . . Divided into three . . .
And just to give my alphabet . . . A sort of final spark . . . I'd
punctuate the sentence with . . . An "!"

MISFORTUNE

Misfortune is a cruel thing . . . That takes us by surprise . . .
Just like a sudden thunderstorm . . . That darkens all the skies . . .
It wipes away the savings we . . . Have tried so hard to keep . . .
And leaves us all unsettled and . . . Incapable of sleep . . . It tears
in two the plans we make . . . It drives us to despair . . . And it
removes the clouds beneath . . . Our castle in the air . . . And yet
misfortune is a thing . . . Almighty God decrees . . . Among so
many other things . . . That are His mysteries . . . We have no
right to question Him . . . Or what He wants to do . . . But if we
keep our faith with Him . . . He helps our dreams come true.

UMBRELLA OF DREAMS

Sometimes I think it rains too much . . . And things get
extra wet . . . But I do not allow myself . . . To worry or to fret
. . . Not just because I realize that . . . I cannot stop the rain . . .
And that I know it does no good . . . To murmur or complain
. . . But in the simple thought that if . . . I try to do my part . . .
No flood can ever sweep away . . . The sunshine in my heart . . .
No shower can extinguish faith . . . No deluge can deny . . . My
happiness when all my hopes . . . Are reaching to the sky . . . And
so I let the rain come down . . . And go my merry way . . . Enjoy-
ing all the sunshine of . . . The dreams that fill my day.

SONG COMPOSER

The song composer is the one . . . Who draws those strange designs . . . That rise and fall and sometimes curve . . . Within a group of lines . . . He manufactures melodies . . . To guide the dancing feet . . . Or gives the highly cultured ear . . . An operatic treat . . . He fashions popular refrains . . . For singers on the air . . . And he prepares the holy hymns . . . For churches everywhere . . . He has to struggle hard at first . . . And many years may pass . . . Before he is considered in . . . The more successful class . . . He tries out all the different notes . . . And when he makes them fit . . . He hopes his composition will . . . Become a current hit.

FRIENDLY TOWN

The little town has many charms . . . With which to gather fame . . . And make its people extra proud . . . To mention it by name . . . And more than all its other traits . . . And qualities combined . . . Is that of being courteous . . . Considerate and kind . . . Of being sympathetic in . . . A manner warm and true . . . Not only in its circle but . . . To every stranger too . . . It smiles and says good-morning and . . . Good-evening and good-night . . . And in so many other ways . . . It strives to be polite . . . It welcomes everybody with . . . Its friendly, open arms . . . And proves a little town can be . . . A place of many charms.

FISHERMAN

The fisherman is anyone . . . With rod and reel and line . . . Who thinks he knows exactly when . . . The fishing will be fine . . . He rows around an endless lake . . . Or wades into a stream . . . And big and many are the ones . . . He catches in his dream . . . He loves to look upon the trout . . . The flounder, perch or bass . . . And where the sea is deep enough . . . The marlin is his class . . . He says it is a game of skill . . . That takes a lot of pluck . . . And yet each time he baits his line . . . He hopes for better luck . . . He may have caught 10,000 fish . . . But he will always say . . . The biggest and the finest was . . . The one that got away.

EVER FORWARD

Another year has run its course . . . Twelve months have come and gone . . . However we have used the time . . . We have to carry on . . . However great our glory now . . . Or ill the wind that blew . . . There is another year ahead . . . With many things to do . . . The hours are not long enough . . . To ponder or regret . . . For there are struggles to be faced . . . And problems to be met . . . Then let us gird ourselves anew . . . And keep our courage high . . . And to the pattern of the past . . . Now briefly say good-by . . . Let us ask God for stronger faith . . . And nobleness of mind . . . Let us go forward in the dawn . . . And never look behind.

NEW GRANDDAD

A man becomes a daddy and . . . His chest expands with pride . . . He walks on air and everywhere . . . He has a healthy stride . . . But have you ever seen the one . . . Who jumps around with joy . . . Because his son or daughter has . . . A baby girl or boy? . . . They call him "gramps" or grandpa or . . . Some other name like that . . . And you can bet his head is twice . . . The size of any hat . . . He used to dread the day when he . . . Would be considered old . . . With nothing more than courtesies . . . And memories to hold . . . But when he sees that baby he . . . Forgets to eat his lunch . . . Because he is a granddad now . . . And just as pleased as punch!

WHEN HE PROPOSES

When he asks for your hand . . . And you gaze in his eyes . . . Do you stop to consider . . . That he is a prize? . . . Does it ever occur . . . To your proud little mind . . . That suitable swains . . . Are not simple to find? . . . That when he appears . . . To be humble and shy . . . He merely is holding . . . Your picture up high? . . . That he has selected you . . . Out of the mass . . . Of maidens of every . . . Description and class? . . . And that when he gives you . . . The rest of his life . . . He gives you the honor . . . Of being his wife?

MY BIRTHDAY PRAYER

I thank You, God, for giving me . . . Another year of life . . . Surrounded by my children and . . . My faithful, loving wife . . . I thank You for the blessings great . . . That we have all enjoyed . . . For health and food and shelter and . . . For keeping me employed . . . My heart is ever grateful for . . . Your comfort and Your aid . . . The little luxuries and for . . . The progress I have made . . . I know that I did not deserve . . . So many things from You . . . And probably You found my prayers . . . Too hasty and too few . . . But, God, however poor my past . . . Performance may appear . . . Please help me live a better life . . . Throughout the coming year.

WIND

I like to listen to the wind . . . That whistles in my ear . . . When I am walking on the street . . . And all the sky is clear . . . I like the wind that howls at night . . . When snow is at my door . . . And burning logs reflect their blaze . . . Upon the cozy floor . . . And then there is the roaring wind . . . That whips and rolls the sea . . . To add a new adventure and . . . A thrilling memory . . . I follow all the winds that blow . . . Across the fields of grain . . . And those that push the smoke away . . . And mingle with the rain . . . But most of all I like the wind . . . That comes along in spring . . . The gentle wind that whispers love . . . And makes me want to sing.

BROKER

The broker gets the goods you need . . . To put upon your shelf . . . And yet he does not handle the . . . Commodity itself . . . He is the go-between who knows . . . How much there is on hand . . . And what percentage it will take . . . To satisfy demand . . . He plays a sort of double game . . . Because he serves the trade . . . By helping merchants and the ones . . . By whom the goods are made . . . Or it may be his specialty . . . To deal in bonds and stocks . . . Where customers may gather wealth . . . Or lose their shirts and sox . . . And as for his reward in life . . . The busy broker gets . . . The kind of reputation and . . . Commission that he nets.

WITH YOU, MY LOVE

I want to be beside you, love . . . Wherever you may go . . . And share with you the sun, the stars . . . And all the winds that blow . . . I long to be your friend for life . . . And give you everything . . . Of beauty and of happiness . . . The golden years can bring . . . My heart is never sad unless . . . Your own is feeling blue . . . And in the magic of your smile . . . My hopes and dreams come true . . . I never want to leave you but . . . I want you for my own . . . Because when you belong to me . . . I never am alone . . . I want to be with you, my love . . . Through hours brief and long . . . And share with you the melody . . . Of every little song.

IF WE WERE RICH

Sometimes my wife and I discuss . . . How pleasant it would be . . . If we were very wealthy and . . . There were no work for me . . . It would be such an easy life . . . With nothing more to do . . . Than eat and sleep and entertain . . . And shop for something new . . . Our comforts would be cared for by . . . The butler, maid and cook . . . And all the other servants in . . . A rich man's story book . . . But then we sit and wonder how . . . My hours would be spent . . . When I would weary of the ways . . . Of my retirement . . . And we agree our life would be . . . More thoroughly enjoyed . . . If I had something that would keep . . . My idle time employed.

DOING WHAT IS RIGHT

As there is glory in the day . . . And beauty in the night . . . So there is something to be gained . . . By doing what is right . . . It may not be so pleasant and . . . There may be times indeed . . . When there are little lessons we . . . Are not inclined to heed . . . But what is there to gain from wrong . . . With reason to rejoice . . . When God has given each of us . . . A conscience with a voice? . . . It may be difficult at first . . . To break the older tie . . . But gradually we struggle free . . . And reach up to the sky . . . And there we find it possible . . . To overcome the odds . . . And share in all the glory and . . . The beauty that are God's.

OUR KINDLY KING

God will forgive our sins if we . . . Are sorry and sincere . . .
And if our mind to make amends . . . Is purposeful and clear . . .
He wants to know we mean it when . . . We promise to be good
. . . And that we will abide by all . . . The principles we should
. . . And then He will bestow on us . . . The strength we always
need . . . To give the best there is in us . . . By thought and word
and deed . . . He longs to help us grow in grace . . . And wisdom
day by day . . . And to depend on us to help . . . Our neighbor
on his way . . . Although He passes judgment while . . . He
watches from above . . . God is our kindly King Who rules . . .
With mercy and with love.

MEMENTO

She must have been a saintly soul . . . Unlike this world of strife
. . . That ever God should call her in . . . The very bloom of life
. . . When youth is reaching out with arms . . . Untouched by
qualm or dread . . . To happiness and beauty and . . . To all that
lies ahead . . . When dreams are in the making and . . . A song
is in the air . . . For him to kiss and her to blush . . . And love
to linger there . . . When hearts are bound together by . . . The
trysts of yesteryears . . . And time is only something to . . . Record
the smiles and tears . . . She must have been a creature fair . . .
With eager eyes and gay . . . For angels of the night to come . . .
And carry her away.

THE FOUR FREEDOMS

Freedom of worship and freedom of speech . . . Freedom from
want and fear . . . These are the things for which we fight . . .
The things we hold so dear . . . Freedom of conscience in choosing
a church . . . And freedom in going there . . . For marriage, bap-
tism, to be confirmed . . . Or silently offer a prayer . . . Freedom of
saying whatever we think . . . Whether in heart or in mind . . .
Voicing opinion for all to hear . . . Passive or cruel or kind . . .
Freedom from hunger and bitter cold . . . Freedom from deep despair . . . From shadow and noose and firing squad . . . Following
everywhere . . . These are the freedoms for which we fight . . .
Wherever we wage the war . . . These out of all the things on earth
. . . Are worth while fighting for.

LAWYER

You talk to him about yourself . . . And what is troubling you . . . And from his law books on the shelf . . . He tells you what to do . . . If he agrees to take your case . . . (With promise of a fee) . . . He searches every legal trace . . . To find your remedy . . . He files the papers, goes to court . . . And strives to prove your claim . . . With references of every sort . . . Including dates and names . . . He does the best he can to draw . . . The jury to your side . . . And patiently expounds the law . . . To have it thus applied . . . He struggles days and studies nights . . . To win the suit for you . . . He is the guardian of your rights . . . Your friend and counselor true.

ONE KINDLY DEED

If I can do one kindly deed . . . For someone else on earth . . . I shall consider that my life . . . Has carried out its worth . . . I do not mean the simpleness . . . Of offering a smile . . . But something generous that would . . . Be so much more worth while . . . Some sacrifice that would portray . . . The good I want to do . . . To prove to someone that I am . . . A faithful friend and true . . . I want to do my very best . . . And give the most I can . . . To ease the heavy burden of . . . My friendly fellow-man . . . To help him walk the weary way . . . That leads him to his goal . . . That God may gain the gratitude . . . Of one more human soul.

CLERK

He walks around or stands behind . . . The counter in a store . . . He spends his hours in a bank . . . Or on an office floor . . . He serves the buying public or . . . He labors at a desk . . . But for the clerk there is no time . . . For leisure or burlesque . . . He has to be on time each day . . . To tackle all his woes . . . And always he must stay until . . . The final whistle blows . . . He does not have a union and . . . He is the hardest hit . . . When prices soar beyond the point . . . Where there is sense to it . . . He may become a president . . . Or owner of a store . . . Or he may struggle as a clerk . . . For 50 years or more.

I SPARE THE ROD

My wife insists our little girl . . . Is willing to obey . . . As long
as I am not at home . . . To play with her all day . . . She tells me
that I do my best . . . To spoil and pamper her . . . By letting her
do everything . . . Her fancy would prefer . . . Well, I will not
deny my guilt . . . Or try to hide my sin . . . Whatever my young
daughter asks . . . I usually give in . . . But after all in years gone
by . . . I spoiled her brothers too . . . And now they are a splendid
pair . . . Of youngsters fine and true . . . And while it may be just
good luck . . . As my dear wife declares . . . I think a child is
better off . . . By all the love it shares.

PARTLY LUCK

I know I struggled to attain . . . The place I hold today . . .
And many hours that I worked . . . I might have spent in play
. . . It never was an easy path . . . And there were times when I
. . . Considered whether I should quit . . . Or keep my courage
high . . . But I would be untruthful if . . . I did not now admit
. . . That there were certain lucky breaks . . . That played a part
in it . . . That God was always at my side . . . And when my
hopes grew dim . . . I found untold encouragement . . . In keeping faith with Him . . . And every time my lips were poised . . .
To drink a bitter cup . . . Some unforeseen event occurred . . . To
lift my spirits up.

I LIVE FOR YOU

When you are lonely and your tears . . . Are difficult to hide
. . . Remember, darling, I would be . . . Forever at your side . . .
When all your other friends are gone . . . (If ever that should be)
. . . Let not your heart forget that you . . . Can still depend on
me . . . And though the deepest tragedy . . . May wander in your
wake . . . You may be sure I live my life . . . For your beloved sake
. . . Because I love you, darling, as . . . A sweetheart and a friend
. . . From every moment now until . . . Eternity may end . . .
Because you fill my heart with joy . . . And make my dreams come
true . . . And you are just so wonderful . . . I think the world of
you.

FRIENDS TO SHARE

Whatever friends I have are yours . . . Wherever they may be . . . And may they be as good to you . . . As they have been to me . . . I hope that you will come to know . . . How much they all have meant . . . And why the very thought of them . . . Has kept my heart content . . . I do not want you to infer . . . That they and I are through . . . But merely that I long to share . . . The best of friends with you . . . They are the ones who never fail . . . In time of need or stress . . . For they are constantly concerned . . . About your happiness . . . They understand and sympathize . . . And they will give or lend . . . And so they show the way in which . . . I want to be your friend.

FOOLISH MAN

He is a foolish man who tries . . . To walk upon this sod . . . Without the aid of others and . . . Without the help of God . . . Who is so learned in his ways . . . That he can do without . . . What anyone might offer him . . . To overcome a doubt . . . He does not try to understand . . . That God is everywhere . . . And only God himself can give . . . The answer to a prayer . . . He is a foolish man who thinks . . . That he can walk alone . . . And be admired by the ones . . . To whom His name is known . . . For everyone should welcome help . . . To get his labor done . . . And only by the grace of God . . . Is any battle won.

TOUCH OF SPRING

A touch of spring is in the air . . . While winter makes a truce . . . The wind is warm, and everywhere . . . The ground is soft and loose . . . The sky is blue, the golden sun . . . Is smiling as before . . . The shadows vanish one by one . . . The snow is now no more . . . The lonely days are in retreat . . . Where happiness commands . . . And there are children in the street . . . With marbles in their hands . . . Beyond the hill the sea is still . . . And waiting at the bay . . . Are they who know their vessel will . . . Be sailing home some day . . . A woman slowly drops her shawl . . . The farmer rests his plow . . . The chimney smoke is gone and all . . . The doors are open now.

YOUR LETTER

The sun is really bright today . . . And all the skies are blue
. . . Because the letter in my hands . . . Is one that came from
you . . . It lifts me to the clouds again . . . And melts away my
fears . . . And only out of happiness . . . Do I have any tears . . .
It just arrived and yet it seems . . . I know it all by heart . . . And
nothing gives me greater joy . . . While we must be apart . . .
Your phrases and your paragraphs . . . Are beautiful designs . . .
And I can read the secret thoughts . . . You wrote between the lines
. . . Each word is like a precious gem . . . That sparkles in the
light . . . And when I see your signature . . . I hear you say good-
night.

DREAM HOUSE

Some day we plan to build a house . . . As tall and long and
wide . . . As we believe would really have . . . The space we need
inside . . . With bedrooms for the children and . . . A playroom
of their own . . . And then a special room or two . . . Where
guests could be alone . . . A dining room and living room . . .
Sufficient in their size . . . To serve and entertain the friends . . .
With whom we socialize . . . A kitchen and a study and . . . A
place where servants stay . . . And quite a large garage in which
. . . To put our cars away . . . Some day the house we plan to
build . . . Will be a dream come true . . . But in the meantime
we will make . . . Our little cottage do.

DOG

He follows you around the house . . . And out upon the street
. . . Wherever you may wander, he . . . Is always at your feet . . .
He wants to just be near you and . . . To get a pat or two . . . And
in return he tries to learn . . . What he's supposed to do . . . Like
being very quiet when . . . Your visitors arrive . . . But set to scare
a stranger or . . . To chew him up alive . . . He plays with you
and wags his tail . . . To let you know it's fun . . . He longs to
make you understand . . . That you're the only one . . . He's
loyal and attached to you . . . Through happiness and strife . . .
And if there were a need for it . . . He'd gladly give his life.

ALONE WITH YOU

I like to sit and talk with you . . . And dream the night away
. . . Nor do I mind if all our plans . . . Are made to go astray . . .
For there is so much pleasure in . . . A simple thought or two
. . . Our notions of tomorrow and . . . The things we want to
do . . . The happiness of seeing you . . . With eyes of beauty
bright . . . Across the dinner table in . . . A quiet gleam of light
. . . The silvery sound that is your voice . . . The gesture of your
hand . . . And something in the way you nod . . . That shows you
understand . . . And every little word you say . . . Whatever it may
be . . . That may not bother you one bit . . . But means so much
to me.

LET ME BE USEFUL

Let not my life be useless, Lord . . . But help my heart to be . . .
Of some enduring benefit . . . To all humanity . . . I want to do
the best I can . . . As long as I am here . . . To light the way for
someone else . . . With kindliness and cheer . . . To do a worthy
deed or two . . . And generously give . . . Whatever I can do without . . . To help my neighbor live . . . I want to be of service, Lord
. . . And answer every call . . . With words of gentle sympathy
. . . And charity to all . . . Enable me to rise above . . . The bitterness of strife . . . And every moment of each day . . . To live a
useful life.

DISH DECISION

When I make up my mind to have . . . A meal at some café . . .
Invariably I am not sure . . . What I shall eat that day . . . I look
the menu up and down . . . And carefully compare . . . The items
for consumption that . . . Comprise the bill of fare . . . I ponder
over meat and fish . . . The salads smooth as silk . . . The
soups, desserts and vegetables . . . And coffee, tea or milk . . .
And then I glance around the place . . . And suddenly I see . . .
Another diner with a dish . . . That looks real good to me . . . And
whether it is high in price . . . Or sure to make me fat . . . I call the
waiter and I say . . . "Just bring me some of that."

FRIENDSHIP HOUSE

The sun is always shining in . . . The home where friendship
lives . . . Where life is measured not by tears . . . But by the joy
it gives . . . Where hands are clasped in greeting and . . . The
warmth of love is shown . . . And every word is spoken in . . .
An understanding tone . . . The flowers are forever fair . . . Where
kindly thoughts abide . . . Where there is never any room . . .
For jealousy or pride . . . Where sympathy and sacrifice . . . And
cheerfulness prevail . . . And smiles of true encouragement . . .
Are like an endless trail . . . The sun is always shining and . . .
The sky is always clear . . . Where friendship lives and sentiments
. . . Are honest and sincere.

BOYS AT THE TABLE

The table manners of my boys . . . Could stand some brushing
up . . . Including how they wield a knife . . . And how they hold
a cup . . . They use their forks at proper times . . . The way most
people do . . . But I regret to say that they . . . Employ their
fingers too . . . Right after grace, in record time . . . They stow
their food away . . . For they are more concerned about . . .
Returning to their play . . . I try to teach them etiquette . . . And
keep my temper sweet . . . But they are not concerned about . . .
The way in which they eat . . . And yet whenever they have dined
. . . In someone else's den . . . Their host reports that they have
been . . . The perfect gentlemen.

GETTING EVEN

There is no comfort to be gained . . . From settling up a score
. . . Except to satisfy our pride . . . When we are good and sore
. . . We tell ourselves how terribly . . . Our feelings have been
hurt . . . Because what someone said to us . . . Was critical and
curt . . . Or maybe in some other way . . . We have sustained a loss
. . . And we consider it unfair . . . To have to bear that cross . . .
But getting even does not change . . . The color of defeat . . . And
in the last analysis . . . Revenge is never sweet . . . It is much better
to assume . . . The sorrow we have met . . . And have the noble
courage to . . . Forgive and to forget.

POPCORN TIME

My wife objects to popcorn when . . . We see a picture show . . .
Though popcorn is my paradise . . . When I agree to go . . . She
tells me that she cannot stand . . . The crackling, crunching sound
. . . And she maintains that it disturbs . . . The patrons all around
. . . But I am never happy when . . . I sit before the screen . . .
Unless I have some popcorn fresh . . . To go with every scene
. . . It seems to me this pleasure is . . . A most important part . . .
Of trying to appreciate . . . The motion picture art . . . Because
a box of popcorn keeps . . . My stomach satisfied . . . Throughout
the time my eyes and ears . . . Are so preoccupied.

PRAYER FOR MOTORISTS

God, give me health and common sense . . . To drive the way I
ought . . . To watch the road and follow all . . . The rules I have
been taught . . . I will observe the signs that say . . . To stop or
lessen speed . . . And when some child appears ahead . . . I will
take special heed . . . I will be careful at each turn . . . Of motions
that I make . . . To let the other drivers know . . . The course
that I would take . . . I will be mindful of the wheel . . . The
pedals on the floor . . . The shift, the mirror, instruments . . .
And tightness of each door . . . I promise to be sober, God . . .
And always drive my best . . . Just give me health and common
sense . . . And I will do the rest.

TRADITION

Tradition is a noble thing . . . That keeps the past awake . . .
And often helps us to avoid . . . A serious mistake . . . It is the
path of pioneers . . . Who found it straight and true . . . And
who left every gate unlocked . . . For others to go through . . .
It is the honored mark of time . . . Upon the brow of earth . . .
For those who struggled yesteryear . . . To prove their better worth
. . . Tradition is a thing that we . . . Should contemplate and
weigh . . . And try to follow in the life . . . We live from day to
day . . . It ought to be our guiding star . . . However high we
climb . . . Unless we find it interferes . . . With progress in our
time.

MY YEAR BOOK

Here is my stewardship, O Lord . . . Of what I tried to be . . .
And how I spent the year You made . . . Available to me . . . I
wasted many hours in . . . Pursuit of idle play . . . While putting
off some urgent task . . . Until another day . . . I could have
spoken kinder words . . . And done a good deal more . . . To serve
Your other servants, Lord . . . Who knocked upon my door . . .
My heart became discouraged and . . . I frequently complained
. . . Because the road was difficult . . . Or just because it rained
. . . But every day I said my prayers . . . However brief and few
. . . And never once throughout the year . . . Did I lose faith in
You.

MY WORLD TODAY

Whenever I relax and I . . . Have time to dream away . . . I like
to think of how the world . . . Is getting on today . . . I do not
mean the nations and . . . The problems that are theirs . . . Or
mighty corporations with . . . Their monetary cares . . . But I refer
to Joe and Tom . . . Who live across the street . . . And if their
wives and children have . . . Enough to wear and eat . . . If Mary
had her baby and . . . The doctor was on time . . . And why my
youngsters have to have . . . A nickel or a dime . . . In other words
whenever I . . . Have time to dream away . . . I dream about the
little world . . . Where I belong today.

NO LOVE RATION

Oh, they can ration gasoline . . . And radios and cars . . . And
they can cut our cake in two . . . But not the moon and stars . . .
Yes, they can give us half a suit . . . And just a single glove . . .
And they can parcel sugar but . . . They cannot ration love
. . . We'll have to use less butter and . . . Go easy on the cream . . .
But who is there to tell us we . . . Are not allowed to dream?
. . . So why be blue and downcast if . . . They give us less to
eat . . . When love is free and plentiful . . . And infinitely sweet?
. . . Why worry over taxes or . . . The luxuries we knew . . .
When there is no priority . . . On happiness for two?

I WANT TO HELP YOU

I want to be the kind of friend . . . That means so much to you
. . . That you will always think of me . . . In everything you
do . . . That you will always call on me . . . When I might be
of aid . . . To help you out or keep your heart . . . From being
too afraid . . . I want you to remember that . . . Wherever I may
be . . . I am prepared to serve you in . . . The least capacity . . .
That I will use my knowledge and . . . What strength I may possess
. . . To make each day along your way . . . A time of happiness
. . . And that it is a joy to me . . . Whenever I can do . . . Some
favor that may pave the path . . . Where all your dreams come true.

GARBAGE MAN

If we turn up our nose at him . . . Who hauls our garbage off
. . . Or if we feel the least inclined . . . To ridicule or scoff . . .
We ought to stop and ask ourselves . . . How we would live today
. . . If no one ever gathered it . . . And carted it away . . . The
odor would be bad enough . . . But also there would be . . . A dire
menace to the health . . . Of our community . . . We ought to be
more conscious of . . . His most important deed . . . Because in
doing what he does . . . He fills a vital need . . . He helps promote
the cleanliness . . . Of houses and cafés . . . And for his service he
deserves . . . Our gratitude and praise.

THE WORLD

The world is a strange and a wonderful place . . . Where everyone comes and goes . . . And everyone has a particular face . . .
With eyes and a mouth and a nose . . . Where everyone stumbles
before he walks . . . And learns how to eat and drink . . . And
everyone jabbers until he talks . . . Of anything he may think . . .
The world is a place where the rain comes down . . . And the tears
are free to flow . . . Where a man may move to another town . . .
And put on another show . . . Where a welcoming hand and a
friendly smile . . . Are the tokens of brotherly love . . . And life
is the length of an endless mile . . . To the silver stars above.

MY WONDERFUL WIFE

My wife is very beautiful . . . And also very smart . . . And that is why I cherish her . . . With all my loving heart . . . She is my earning power and . . . My money in the bank . . . And if I have a claim to fame . . . I have my wife to thank . . . She is my inspiration and . . . The key to my success . . . And everything she ever does . . . Is for my happiness . . . She cleans the house and cooks the meals . . . And faithfully attends . . . To all the social niceties . . . Of entertaining friends . . . She keeps the children healthy and . . . Encourages their fun . . . Indeed my wife is wonderful . . . Beyond comparison.

DREAM OF DELIGHT

I look at the stars in their heavenly height . . . And I wander the ocean blue . . . For the wonderful dream that I dream tonight . . . Is a dream of delight with you . . . And the marvelous glow of the crystal snow . . . Wherever the paths divide . . . Is a beautiful thing that only the spring . . . Is ever prepared to hide . . . I gaze in your eyes and I gather your sighs . . . And I wonder what fortunate fate . . . Invited me here to the atmosphere . . . Of the roses around your gate . . . And always I dream in the gleam of the stars . . . Of the day when my dream will come true . . . And my heart may abide in the joy and the pride . . . Of being together with you.

COMMAND ME, LORD

Whatever You may ask of me . . . I am at Your command . . . Because I want to serve You, Lord . . . With heart and soul and hand . . . I want to do Your holy will . . . Whatever day or night . . . And thereby try to make myself . . . More worthy in Your sight . . . I owe so much to You, O Lord . . . For all that You have done . . . Especially in crowning me . . . With battles I have won . . . For all the comfort and the grace . . . That You have given me . . . To help me on my way to Your . . . Sublime eternity . . . And so if there is anything . . . That I can ever do . . . Please let me know, O Lord, because . . . I owe my life to You.

SO YOUNG, SO GOOD

A smiling lad of 13 years . . . So good in every way . . . Obedient and diligent . . . And courteous and gay . . . A brilliant little scholar and . . . A pious altar boy . . . He made his parents proud of him . . . And gave them every joy . . . No task, however difficult . . . Could stay his forward stride . . . Before his soul was summoned by . . . The God of time and tide . . . The God Who knows and Who alone . . . Can tell the reason why . . . Some men grow old and weary while . . . A youngster has to die . . . A youngster on his way from church . . . Where holiness begins . . . And where he asked forgiveness for . . . The things he thought were sins.

CARTOONIST

He draws the comic characters . . . We look for every day . . . To find a brighter moment as . . . We go along our way . . . He may prepare a story strip . . . Or just a single pose . . . But always he is helping us . . . To put away our woes . . . He draws our daily incidents . . . However old or new . . . And causes us to chuckle at . . . The funny things we do . . . His style is very simple but . . . If he is really good . . . His work is human, to the point . . . And quickly understood . . . He sketches out the misery . . . Of struggle and of strife . . . And substitutes the humorous . . . And happy side of life.

BUY A BOND

If those little tears have started . . . And you're blue because you've parted . . . With a blonde . . . Just forget about that honey . . . Let your smile be bright and sunny . . . And with what you save in money . . . Buy a bond . . . If your profits are not steady . . . And your clerk is getting ready . . . To abscond . . . Don't be grumbling and complaining . . . Just forget that it is raining . . . And with what you have remaining . . . Buy a bond . . . When you hear your country calling . . . It is time to quit the stalling . . . And respond . . . Don't depend upon your mother . . . On your sister or another . . . Just get out your cash and, brother . . . BUY A BOND!

Good fortune brought me to your door . . . And when you heard me knock . . . I was invited in without . . . The turning of a lock . . . Your welcome was as warm as if . . . You had expected me . . . And just as if your heart had longed . . . To have my company . . . You wore the smile of friendship and . . . You made me feel at ease . . . And in so many other ways . . . You did your best to please . . . And when I saw your kindly eyes . . . And touched your helping hand . . . I knew that you would always be . . . The one to understand . . . I knew that I could go to you . . . However long the night . . . And you would always comfort me . . . Until the morning light.

BOOKKEEPER

The books he keeps are those that make . . . A gay or gloomy boss . . . According to the tale they tell . . . Of profit or of loss . . . They show how much is taken in . . . And what is spent each day . . . Including that percentage small . . . That constitutes his pay . . . He enters all the items from . . . A carload to a stamp . . . While he adjusts his eyeshade to . . . The brilliance of the lamp . . . He checks the inventory and . . . The value of each chair . . . And charges off the dusty debts . . . When debtors cease to care . . . His knowledge of the business books . . . Makes him a priceless gem . . . As long as he is dutiful . . . And does not juggle them.

SNUGGLE-BEAR

Kristina snuggles up to me . . . Upon the couch or chair . . . And that is why I call my girl . . . My little Snuggle-Bear . . . There are a lot of other names . . . I call my daughter dear . . . Including Woopsie, Baby Doll . . . And Buttercup of Cheer . . . But she is always happiest . . . And proud as she can be . . . Whenever I say Snuggle-Bear . . . And hug her close to me . . . She keeps reminding Mommy and . . . Her brothers of that name . . . As though it were her calling card . . . To everlasting fame . . . Kristina is my Snooksie and . . . My Texas Flower fair . . . But more than any other thing . . . She is my Snuggle-Bear.

PRAYER FOR EVERY DAY

Today, O God, I want to rise . . . And give my thanks to You
. . . For having helped me yesterday . . . In all I tried to do . . .
And then I want to ask You for . . . Your grace again today . . .
That I may not be weak enough . . . To waste my time away
. . . That I may keep my vision clear . . . And recognize my
goal . . . And do whatever else I should . . . To sanctify my soul
. . . I want to ask You to bring out . . . The better things in me . . .
That I may be a worthy part . . . Of my community . . . That I
may not go selfishly . . . In search of foolish fame . . . But live my
life for this one day . . . In honor of Your name.

VASE

A vase is used for flowers fair . . . To keep them fresh and bright
. . . And stand them in a special place . . . For everyone's delight
. . . But now and then the vessel is . . . Of greater use than
these . . . For those who live in hopes and dreams . . . Or dwell
in memories . . . It is the fond remembrance of . . . A gift from
someone dear . . . Or it has held the roses of . . . A sweeter yesteryear . . . It is a palace on the path . . . Of promises and plots . . .
Where love belongs to lilacs or . . . The soft forget-me-nots . . . A
vase may be a place to keep . . . The flowers fresh and bright . . .
Or it may be a loving cup . . . Of silver stars at night.

FARMER AT WAR

The farmer's rifle is his plow . . . His tractor is his tank . . . His
uniform of overalls . . . Denotes his worthy rank . . . His cotton
and his corn and wheat . . . And all the crops he sows . . . Comprise the ammunition for . . . His devastating blows . . . His
irrigation ditches are . . . The trenches that he digs . . . And he is
sounding reveille . . . When calling to his pigs . . . His fences are
entanglements . . . To keep the foe away . . . His windmill is the
beacon light . . . That guides the ships to bay . . . And when he
sells his milk and eggs . . . And buys a bond or two . . . He shows
he is a soldier and . . . A sailor through and through.

FRIENDLY DOOR

The friendly door is that approach . . . Where no one has to knock . . . And any key of kindly thought . . . Will turn the only lock . . . It is a door that opens wide . . . And seems to say hello . . . However cold may be the rain . . . Or wild the winds that blow . . . It warmly welcomes everyone . . . Who may be passing by . . . Without regard to name or fame . . . Or even whence or why . . . The friendly door swings back and forth . . . Without a squeak or creak . . . Or barrier to anything . . . The visitor may seek . . . It is the door to pleasure in . . . A palace or a hut . . . Except for those who wear a frown . . . And try to slam it shut.

KRISTINA'S BED

Kristina has her little bed . . . In which she sleeps at night . . . And where she always takes her nap . . . On rainy days and bright . . . She likes it very much and when . . . Her lunch is stowed away . . . She lets me put her in there for . . . A portion of the day . . . But when the silver stars appear . . . Around her curly head . . . She wants to go to Sleepy Town . . . On Mommy's cozy bed . . . And so she takes her dolls in there . . . To keep her company . . . And then she says good-night to God . . . And hugs and kisses me . . . And after she is sound asleep . . . I take her up from there . . . And put her in her little bed . . . And in God's loving care.

THE THINGS WORTH WHILE

I have been trying to decide . . . What things are most worth while . . . And these I think are all of them . . . A prayer, a deed, a smile . . . A prayer to God in gratitude . . . For all that He has done . . . And to petition Him for strength . . . In battles to be won . . . A faithful deed to serve each need . . . And answer every call . . . Especially for charity . . . However great or small . . . And just to have the friendly smile . . . That brightens up the day . . . And does so much to lighten cares . . . And take the clouds away . . . Yes, these I think are all of them . . . A prayer, a deed, a smile . . . To fill the world with happiness . . . And make this life worth while.

I OFFER YOU MY HEART

I cannot promise you success . . . With pockets full of gold . . .
Or everlasting happiness . . . For you to have and hold . . . I cannot give the heavens blue . . . The waves that rise and fall . . .
I have my heart to offer you . . . And that is all . . . I do not own
a large estate . . . Or any part of fame . . . And there is nothing
really great . . . Connected with my name . . . I do not have a
palace new . . . With pleasures to enthrall . . . I have my heart to
offer you . . . And that is all . . . So many others can provide
. . . The luxuries there are . . . And be forever at your side . . .
As constant as a star . . . But I may never be so true . . . Or build
a house so tall . . . I have my heart to offer you . . . And that is all.

LITTLE CHURCH

I like the little church that stands . . . Upon a humble street . . .
Or in the quiet country where . . . The friendly farmers meet
. . . It may not have a gilded dome . . . Or spires grand and tall
. . . Or any wonderful design . . . To grace the door or wall . . .
It may not boast of windows stained . . . With scenes of holy
art . . . But always it extends to all . . . A welcome from the
heart . . . I like the little church because . . . It struggles every day
. . . To keep on going and to serve . . . The gentle souls that
pray . . . And most of all because it has . . . That sweet and peaceful air . . . In which we cannot help but feel . . . That God is
really there.

UNANSWERED LETTERS

They are the silent calling cards . . . Upon a silver tray . . .
That gather dust the while the host . . . And hostess are away . . .
They are as weary travelers who . . . Keep knocking at your door
. . . Beseeching you to look at them . . . And read their thoughts
once more . . . Or much as friends who hail you when . . . They
see you passing by . . . And hope that you will favor them . . .
With some polite reply . . . They are the ghosts that haunt your
room . . . At night when you undress . . . And constantly remind
you of . . . Your social tardiness . . . They are the only answer to
. . . The question why you fail . . . To slow the postman's footsteps and . . . To gather in more mail.

TOAST TO LIFE

I count my disappointments and . . . I add my pleasures up . . .
I mix them all together and . . . I pour them in a cup . . . And
then I drink a toast to life . . . For such as it may be . . . And to
the pattern that is part . . . Of every memory . . . The laughter and
the little tears . . . The sunshine and the rain . . . The summer
sky, the winter snow . . . Beyond the window pane . . . The magic
nights I spent with you . . . When stars were overhead . . . And
all the plans we made and all . . . The promises we said . . . I
drink a toast to life and love . . . And everything they hold . . .
And to the memories to be . . . Some day when I am old.

NEXT DOOR TO US

The folks who live next door to us . . . Are not so far away . . .
In fact we often overhear . . . Whatever words they say . . . We do
not mean to listen to . . . The things that they discuss . . . And
we are not concerned when they . . . Decide to have a fuss . . .
But when we occupy our porch . . . Our ears are never more
. . . Than just a dozen feet or so . . . From their own kitchen
door . . . Their gossip always reaches us . . . Across that little space
. . . Unless we play the radio . . . Or go some other place . . .
And that is why we plan to buy . . . A vast amount of ground . . .
So we may live in privacy . . . And never hear a sound.

BECAUSE OF YOU

If life is wonderful today . . . And hope is born anew . . . If I
am happy in my heart . . . It is because of you . . . It is because I
tell myself . . . That you have faith in me . . . And your devotion
and your love . . . Are boundless as the sea . . . If every struggle is a joy . . . And every task is light . . . It is because the
thought of you . . . Makes every moment bright . . . It is because
you comfort me and . . . When you hold my hand . . . I know
without a word from you . . . How well you understand . . .
And if my humble efforts help . . . To make your dreams come
true . . . It is because my grateful heart . . . Is so in love with you

I THANK YOU, GOD

This prayer, O God, is not to ask . . . For blessings great or small
. . . For comfort, happiness, success . . . Or anything at all . . .
But just to let You know, O God . . . My gratitude today . . . For
everything that You have done . . . To help me on my way . . .
To thank You for the strength of heart . . . That You have given
me . . . And for protecting me from harm . . . And painful injury
. . . For faith and freedom, work and rest . . . Enough to eat and
drink . . . And words of wisdom from Your lips . . . To guide me
when I think . . . A prayer to thank You and to say . . . That I
will try to do . . . The best I can to show You, God . . . I mean
my thanks to You.

TELEGRAM

The message sent by wire is . . . An expeditious way . . . To tell
a friend or relative . . . The words we want to say . . . It is the
flying messenger . . . Of thoughts that we express . . . To offer love
and sympathy . . . Or wish for happiness . . . To open up and close
a deal . . . Or just negotiate . . . And say the plane, the bus or train
. . . Will be on time or late . . . A telegram may be concerned . . .
With anything on earth . . . From death or graduation to . . . A
wedding or a birth . . . It is a speedy means by which . . . To get
our message through . . . And know that there will always be . . .
A record of it too.

SIGNS OF SPRING

The leaves are turning green again . . . The snows are disappear-
ing . . . And soon the spring will come again . . . With all its
charms endearing . . . The birds will sing their songs again . . .
And children will be playing . . . The flowers will be beautiful
. . . With petals gently swaying . . . And everywhere will be the
signs . . . That tell about this season . . . When maidens blush
and gentlemen . . . Are less inclined to reason . . . The moon will
grow romantic and . . . The stars a little brighter . . . Young lips
will meet and gentle arms . . . Will squeeze a little tighter . . .
But husbands will remain the same . . . And they will know the
meaning . . . Of certain signs that indicate . . . The house will get
a cleaning.

MEASURE OF LIFE

What does it matter if I live . . . For 50 years or one . . . As long as I have time enough . . . To get my duty done? . . . The more important thing in life . . . Is trying to decide . . . What talent I possess and how . . . It ought to be applied . . . How I can use that gift from God . . . (As everybody should) . . . To bring about more happiness . . . And do the greatest good . . . To help my neighbor and to serve . . . My country in its need . . . With kindness and sincerity . . . In every word and deed . . . It matters not to me how long . . . I dwell upon this sod . . . I merely do the best I can . . . And leave the rest to God.

SUN ON MY SADDLE

The sun is on my saddle and . . . The spur is on my boot . . . The wind is at my elbow and . . . My gun is set to shoot . . . But I am not for hunting and . . . My aim is not to kill . . . For I am riding to my love . . . Who lives on yonder hill . . . And I am bringing flowers and . . . Some candy from the store . . . To let her know my feelings when . . . I ride up to her door . . . I want to see her standing in . . . Her pretty apron there . . . And try to get up nerve enough . . . To tell her that I care . . . And when the stars are shining and . . . My horse is sound asleep . . . I want to hear her lips declare . . . That she is mine to keep.

IF I COULD PAINT

If I could paint the mountains . . . The heavens I have seen . . . The swirling, sparkling rivers . . . The rolling fields of green . . . The snow that flies in winter . . . The soil that turns in spring . . . The sunshine of the summer . . . The nightingales that sing . . . If I could etch the raindrop . . . That gently splatters down . . . The autumn leaves in festive garb . . . Of yellow, red and brown . . . The rose so rich in redolence . . . Beside a garden wall . . . The golden moon, the silver stars . . . And all the winds that call . . . I'd linger in a meadow where . . . The weeping willow nods . . . And fashion you a picture of . . . The beauty that is God's.

OUR FAMILY PRAYER

Almighty God Who gave us life . . . To You we humbly pray
. . . To You we dedicate our deeds . . . And all our dreams today
. . . To You we turn for counsel and . . . The grace to do Your
will . . . And to respect the vows that we . . . Have chosen to
fulfill . . . Please be the guardian of our home . . . Watch over us
and bless . . . Each member of our family . . . With health and
happiness . . . Give us the richness of this life . . . And guide our
steps with care . . . That we may never fail You, God . . . Or
falter anywhere . . . Teach us to live as Christians in . . . Obscurity
or fame . . . And so bring everlasting praise . . . And glory to
Your name.

CHAIRMAN

A chairman is the chosen head . . . Of some directors' board . . .
Whose job it is to stimulate . . . A spirit of accord . . . Or he is one
whose duty is . . . To rule a meeting hall . . . And listen to the
arguments . . . Advanced by one and all . . . He supervises pro-
grams and . . . Proposes certain tasks . . . And tries to answer
everything . . . That anybody asks . . . If there is too much noise
he pounds . . . The gavel in his hand . . . In order to remind the
crowd . . . That he is in command . . . He has to be a patient soul
. . . Equipped with common sense . . . And he must be a leader
who . . . Inspires confidence.

SEWING MACHINE

Of all the articles we own . . . The most productive one . . . Is
that machine on which my wife . . . Gets all her sewing done . . .
It hums from morning until night . . . To make the dresses fair
. . . Our little daughter models for . . . And loves so much to
wear . . . It patches pants for little boys . . . Who have to go to
school . . . And makes pajamas that will keep . . . Their bodies
warm or cool . . . It hems the curtains and it mends . . . My trou-
ser pockets too . . . To keep what little change I have . . . From
ever slipping through . . . Indeed it is an instrument . . . That
adds a lot to life . . . And sews up my affection for . . . My very
busy wife.

YOU LOVE HIM

I know you are in love with him . . . I see it in your eyes . . .
And all your cynical remarks . . . Are only a disguise . . . You do
not want to have your love . . . Exposed beneath the sun . . . As
long as he has never said . . . You are his only one . . . But always
you remember him . . . And constantly you care . . . And in your
search to find his face . . . You wander everywhere . . . You look
for him along the street . . . And on the moonlit beach . . . Sometimes you think you see him but . . . His heart is out of reach . . .
You love him and you dream of him . . . And yet what will you
do . . . If some day you discover he . . . Is not in love with you?

PERFECT EVENING

The perfect evening is the one . . . When people ring your bell
. . . And sunny smiles are all the things . . . They ever want to
sell . . . When everything that you discuss . . . Is full of friendly
cheer . . . And every little compliment . . . Is honest and sincere
. . . You talk about tomorrow and . . . The plans that you have
made . . . Including all the doubts there are . . . That make you
half afraid . . . You listen to the tales they tell . . . And then you
tell your own . . . And you discover that you have . . . No cause
to feel alone . . . And so the perfect evening is . . . The one that
starts and ends . . . With those who share their thoughts with
you . . . And show that they are friends.

SPEAKING OUT

Sometimes we need our courage to . . . Express the thoughts we
think . . . By word of mouth, by telegraph . . . Or with our pen
and ink . . . We hesitate to tell the world . . . Exactly how we feel
. . . In fear of being criticized . . . For what we may reveal . . .
But also there are times in life . . . When it is truly well . . . To
have the courage to conceal . . . Whatever we would tell . . . The
courage to refrain at last . . . From uttering our mind . . . Whenever our expressions might . . . Be cruel or unkind . . . And so
for everything we say . . . The rule appears to be . . . That we
should speak with fortitude . . . And with diplomacy.

SHAKING HANDS

It is an ordinary thing . . . To shake a person's hand . . . It's done by commoner and king . . . In almost every land . . . In this uncompromising way . . . Our welcome we extend . . . And somewhat casually display . . . The feeling of a friend . . . It seals the making of a bet . . . And always comes before . . . A pair of pugilists get set . . . Upon the canvas floor . . . It says hello, it means good-by . . . It shows we are not rude . . . It causes us to wonder why . . . We ever had a feud . . . It's more than just a way to be . . . Polite and quite in style . . . It signifies true sympathy . . . And it is worth the while.

ST. PATRICK

The story of St. Patrick is . . . A story told before . . . Of how he banished all the snakes . . . From Ireland's sunny shore . . . But whether we believe the tale . . . Or think it very odd . . . His name is one that represents . . . The men who honor God . . . For he taught Christianity . . . Wherever he appeared . . . And his divine Creator was . . . The only One he feared . . . He spread the gospel fervently . . . That everyone might live . . . In all the love and charity . . . The world could ever give . . . And so no matter what his creed . . . Or how he chose to pray . . . He honored God and that is why . . . We honor him today.

UNHAPPY AT WORK

Few things in life cause more concern . . . Or do so much to irk . . . Than just the knowledge that we are . . . Unhappy in our work . . . The thought that someone over us . . . Is anything but fair . . . And that the credit we deserve . . . Is not for us to share . . . Or when we have to struggle and . . . Our mind is never free . . . Because some fellow-worker has . . . A petty jealousy . . . It makes for poor production and . . . It surely takes away . . . The least incentive we may have . . . To really earn our pay . . . And too it makes us wonder why . . . We linger there at all . . . And tolerate the ones who are . . . So selfish and so small.

LADY IN WHITE

She tends the needs and comforts of . . . A world with sickness fraught . . . And fosters peace and happiness . . . In feeling and in thought . . . Unselfishly she tries to soothe . . . And ease the slightest pain . . . And usher in the sunshine when . . . The skies begin to rain . . . An angel spreading mercy in . . . The darkness of the night . . . Restoring broken bodies with . . . A new and healing light . . . Returning strength to flesh fatigued . . . And to the weary mind . . . She is the feet for all the lame . . . The eyes for all the blind . . . She is the albatross that guides . . . The storm-encircled ships . . . And she is every smile that parts . . . A youngster's pallid lips.

THE CHEERFUL SIDE

The cheerful side of everything . . . Is all I ever seek . . . Including all the kindly thoughts . . . My friendly neighbors speak . . . I hope to see the morning sun . . . When I get up and dress . . . And every hour of the day . . . I hunt for happiness . . . There is no glory to be gained . . . From bitterness and tears . . . And selfishness does nothing to . . . Improve the passing years . . . And yet I do not mind the rain . . . Because I always know . . . It helps the grass and flowers and . . . The farmer's crops to grow . . . And frequently I find there is . . . A rainbow in the sky . . . And all around the dreams I dream . . . To keep my spirits high.

JIMMIE'S GOAL

I try my best to figure out . . . What Jimmie wants to be . . . But at the moment I confess . . . It rather puzzles me . . . He starts to make a model plane . . . Like those the soldiers fly . . . And so a great career is carved . . . For combat in the sky . . . But then he builds a radio . . . From which it would appear . . . He has a strong desire to . . . Become an engineer . . . And then again he takes his pen . . . And draws cartoons all day . . . Or else he makes up funny songs . . . To while the time away . . . And so the only thing that seems . . . To get more clear to me . . . Is that I cannot figure out . . . What Jimmie wants to be.

IF THERE BE GOOD IN ME

Dear God, if there be good in me . . . Let all of it come out . . .
If I have love and sympathy . . . Let no one be in doubt . . . If I
can do some kindly act . . . Please give me strength to make . . .
My effort an accomplished fact . . . For someone else's sake . . .
Inspire me to give my best . . . In everything I do . . . And never
let my spirit rest . . . Until I see it through . . . Whenever there
are clouds of gray . . . And heavy hang the years . . . Help me
help someone on his way . . . And help me dry his tears . . . Dear
God, be always with me and . . . If there be good in me . . . Let it
go out to every land . . . And all humanity.

ONE AT A TIME

Some people think in terms of all . . . The jobs they have to do
. . . Instead of taking one of them . . . And carrying it through
. . . They visualize the duties that . . . Confront them every
day . . . And feel it is impossible . . . To put them all away . . .
But if they did them one by one . . . With diligence and care . . .
In time their obligations would . . . Be vanishing in air . . . Because it is the steady grind . . . Of taking things in turn . . . That
does the job and cultivates . . . The laurels that we earn . . . A
task is not so difficult . . . When one at last begins . . . And daily
perseverance is . . . The only thing that wins.

OLD MAN WITH FIDDLE

He stood at the curb . . . In the traffic din . . . And started to
play . . . His violin . . . It may be that music . . . Has charms, as
they say . . . Or perhaps it was how . . . I was feeling that day
. . . It might have been he . . . With his beard flowing white . . .
The years he had lived . . . And his pitiful plight . . . It could have
been something . . . I tried to recall . . . A vague little something
. . . Or nothing at all . . . But I know that I stood . . . And I
listened to him . . . And my cheeks they were moist . . . And my
eyes they were dim . . . And the people around me . . . Were
silent and sad . . . Or possibly wistful . . . And quietly glad . . .
For he smiled to us all . . . As he stood in the street . . . And we
showered our coins . . . At his tired feet.

COMPLIMENT

A compliment can do so much . . . To brighten up the day . . .
To lift a fellow's spirit up . . . And help him on his way . . . It is
a friendly luxury . . . We all can well afford . . . And one that is
as like as not . . . To bring us some reward . . . It only takes a
kindly thought . . . Some words of simple choice . . . And just
the little energy . . . Of turning on our voice . . . It may be more
than we believe . . . He honestly deserves . . . And he may even
be a bit . . . Disturbing to our nerves . . . But all of us throughout
this world . . . Would make a better grade . . . If we would just
make certain that . . . More compliments were paid.

DEAR SERVICE MAN

This letter is to let you know . . . That we at home are well
. . . And things are rolling right along . . . Without an idle spell
. . . We have sufficient clothing and . . . An ample food supply . . .
And all the comforts we could ask . . . To keep our spirits high . . .
Our factories are humming and . . . The planes and tanks you
need . . . Are leaving our production lines . . . With extra special
speed . . . Both men and women are at work . . . With all their
brain and brawn . . . And even youngsters do their part . . . To
help us carry on . . . So keep on fighting, Service Man . . . And
rest assured that we . . . Are holding up the front at home . . . For
life and liberty.

BE MINE, MY LOVE

I offer you my love again . . . With every new-born day . . .
And hope with all the heart in me . . . You will not turn away . . .
I may not have as much to give . . . As others hold in hand
. . . But I shall always sympathize . . . And I shall understand . . .
I shall be there to comfort you . . . When shadows cross your
path . . . And I shall never show a sign . . . Of jealousy or wrath
. . . I shall be glad to wait on you . . . And serve your every need
. . . While every wish you ever make . . . Will be my daily
creed . . . So please accept my offer now . . . And make my dreams
come true . . . By giving me the happiness . . . Of being one with
you.

DENTIST

His tools explore your open mouth . . . For teeth that need repair
. . . From east to west and north to south . . . His hands move
everywhere . . . He finds a cavity or two . . . He thinks he ought
to fill . . . And for a dreadful moment you . . . Are fearful of his
drill . . . He comes across an empty space . . . And recommends
a tooth . . . To brighten up your weary face . . . And magnify
your youth . . . He cleans your teeth, he pulls them out . . . From
places dark and deep . . . And if he thinks your lungs will shout
. . . He puts your eyes to sleep . . . With porcelain cap and golden
crown . . . He gives you greater style . . . And looks to you for his
renown . . . Each time you show your smile.

ANOTHER HOME

The building trade is booming now . . . And everywhere it
seems . . . Some architect is trying out . . . His home and office
schemes . . . I like to watch a structure rise . . . To beautify some
space . . . Or see an old establishment . . . Take on a brighter
face . . . The movie, store and restaurant . . . Are practical and
good . . . But homes are more important to . . . The growing
neighborhood . . . And nothing like another house . . . Appeals so
much to me . . . Because I know it will embrace . . . Another
family . . . Because I know there will be love . . . And golden
dreams to share . . . And happy children's laughter will . . . Be
echoing from there.

ETERNAL THANKS

I am so grateful to You, God . . . For all that You have done . . .
From every golden dawn until . . . The setting of each sun . . .
For every little favor and . . . The goals that I have gained
. . . And even for my loneliness . . . Whenever it has rained . . . I
thank You for the beauty of . . . The life You let me live . . . And
for the opportunity . . . To borrow and to give . . . The chance
to gather happiness . . . Wherever I may go . . . And in the
wisdom of the world . . . To contemplate and grow . . . I am
forever grateful for . . . The blessings I receive . . . And pray
that I will never cause . . . Your loving heart to grieve.

WISH FOR WEALTH

I hope I shall be rich some day . . . Beyond my fondest dreams
. . . But only for the purpose of . . . Fulfilling certain schemes . . .
I want to give my family . . . The things they need so much . . .
And after that some luxuries . . . To add a special touch . . . And
when they are provided for . . . By all the different stores . . . I
want to go around and knock . . . On other people's doors . . . I
want to ease their common cares . . . And help them to be gay
. . . By showing them the sunshine and . . . The beauty of the
day . . . I want to teach them charity . . . Beyond the slightest
doubt . . . By doing everything I can . . . To really help them out.

DRIVE SAFELY

A minute may be valuable . . . In getting something done . . .
But not to cut down driving time . . . On business or for fun . . .
There is no place that we must reach . . . So quickly in our car
. . . That one more minute will not serve . . . To get us just as far
. . . Our lives are more important than . . . The keeping of a
date . . . And we may never get there if . . . Our hurry is too
great . . . So let us be more careful on . . . The highway and the
street . . . And let us use good common sense . . . To guide our
hands and feet . . . Let us be sober and alert . . . And patiently
obey . . . The traffic laws that govern speed . . . And rule the
right-of-way.

GRAND OLD MAN

In Lincoln County he is known . . . To all his friends as Bill
. . . This grand old man who finds that life . . . Is still a mighty
thrill . . . His 90 years of energy . . . Of struggle and success . . .
Are proof enough that honest work . . . Will bring you happiness
. . . And watching him behind his team . . . Of horses, you can
see . . . A man is never older than . . . He really wants to be . . .
But most of all we love him for . . . The democratic style . . . In
which he greets the fellows with . . . A handshake and a smile
. . . And most of all we wish him luck . . . And years of healthy
days . . . And may his heart be joyful in . . . A thousand different
ways.

SUCCESS

Success is measured not by wealth . . . Or everlasting fame . . .
Or by the winning score we make . . . In any single game . . . It
is not gathered up at will . . . Or fashioned overnight . . . And it
can never be retained . . . Without a constant fight . . . Success is
slowly harvested . . . By energy and toil . . . And it can only
come to life . . . If there is fertile soil . . . It is the house where
glory lives . . . And perseverance knocks . . . And faith and courage are the keys . . . That turn the master locks . . . It is the real
and rich reward . . . That waits from year to year . . . For those
whose hearts are honest and . . . Whose efforts are sincere.

MY SPECIAL BOOKS

The books I have upon my shelf . . . Are very few indeed . . .
But they are all the special books . . . I ever really need . . . Because
they are the volumes that . . . My friends have given me . . . And
therefore each one represents . . . A cherished memory . . . They
are inscribed with greetings and . . . With compliments of gold
. . . But far more gratifying are . . . The signatures they hold . . .
The names of those who speak to me . . . Across a silent stage . . .
In kindly tones that linger on . . . Beyond the printed page . . .Who
comfort me and urge me on . . . With faith that never ends . . . By
giving me the happiness . . . Of calling them my friends.

LET US SALUTE

Let us salute the Stars and Stripes . . . On this important day
. . . That we have chosen for the flag . . . Of our great U. S. A.
. . . The stars that represent the states . . . The stripes of red and
white . . . That praise the colonists who fought . . . For every
human right . . . Today is Flag Day and today . . . We tell the
world again . . . The story of our country and . . . Our patriotic
men . . . The story of America . . . In red and white and blue
. . . And all that we have done and all . . . We are prepared to
do . . . Let us salute Old Glory and . . . Repeat our pledge once
more . . . That liberty will always be . . . Our goal in peace and
war.

MADAM MOTORMAN

She operates the city bus . . . And makes the trolley go . . . To take us to our daily work . . . Or to the picture show . . . She changes cash, collects the fares . . . And issues transfer slips . . . And washes down a hasty lunch . . . Between a pair of trips . . . She does each portion of her job . . . The way the men would do . . . And does it so efficiently . . . It seems like nothing new . . . Whatever we may think of her . . . We have no right to squawk . . . Because without her wartime help . . . We might be forced to walk . . . And let us realize when we feel . . . Inclined to laugh or scoff . . . That she can tell the customer . . . Just where he should get off!

WELCOME GUEST

The guest is always welcome in . . . The home of smallest size . . . As long as there are friendly smiles . . . To brighten up the skies . . . As long as there are kindly souls . . . To offer warmth and cheer . . . And every spoken sentiment . . . Is honest and sincere . . . It matters not how crowded and . . . Confined the folks may be . . . There always is an extra place . . . In such a family . . . Because their space in which to live . . . Is measured not by feet . . . Or any form of figuring . . . Where engineers may meet . . . But only by their willingness . . . To do their friendly part . . . And all the measurements that show . . . Unselfishness of heart.

CLOCK-WATCHER

Invariably he comes in late . . . And then he finds a way . . . To stall around and kill some time . . . Before he starts the day . . . He stares at all the work there is . . . And with a heavy sigh . . . He wonders why it never ends . . . And bosses never die . . . At every opportunity . . . He goes to get a drink . . . And on each young stenographer . . . He lavishes a wink . . . He sharpens pencils, fills his pen . . . And bothers everyone . . . But what he is supposed to do . . . Is always left undone . . . He greets the final whistle with . . . A weary stretch and yawn . . . And just a second later he . . . Is definitely gone.

144

EMPTY LETTER

I want to write some lines to you . . . But what is there to say?
. . . You know the things I always do . . . To occupy the day . . .
You know I eat my breakfast eggs . . . And gulp my coffee down
. . . Before I urge my tired legs . . . To get me into town . . . You
know I work and have my lunch . . . And then I work some more
. . . Until I give the clock a punch . . . And hurry from the
store . . . I ride the trolley home again . . . And as you also know
. . . I dine and rest, I read and then . . . To bed once more I
go . . . The weather hasn't changed a bit . . . The stars are just
as bright . . . So when you come right down to it . . . What can a
person write?

MAN OF GOD

He is a man of God on earth . . . Who sacrifices all . . . And
lives in princely poverty . . . To heed his church's call . . . Who
ministers to all the needs . . . Of both the rich and poor . . . And
guides them in the struggle and . . . The strife they must endure
. . . He teaches them to think of God . . . Instead of worldly
gain . . . And why the sun must share the sky . . . With clouds
that carry rain . . . He undertakes to heal the sick . . . To help
the blind to see . . . And show the lame the way to walk . . . In
love and sympathy . . . And when he does his duty well . . . He
sanctifies the sod . . . And by his good example proves . . . He is
a man of God.

MY CHILDREN, GOD

I have three lovely children, God . . . As You are well aware
. . . And naturally I want them all . . . To have the best of care
. . . I want my sons to be young men . . . Who walk the righteous
path . . . Devoted to humanity . . . And given not to wrath . . .
I want my darling daughter to . . . Be beautiful and gay . . . But
also kind and generous . . . In every little way . . . And while I
can to some extent . . . Contribute my support . . . I know somewhere along the line . . . My efforts must fall short . . . And that
is why I turn to You . . . In this my time of need . . . And ask
You, God, with all my heart . . . To help them to succeed.

THE SONG I WROTE FOR YOU

Last night I wrote a song for you . . . To take your tears way . . .
And color with the brightest blue . . . The heavens that were gray
. . . I fashioned it with golden bars . . . And for each magic
note . . . I took the silver of the stars . . . And with my heart I
wrote . . . The words that say, "I love you, dear . . . And want you
for my own . . . Each yesterday and yesteryear . . . I too have
been alone . . . In every dream I saw your face . . . So beautiful
and fair . . . And though I wandered every place . . . I could not
find you there . . . But now we are together, dear . . . And all
the skies are blue . . . Oh, come into my arms and hear . . . The
song I wrote for you."

ASSISTANT

He is the one below the boss . . . Who toils throughout the
day . . . To help the boss pretend he is . . . Deserving of his pay
. . . He takes a pride in every task . . . He has the chance to do
. . . And his important title he . . . Would emphasize to you . . .
Of course he has to take the blame . . . When anything goes
wrong . . . But in so many other ways . . . His life is like a song
. . . Because when his superior . . . Is ill or out of town . . . He
wields the mighty gavel and . . . He wears the royal crown . . .
And he is fairly confident . . . That he will rule the roost . . . The
day the boss retires or . . . His title gets a boost.

SEWING BASKET

It holds so many spools of thread . . . And balls of colored yarn
. . . The needles used for sewing and . . . The kind employed to
darn . . . A thimble and a wooden egg . . . Some buttons, snaps
and beads . . . Elastic, ribbon, zippers and . . . The pins to fill all
needs . . . Its contents are the handy tools . . . For making pretty
frocks . . . For patching pants that go to school . . . And mending
grown-up sox . . . The sewing basket is the place . . . Where tired
hands reach in . . . When other daily tasks are done . . . And this
one must begin . . . Where weary eyes and fingers toil . . . Until
they go to bed . . . And leave a basket filled with dreams . . . Of
happy years ahead.

PRAYER FOR CHARITY

I ask You, Lord, for many things . . . To bless and better me . . .
But most of all I want to learn . . . To live in charity . . . I want
to be of service to . . . My neighbor and my kin . . . And help
them reach the worthy goals . . . They try so hard to win . . . To
cheer and comfort those who feel . . . Their efforts have been
spent . . . When all they need is just a word . . . Of real encouragement . . . To counsel those who sorrow and . . . Whose
eyes are dimmed by tears . . . That they may see the uselessness
. . . Of weeping through the years . . . I want to be the perfect
kind . . . Of friend You are to me . . . That others may appreciate
. . . Your generosity.

THE GOOD OF LIFE

I know that every time I smile . . . And really look around . . .
The sun is all that ever makes . . . The shadows on the ground
. . . I mean there is no darker side . . . That is not something
good . . . If only it is analyzed . . . And really understood . . .
The hours may be lonely and . . . The heavens overcast . . . But
rain or wind however wild . . . Is never one to last . . . Today my
troubles multiply . . . Tomorrow they divide . . . I take away my
tears and add . . . A world of joy and pride . . . And so it goes
from year to year . . . If only I can see . . . That everything is
meant to bring . . . Some benefit to me.

TOUCHY

Some people have a strange idea . . . Of how to have some fun
. . . They laugh at jokes they tell themselves . . . But hate to hear
a pun . . . They play their tricks on others and . . . Consider each
a gem . . . But they are always furious . . . When one is tried on
them . . . Their meager sense of humor is . . . Forever in reverse
. . . And when the truth is told to them . . . It only makes it
worse . . . They are the simple-minded who . . . Are grouchy all
the day . . . Unless the world is in accord . . . With their peculiar
way . . . Invariably they think themselves . . . Endowed with
wondrous wit . . . And while they dish it out they are . . . Opposed
to taking it.

OUR GARDEN

I always show our garden to . . . The friends who come to call
. . . And with the greatest pride display . . . The flowers one and
all . . . And thrive upon the compliments . . . They pass along to
me . . . Their praises for my patience and . . . My toil and energy
. . . And everything is wonderful . . . Until they meet my wife . . .
And get to know the awful truth . . . About my "double life" . . .
And then I must confess that I . . . Have never used a hoe . . . A
spade or any implement . . . That helps a garden grow . . . And
painfully acknowledge with . . . A very guilty look . . . Our garden
is the product of . . . My manager and cook.

BARGAIN

A bargain is an article . . . We have the chance to buy . . . When
it appears the price thereof . . . Is anything but high . . . We may
not need it at the time . . . Or some near future date . . . But if
we wait to get it we . . . May find it is too late . . . It need not be
some little thing . . . We order from afar . . . For there are bargains
in a home . . . Piano or a car . . . The seller may be overstocked
. . . And somewhat in distress . . . And possibly next week the
price . . . May even be much less . . . But if the cost is low today
. . . And we sincerely feel . . . We want to buy the item, then . . .
It is a bargain real.

MY LETTERS TO YOU

The letters I address to you . . . Are filled with words of love . . .
About your hair, your eyes and all . . . The silver stars above
. . . They talk about how nice you are . . . And how I picture you
. . . As my eternal partner in . . . A cottage built for two . . . They
tell how much I miss you when . . . You are away from me . . .
And all the joy of being in . . . Your friendly company . . . They
are the music of my heart . . . With which I try to say . . . That you
are in my dreams at night . . . And in my mind all day . . . The
letters I address to you . . . Are like an endless trail . . . I only wish
I had the nerve . . . To put them in the mail.

WHEN I RETURN

When I return from all this war . . . I hope that I shall find . . .
A life as good and pleasant as . . . The one I left behind . . . I do
not seek the neighbors' thanks . . . Their sympathy or praise . . .
Nor do I care to hear them ask . . . About my service days . . . I
only want to see my home . . . The way it was before . . . The
same old gate and garden path . . . The latch upon the door . . .
The tables, chairs and curtains and . . . The pictures on the wall
. . . The old and tattered rug on which . . . I used to trip and
fall . . . I hope my mom will scold me if . . . I do not eat enough
. . . And make me tidy up my room . . . And put away my stuff
. . . I want my dog to wag his tail . . . And jump all over me . . .
I want to find my life at home . . . Just like it used to be.

HOCKEY PLAYER

The hockey player has to have . . . A hockey stick and puck . . .
A pair of skates, a uniform . . . And not a little pluck . . . He need
not be a champion or . . . An artist on the ice . . . But speed and
strength are qualities . . . He cannot sacrifice . . . He really has
to get around . . . And keep the goal in view . . . And when he
makes his lightning shot . . . His timing must be true . . . He
must refrain from fouling when . . . Another player blocks . . . Or
he may pay a penalty . . . By sitting in the box . . . But if he plays
correctly he . . . Will never be a wreck . . . Unless he tries to
stop the puck . . . By sticking out his neck.

MISSING THE BUS

Sometimes when I begin the day . . . I feel inclined to cuss . . .
Because however fast I run . . . I miss the early bus . . . Of course
I know the schedule and . . . What time I should be there . . . And
just how long it takes to bathe . . . And brush my teeth and hair
. . . I know what minutes I must have . . . For coffee and for eggs
. . . Before I grab my hat and coat . . . And exercise my legs . . .
But even though I rise before . . . The old alarm clock rings . . .
The time gets short as I perform . . . A dozen extra things . . . And
even though I dash from home . . . And down the street I fly . . . I
turn the corner just in time . . . To see the bus go by.

TODAY'S HOURS

The hours of today are mine . . . To use in any way . . . But I must use them all before . . . Another day . . . I cannot lock them in a vault . . . Or stack them on a shelf . . . To save them up for someone else . . . Or for myself . . . I cannot turn them in and get . . . A credit on the books . . . No matter how uncertain now . . . The future looks . . . I cannot trade them in for time . . . Of less or greater worth . . . Or shorten or prolong their life . . . Upon this earth . . . Although each one in passing leaves . . . A deep, enduring track . . . When they are gone, there is no way . . . To bring them back.

PRAYER FOR A FAVOR

Dear God, I know that I have asked . . . So many things of You . . . To give me comfort in this life . . . And make my dreams come true . . . And I have not deserved the grace . . . You have bestowed on me . . . Or properly prepared myself . . . For Your eternity . . . But this one time I need Your help . . . More surely than before . . . To be courageous and to keep . . . Disaster from my door . . . Dear God, You know my problem and . . . The answer I must find . . . And there are certain promises . . . I cannot leave behind . . . So I beseech You once again . . . To hear the prayer I say . . . And grant the favor I request . . . To help me out today.

FAIR EXCHANGE

My darling wife dislikes the task . . . Of cleaning house each day . . . But she delights in cutting grass . . . And planting flowers gay . . . She really would prefer to let . . . The dishes stand all night . . . And bother not to keep the dust . . . And cobwebs out of sight . . . While I am more than willing to . . . Perform the household chores . . . To wash the dishes, make the beds . . . And polish all the floors . . . And so we have agreed to do . . . The tasks that we prefer . . . I manage everything inside . . . And leave the rest to her . . . Except of course the cooking job . . . Which all of us agree . . . Must have her super-duper touch . . . To please the family.

YOUR EYES

I love your eyes for what they say . . . Each time they look at me
. . . Because they speak in sentences . . . Of love and sympathy . . .
Because I know their language and . . . It is the same as mine
. . . The language of companionship . . . And friendliness divine
. . . I love your eyes because they say . . . The secrets of your
heart . . . Including all your loneliness . . . If ever we should part
. . . Including all the hopes we hold . . . And all the dreams we
share . . . And what it always means to me . . . To realize that you
care . . . I love your eyes so much because . . . They tell me you
are true . . . And just to look at them I know . . . I am in love
with you.

POST-GRADUATE

When we complete our college course . . . And pocket our de-
gree . . . Invariably it means good-by . . . To books and faculty
. . . But some of us are not inclined . . . To let our studies down
. . . Because we really want to rise . . . To scholarly renown . . .
And so we keep on learning all . . . The things there are to know
. . . And in the world of wisdom we . . . Proceed to grow and
grow . . . We qualify as masters or . . . As doctors tried and true
. . . And take our places rightfully . . . Among the chosen few
. . . And then we are regarded as . . . The experts in our fields . . .
And many are the glories that . . . Our education yields.

BUDGET

A budget is that certain thing . . . We promise we will keep . . .
And over which we are inclined . . . To lose a lot of sleep . . . It
is tomorrow's record of . . . The bills that come our way . . . And
just how much we think we can . . . Afford to spend today . . . It
measures out the groceries . . . Insurance, clothes and rent . . . And
all the luxuries that make . . . The hours more content . . . It figures to that future day . . . When labor should be done . . . And
we should live a life of ease . . . And have a world of fun . . . But
always when tomorrow comes . . . Our budget needs a change . . .
To fit the master plan that seems . . . To slip beyond our range.

HOUSES ON THE STREET

I walk along the street and count . . . The houses one by one . . .
And watch the smoke from chimneys rise . . . Against the setting
sun . . . I walk and wonder to myself . . . What people are in
there . . . What dialogues and kitchen smells . . . Are mingling
in the air . . . What little things went wrong today . . . What progress found its mark . . . What disappointments came, what hopes
. . . Are shining through the dark . . . I wonder what they think
about . . . And what they do to spend . . . These hours that are all
their own . . . Until their very end . . . I wonder what they dream
about . . . And what they have to tell . . . And then I hear the
children laugh . . . And know that all is well.

THEY DO NOT KNOW

I feel so sorry for the ones . . . Who do not understand . . . Or
in the least appreciate . . . The humble of the land . . . Who think
that they are better than . . . The ordinary run . . . And wiser in
the ways of life . . . To welcome or to shun . . . And who will
even undertake . . . To name the daily need . . . Of what the
people ought to think . . . And what they ought to read . . . Instead of having them decide . . . What they consider best . . . And
letting time enough go by . . . To make an honest test . . . Because
if they were learned they . . . Would realize at the start . . . That
they might sway the simple mind . . . But not the human heart.

MIRACLES

A miracle is nothing new . . . According to my book . . . Because I see one everywhere . . . I turn my eyes to look . . . Some
person is alive today . . . Although his car is wrecked . . . And
some poor fellow finds a job . . . He never could expect . . . The
mailman brings some money that . . . Enables me to meet . . . The
payment on a debt that would . . . Have left me on the street . . . A
baby keeps on breathing with . . . The blood that someone gives
. . . And somehow in this selfish world . . . The lowly beggar lives
. . . Which goes to show that miracles . . . Are part of every
day . . . And they are part of God's design . . . To help us on our
way.

GOD'S DESIGN

Each human being has a will . . . That he may call his own . . .
And yet God does not leave a soul . . . Entirely alone . . . He sees
to it that righteousness . . . And decency prevail . . . And that the
avaricious mind . . . Eventually will fail . . . And that is why we
won the war . . . And why we made the grade . . . In first discovering the way . . . The atom bomb is made . . . He will allow
an evil force . . . To reach a certain height . . . But only to remind
us of . . . The sins we ought to fight . . . It is His warning to the
world . . . To keep away from strife . . . And live in humble
harmony . . . To gain eternal life.

THANKS TO LABOR

Today belongs to workers and . . . The cause for which they
fight . . . Whatever their approach may be . . . And whether
wrong or right . . . It is their day to celebrate . . . And hold a
huge parade . . . To glory in their struggle and . . . The progress
they have made . . . The men and women of the shop . . . Who
turn the crane and wheel . . . To build a better world for us . . .
With iron, wood and steel . . . Whose daily sweat enables us . . .
To conquer land and sea . . . And in a thousand ways to live . . .
A life of luxury . . . So let us honor them today . . . And let us
thank them too . . . Because we owe so much to them . . . For
everything they do.

WILL YOU MARRY ME?

My darling, will you marry me . . . And share my humble life?
. . . Will you declare yourself to be . . . My own beloved wife? . . .
Will you be ever at my side . . . In sickness and in health . . . With
courage and with equal pride . . . In poverty and wealth? . . . Will
you inspire me to fame . . . However dark the sky? . . . Will you
do honor to my name . . . Until the day I die? . . . Will you adore
our children and . . . Protect them day and night . . . And guide
them with a loving hand . . . To live for what is right? . . . Then
take me, darling, for your own . . . And put your faith in me . . . I
shall be loving you alone . . . For all eternity.

FAITHFUL FRIEND

One all-important part of life . . . Is that of being true . . . In every way to everyone . . . Who is a friend to you . . . To show appreciation by . . . Returning kindly deeds . . . And being quite concerned about . . . The other person's needs . . . By being honest and sincere . . . Dependable and fair . . . And thereby letting it be known . . . How much you really care . . . Because the path of friendship is . . . A path that never bends . . . A path that does not rise or fall . . . And one that never ends . . . And whether joy or tragedy . . . Is knocking on the door . . . The friendship that is faithful will . . . Endure for evermore.

WASHINGTON

The father of our country, he . . . Was all that greatness meant . . . The leader of our army and . . . Our noble President . . . He won the Revolution and . . . Secured our nation's name . . . Indeed he well deserves to be . . . Within the hall of fame . . . He led us through the darkness of . . . Those early days of strife . . . And gave the people confidence . . . In government and life . . . And equally important to . . . The welfare of the land . . . Exemplified a principle . . . On which we ought to stand . . . And that, as history recalls . . . Was in his early youth . . . When, having chopped the cherry tree . . . He promptly told the truth.

THE DAY WILL COME

The day is sure to come when all . . . The countries will be free . . . And shortages of this and that . . . Will sleep in history . . . There will be gum and chocolate bars . . . And gasoline galore . . . And all the other luxuries . . . We had before the war . . . The butcher will be begging us . . . To buy a steak or two . . . And coupons will be needless when . . . Selecting footwear new . . . The motorist will cuss again . . . The radio will blare . . . And cuffs will grace the trousers smart . . . Both men and women wear . . . New homes will be as plentiful . . . As uniforms and jeeps . . . The rents will drop and OPA . . . Will lose its job for keeps!

BARBER

He prunes the foliage on your head . . . And trims around the
ear . . . So you will look respectable . . . Wherever you appear . . .
With special shears he thins your hair . . . Then washes it with
soap . . . Or uses some restoring stuff . . . To give you added hope
. . . If you declare you want a shave . . . He lets your back repose . . . And puts hot towels on your face . . . (Except of course
your nose) . . . His razor strokes are smooth and sure . . . And
after he gets through . . . You wonder if the looking-glass . . . Is
telling lies to you . . . They say he used to talk so much . . . It
gave a guy a fit . . . But now he seldom says a word . . . Unless you
ask for it.

I LOOK TO GOD

I look to God for everything . . . I need upon this earth . . . My
shelter, food and clothing and . . . Whatever I am worth . . . Of
course I have to go to work . . . And do my certain share . . . And
I must recognize my God . . . And tell Him that I care . . . But
on the other hand I know . . . No matter what I do . . . I must
depend upon my God . . . To help me see it through . . . Because
no matter how I try . . . I cannot ever be . . . The least bit stronger
than the strength . . . My God has given me . . . And that is why
I look to God . . . For everything I need . . . Including inspiration
for . . . My every word and deed.

SILENCE OF NIGHT

In all the silence of the night . . . I never feel alone . . . Because
the very silence is . . . A thing I call my own . . . Within its walls
I know that I . . . Am undisturbed and free . . . And when I
speak my thoughts to it . . . It whispers back to me . . . It fills my
mind with peace and calm . . . Throughout the hours long . . .
And sometimes it is almost like . . . A soft, endearing song . . . I
seek the silence of the night . . . Because it seems to say . . . The
many things I cannot hear . . . When I endure the day . . . It helps
me to appreciate . . . That I am still on earth . . . And in the comfort it bestows . . . It is of golden worth.

DAD

He is the one who shaves each morn . . . And leads the breakfast prayer . . . Then kisses all the family . . . And dashes down the stair . . . He works all day in some big place . . . Upon a busy street . . . At dusk he hurries home to bring . . . His little ones a treat . . . He reads the paper, smokes a pipe . . . And talks so very wise . . . He drives the car, he mows the lawn . . . And walks for exercise . . . He never seems to have enough . . . To pay the bills on hand . . . And yet he manages to meet . . . Each family demand . . . His kindness and his goodness are . . . His every thought and deed . . . He's always where he's needed and . . . He always fills the need.

MOTHER

She rocks you in your cradle and . . . She helps you learn to walk . . . She teaches you to dress and play . . . And even how to talk . . . She cleans the house and cooks the meals . . . She mends the clothes you wear . . . She nurses you in sickness with . . . The tenderest of care . . . She counsels you and guides you in . . . The things you want to do . . . But does not try to interfere . . . Or force her will on you . . . Her happiness is in your smile . . . Her sorrow in your tears . . . Her memories are all your words . . . And actions through the years . . . Your safest place in trouble is . . . The haven of her hands . . . And somehow if you're in the wrong . . . She always understands.

YOUR HAPPINESS

Of all the greetings and the gifts . . . The world could send my way . . . Your happiness would be the best . . . To brighten Christmas Day . . . Because when you are happy, dear . . . I have no tears to hide . . . But in the knowledge of your joy . . . My soul is satisfied . . . And that is why I hope your life . . . Will be an endless song . . . In every way this Christmas Day . . . And all the new year long . . . I offer you my lasting love . . . And oh, I promise you . . . That I will never leave your side . . . Or ever be untrue . . . You are the dearest to my heart . . . And you will always be . . . The only one whose happiness . . . Can mean so much to me.

THANK GOD TODAY

Let us be thankful on this day . . . For all that we possess . . .
A home, a job and time enough . . . For extra happiness . . . Our
freedom of religion and . . . The right to speak our mind . . . And
for the constant friendliness . . . Of neighbors good and kind . . .
Let us give thanks to God again . . . That we are not at war . . .
And in all likelihood we have . . . Prosperity in store . . . That we
have clothes and food and drink . . . To keep ourselves content . . .
And we may vote as we prefer . . . For better government . . . Let
us give gratitude for all . . . The ways in which we thrive . . . And
more especially that we . . . Are healthy and alive.

GUEST NOTE

It sure was mighty good of you . . . Inviting me to call . . . To
spend the evening and to have . . . Some dinner with you all . . .
To sit around and smoke and talk . . . And sip a glass or two
. . . Recalling days of long ago . . . And dwelling on the new . . .
It was a grand occasion and . . . I could not help but sigh . . .
When suddenly I realized it . . . Was time to say good-by . . .
Your hospitality was just . . . As warm as it could be . . . And al-
ways it will linger as . . . A pleasant memory . . . And so I am
delighted you . . . Invited me to call . . . And in reply can only
say . . . I sure do thank you all.

FIREMAN

Sometimes for hours he is free . . . To occupy a seat . . . But
when the bell starts ringing he . . . Is right upon his feet . . . He
dons his helmet, grabs his ax . . . And jumps aboard the truck . . .
In bravery he never lacks . . . Although he hopes for luck . . . He
knows the danger he must face . . . Wherever flames appear . . .
And yet he hurries to the place . . . Without a sign of fear . . . He
knows the smoke may steal his sight . . . The blaze may hem him
in . . . The crumbling walls may crush his might . . . But still he
strives to win . . . Sometimes for hours he is free . . . But always
he is there . . . To save the lives and property . . . Of people everywhere.

BEYOND THE STARS

Beyond the stars of all the skies . . . There must be something
true . . . There must be something beautiful . . . And wonderful
as you . . . There must be something greater than . . . The feeling
of a friend . . . There must be dreams of life and love . . . That
never seem to end . . . And if I ever pass beyond . . . The hill that
winds caress . . . I know that I shall find the way . . . To lasting
happiness . . . I know that I shall find you there . . . As lovely as
before . . . The picture of perfection when . . . The sun is at my
door . . . I know that somehow you will smile . . . The smile you
meant for me . . . And you and I shall live in love . . . For all
eternity.

SUNDAY OFFERING

On Sunday when the plate or box . . . Is passed around in church
. . . We should not hesitate to give . . . Or fumble in our search
. . . There is no rule that specifies . . . How much we have to
bring . . . And it is not the payment of . . . A price for anything
. . . But it is simply that amount . . . With which we gladly
part . . . According to our pocketbook . . . And magnitude of
heart . . . It is our way of thanking God . . . That we may meet
in prayer . . . And help our missionaries spread . . . The gospel
everywhere . . . Instead of a "collection" it . . . Is more precise
to state . . . Our offering is placed upon . . . A contribution plate.

TIME FOR BED

I'm not the least bit tired in . . . My body or my head . . . And
yet according to the clock . . . I ought to go to bed . . . I know
I ought to get some rest . . . Before the dawn comes up . . . Or else
at breakfast I may doze . . . Beside my coffee cup . . . I do not
want to sleep right now . . . But what am I to do? . . . The hands
of time are reaching far . . . Beyond the stroke of two . . . I am
not ready for the dreams . . . My pillow holds for me . . . My
mind is not prepared to meet . . . Its maze of memory . . . But I
must get to work on time . . . And have a steady head . . . The
clock is quite correct and so . . . I guess I'll go to bed.

GRANDMA

Dear Grandma is a good old soul . . . On whom we all depend
. . . Because she always helps us when . . . We really need a
friend . . . She understands our problems and . . . She tells us what
to do . . . If we would face the future days . . . And see them
safely through . . . And yet she does not interfere . . . Or criticize
our deeds . . . But constantly considers our . . . Desires and our
needs . . . She treats our little children with . . . The greatest love
and care . . . Especially if we should be . . . Invited anywhere
. . . As long as she is close at hand . . . We never feel alone . . .
Because she makes us feel we are . . . Entirely her own.

HIS HAPPY HOME

His home may look quite humble and . . . His comforts may be
few . . . But if he moved he would become . . . Dissatisfied and
blue . . . Because there is no city and . . . There is no street address . . . That ever could be equal to . . . His present happiness
. . . For years his steps have guided him . . . To those familiar
stores . . . And all along the way his friends . . . Are counted by
the scores . . . He loves the dear old neighborhood . . . Each
flower, tree and stone . . . And if he ever left it he . . . Would feel
so all alone . . . There is no castle in the clouds . . . Or palace
bright and gay . . . That could replace the happy home . . . He
calls his own today.

TAKE IT IN STRIDE

We have no right or reason to . . . Expect a perfect life . . . But
we must undergo our share . . . Of struggle and of strife . . . We
cannot look for everything . . . To work out quite all right . . .
With sunshine in the sky all day . . . And silver stars at night
. . . But sometimes we must have a tear . . . A sorrow or regret . . .
Or some unfortunate affair . . . We wish we could forget . . . And
so the best that we can do . . . Is try to be prepared . . . For any
disappointment or . . . Distress that must be shared . . . To go
along from day to day . . . With courage at our side . . . And take
whatever happens in . . . Our ordinary stride.

FREE FRANCE, TO ARMS!

The Marseillaise resounds again . . . Across the fields of France
. . . That brothers of equality . . . May have another chance . . .
The flag is on the mast again . . . The new-born voices cheer . . .
The underground is rising up . . . And shaking off its fear . . . The
cannons roar, the bombers dive . . . Beyond the hills of France
. . . The soldiers of fraternity . . . Are gathered to advance . . .
The glory that was Bonaparte . . . The fame of Lafayette . . . And
Joan of Arc are there today . . . That no one may forget . . . Red
run the rivers through the towns . . . And villages of France . . .
But now the sons of liberty . . . Cast not a backward glance . . .
Free France is on the march again . . . Her head no longer bowed
. . . A comrade to united men . . . Supremely brave and proud!

DOORMAN

He stands erect in uniform . . . Prepared to hold the door . . .
While you go in the hostelry . . . The theater or store . . . He meets
your auto at the curb . . . And from his lofty height . . . He even
gives a smart salute . . . To show he is polite . . . And if you need
a taxi or . . . Directions here and there . . . He serves you promptly
with his fine . . . Aristocratic air . . . It always warms his heart to
get . . . A friendly word or smile . . . Especially from patrons who
. . . Are socially in style . . . And when he plays his part in life
. . . Without the slightest slip . . . He naturally appreciates . . .
The kindness of a tip.

I MUST REMEMBER —

The silent night is lonely and . . . There is no golden dawn . . .
Because I must remember, love . . . That you are really gone . . .
I must remember in my heart . . . The happiness we knew . . .
And that my only world was one . . . In which I lived with you
. . . There is no breath of fragrance in . . . The flowers that I
press . . . And if I call your name I hear . . . The sound of empti-
ness . . . I roam the house from room to room . . . I gaze beyond
the sea . . . But there is nothing I can do . . . To bring you back
to me . . . I have to tell myself again . . . That you are really
gone . . . And I can only ask The Lord . . . For strength to carry
on.

I never could measure my love for you . . . For it reaches beyond the sun . . . It is wider than width and deeper than depth . . . And longer than distances run . . . It flows from the highest mountain top . . . To the field in the valley below . . . It extends from the sky to the bed of the sea . . . And as far as the wind may blow . . . It is soft as a kiss, it is stronger than steel . . . It is richer than any gem . . . It is constant as ever the stars above . . . And brighter than all of them . . . No, I never could measure the scope of my love . . . By anything old or new . . . But I know it is endless as time itself . . . And it all belongs to you.

PRAY FOR THEM

Let us respect the souls of all . . . Who sleep beneath the sod . . . And pray that they are safely and . . . Eternally with God . . . The mighty and the humble ones . . . The selfish and the kind . . . The wealthy and the poor and all . . . Who left the world behind . . . They have no earthly riches now . . . They hold not any hate . . . And if their task remains undone . . . They know it is too late . . . But God will give them credit for . . . The struggles of their day . . . And surely He will listen to . . . The fervent prayers we say . . . So let us intercede for those . . . Who walk the way alone . . . And pray that God will comfort them . . . And claim them for His own.

FAVOR

A favor is that kindly deed . . . Beyond a friendly smile . . . That comforts someone else on earth . . . And makes this life worth while . . . It may involve a fortune or . . . The fraction of a cent . . . Or just some little effort that . . . Is generously spent . . . We may be asked to do it or . . . The thought may be our own . . . In any case it is the way . . . Our charity is shown . . . It is a little sacrifice . . . That we are glad to make . . . To brighten up the sky a bit . . . For someone else's sake . . . And often we consider it . . . A privilege to extend . . . Because there is no greater deed . . . Than helping out a friend.

BORROWING BUG

Some neighbors borrow sugar or . . . A loaf of bread or two . . .
While others look for garden tools . . . To see the summer through
. . . And then there are the ones who want . . . A car in which to
ride . . . And someone good to watch the child . . . Who is their
joy and pride . . . Of course they all are asking for . . . The sort
of help they need . . . And many of us like to do . . . A kind and
friendly deed . . . But every time we call on them . . . For something they might share . . . It seems their hands are empty and . . .
Their cupboards all are bare . . . While they go right on borrowing
. . . From everyone until . . . They use up everything they can . . .
Including their good will.

FAITHFUL SERVANT

The faithful servant is the one . . . Who does his duty well . . .
And by his very faithfulness . . . Forever will excel . . . Who keeps
the promises he makes . . . However great they are . . . And even
though fulfilling them . . . May cover up his star . . . He never
misses meetings when . . . He says he will be there . . . And when
the work is passed around . . . He gladly takes his share . . . He
does not mumble or complain . . . When things are not all right
. . . But he is always brave enough . . . To carry on the fight . . .
He is not one who changes with . . . The weather of the day . . .
But he may be depended on . . . In every single way.

DATE WITH DONNIE

My Donnie likes to come downtown . . . And keep me company
. . . On days when he is not in school . . . And I am somewhat
free . . . He likes to ride the trolley car . . . And have a chance to
stare . . . At all the folks and things along . . . The busy thorough-
fare . . . He always goes to lunch with me . . . And it is evident
. . . His appetite is healthy and . . . His conduct excellent . . .
Well, after lunch he offers me . . . A choice of where to go . . .
The 10 cent store, to buy a toy . . . Or to a picture show . . . And
by the time he heads for home . . . He is prepared to say . . . That
he has had a busy and . . . A profitable day.

FACE AT THE WINDOW

She drew her shawl about her, she . . . Who was so very old . . .
For on this lonely winter night . . . The wind was wild and cold . . .
And as she tottered down the street . . . She shivered and she shook
. . . And in her failing eyes there was . . . A weary, frightened
look . . . She stopped before a certain house . . . But did not ring
the bell . . . Instead she gazed inside to see . . . What story it
might tell . . . And when she drew away again . . . The frightened
look was gone . . . Her steps seemed somewhat lighter then . . . As
she continued on . . . The shawl around her shoulders slim . . .
Fell lightly from its place . . . And passing strangers marveled at
. . . The smile upon her face.

WHEREVER WE LIVE

It does not matter where we live . . . Or how the climate seems
. . . As long as we are trying to . . . Fulfill our daily dreams . . .
As long as we have faith and hope . . . And give our very best . . .
And we appreciate the ways . . . In which our lives are blessed
. . . There may be some unpleasant things . . . That bother and
annoy . . . And possibly some other place . . . Would bring us
greater joy . . . But we have no assurance of . . . A perfect spot on
earth . . . And every neighborhood presents . . . Its own peculiar
worth . . . So why should we be looking for . . . A more inviting
site . . . When everything the way it is . . . Is probably all right?

I LIKE TO DREAM

Among the pastimes I like best . . . Is just to sit and dream . . .
And ponder things not as they are . . . But as they sometimes seem
. . . To look behind the clouds of gray . . . And try to find the
sun . . . That it may brighten all my hopes . . . In battles to be
won . . . I tell myself that everything . . . Cannot be always bad
. . . But somewhere I shall gather smiles . . . To make my spirits
glad . . . I figure up the odds in life . . . And it appears to me . . .
There has to be some happiness . . . For every misery . . . And so
I pass the time of day . . . When it is mine to spend . . . And all
my dreams and memories . . . Are songs that never end.

TO A WAR BRIDE

You loved him and you married him . . . And now you have to
wait . . . Until the war is over and . . . There is an end to hate
. . . You said you would prefer to be . . . His wife for just a
day . . . Than not to have his loving arms . . . Before he went
away . . . And well you do your duty now . . . To write him
every night . . . To pray for him and dream of him . . . When
you put out the light . . . You are a brave, determined girl . . . To
keep your chin up high . . . To watch the battlefronts, to hear . . .
The thunder in the sky . . . And surely God will bless you for
. . . Your faith and courage true . . . And surely God will keep
him safe . . . And bring him back to you.

ORGANIST

The organist provides the world . . . With music soft and sweet
. . . Except the one who grinds it with . . . A monkey on the
street . . . And sometimes too except the one . . . Who plays it
with his breath . . . And being just an amateur . . . He bores a
guy to death . . . But in the theater, at home . . . In school or in
the church . . . His talent is a thing for which . . . All audiences
search . . . He gives to every melody . . . That deep, impressive
sound . . . That rises to the rafters and . . . That echoes all around
. . . And when his fingers touch the keys . . . Wherever people
pray . . . The angels seem to catch his tune . . . And carry it away.

TIME TO PRAY

It is not difficult to pray . . . When we are faced with fears . . .
Or when the shadows climb the walls . . . And tragedy appears
. . . Our voices rise above the roar . . . Of every raging sea . . .
And words of sudden eloquence . . . Present our tearful plea . . .
But when there is no storm and when . . . We have a perfect day
. . . We seldom turn our thoughts to God . . . Or take the time to
pray . . . And if it is a duty then . . . It also is a task . . . To thank
Him or to let Him know . . . The miracles we ask . . . And yet
a daily prayer to God . . . Is such a little thing . . . Compared to all
the comfort and . . . The blessing it can bring.

GRAMMAR SCHOOL

The subjects taught in grammar school . . . Are not the ones we pick . . . For we must learn to read and write . . . And do arithmetic . . . We have to study spelling and . . . The way each word must sound . . . And we are made to understand . . . The world is really round . . . We memorize a lot of dates . . . And names and places too . . . From Bunker Hill to Tokyo . . . And all the oceans blue . . . While in between we come across . . . The principles of youth . . . Obedience and bravery . . . And loyalty and truth . . . And so we find ourselves prepared . . . To start in junior high . . . And to the land of childhood dreams . . . We say a brief good-by.

FAITH IN GOD

My faith belongs to God because . . . He is so good to me . . . And just because each day and night . . . He keeps me company . . . I know that He is present when . . . I see the morning sun . . . And all throughout the afternoon . . . Until the day is done . . . I feel His presence at my side . . . When silver stars appear . . . And when I close my eyes in sleep . . . I know that He is near . . . Whatever glory calls my name . . . Or tragedy may knock . . . He has the magic key I need . . . For every kind of lock . . . God never fails my humble heart . . . But He is always there . . . To listen to my troubles and . . . To answer every prayer.

SECRETARY

In many ways on business days . . . The boss depends on her . . . This lady who is more than just . . . A good stenographer . . . For she not only has to type . . . And write in shorthand style . . . And she not only has to know . . . Exactly how to file . . . But she must have some business sense . . . And when she is alone . . . She has to handle everything . . . As though it were her own . . . She has to deal with those who call . . . In person or by mail . . . And help the firm make money so . . . The business will not fail . . . Her problems are innumerable . . . And some of them get old . . . But she who does her duty well . . . Is worth her weight in gold.

TEN YEARS TOGETHER

You've cooked and sewed and kept our house . . . For 10 delightful years . . . You've shared with me each victory . . . And kissed
away the tears . . . You've urged me on to greater goals . . . With
courage, faith and pride . . . In time of stress or happiness . . .
You've never left my side . . . You've given me two little boys
. . . The handsomest in life . . . And borne with love the duties
of . . . A mother and a wife . . . You've never found a sacrifice
. . . Too difficult to make . . . Each song and sigh has been for my
. . . And for the children's sake . . . And so each year, to honor
you . . . I set this day apart . . . And humbly come to thank you
from . . . The bottom of my heart.

TWO PRAYERS

There are two special prayers that we . . . Should take the time
to say . . . In striving for accomplishments . . . To glorify the day
. . . A prayer when we are starting out . . . To do a certain deed
. . . That we may have the guidance and . . . The courage to succeed . . . And secondly a prayer of thanks . . . For all the strength
and grace . . . With which The Lord enables us . . . To run a
worthy race . . . We may not be triumphant but . . . We ought to
be aware . . . That out of every gain we make . . . The Lord deserves His share . . . And He is just as eager to . . . Receive our
grateful praise . . . And He is glad to help our hearts . . . To strive
for better days.

IF ONLY TONIGHT

If I could touch your hand tonight . . . And hold you in my
arms . . . And if your lips were mine to kiss . . . With their
eternal charms . . . If I could walk beside you now . . . Beyond
the garden gate . . . Without a shadow in my heart . . . Or any
fear of fate . . . I would not mind the weather with . . . Its rain
and snow and sleet . . . Or when the sun is beating down . . .
Upon a thirsty street . . . I would not think about the past . . .
With all its beauty bright . . . I would not dream of days to come
. . . But only of tonight . . . I would be counting minutes and . . .
The seconds they embrace . . . In all of which I might behold
. . . The beauty of your face.

I WRITE FOR YOU

I write of love and beauty and . . . The silver stars at night . . .
The seasons and the wind and rain . . . And morning clear and
bright . . . Of children's laughter echoing . . . Behind a friendly
door . . . The farmer in his harvest field . . . And men who march
to war . . . I paint the passing smiles and tears . . . In moods of
memory . . . And say my gratitude to God . . . For giving life to
me . . . May you derive some pleasure from . . . Each offering
in rhyme . . . Some peace and consolation and . . . A smile from
time to time . . . I write these lines not only to . . . Pursue my daily
art . . . But all the more to share with you . . . The feeling in my
heart.

MAKING MISTAKES

At one time or another we . . . Commit a sad mistake . . . That
may embarrass us or cause . . . Some other heart to break . . . We
may not mean to do it and . . . We may be all upset . . . And we
may tell ourselves it is . . . An error we regret . . . But what is
more important is . . . Our will to make amends . . . To show that
we are sorry and . . . We want to keep our friends . . . For they
will surely overlook . . . The poorness of the past . . . If we are
willing to improve . . . And make our promise last . . . So let us do
the best we can . . . And when mistakes are made . . . Let us correct them one by one . . . Alone and unafraid.

LITTLE BUILDER

Kristina builds a big garage . . . A fence or other thing . . . And
that is very well until . . . A caller tries to ring . . . Because her
workshop occupies . . . The sidewalk out in front . . . And getting
through that maze of stuff . . . Requires quite a stunt . . . Her
little chairs and table take . . . A vast amount of space . . . And
dolls and toys contribute to . . . A mighty crowded place . . . She
says we have to walk around . . . Or else we have to wait . . .
Until Kristina comes along . . . To open up the gate . . . And
while we want our little girl . . . To exercise and play . . . We wish
that her construction craze . . . Would quickly pass away.

GOLD STAR MOTHER

She gave him birth and watched him grow . . . And dressed him up from top to toe . . . She taught him how to smile and walk . . . To eat and drink and how to talk . . . She made his lunch for school each day . . . And showed him how to work and play . . . She urged him on and helped him choose . . . And nursed each cut and bump and bruise . . . She guided him from wrong to right . . . And told him when and how to fight . . . But most of all, right from the start . . . She gave her boy her loving heart . . . While he, in turn, was more than glad . . . To give up all he ever had . . . That you and I and other sons . . . Might never meet the blazing guns . . . So let us pay our deep respect . . . And solemnly let us reflect . . . Upon the grave she gave that we . . . Might carry on to victory.

BE WITH ME, GOD

Be with me, God, when I am glad . . . And all the skies are blue . . . And never let me fail to give . . . My gratitude to You . . . Be with me when the night is dark . . . And shadows cross my heart . . . That I may always keep the faith . . . And never grow apart . . . Let not my mind be lonely or . . . My footsteps go astray . . . But teach me how to live my life . . . According to Your way . . . Be with me, God, when I am home . . . And when I travel far . . . And help me to appreciate . . . The beauty of a star . . . Be my companion everywhere . . . In happiness and tears . . . Be with me, God, and give me grace . . . Through all my earthly years.

THE KINDLY DEED

I never knew how beautiful . . . This life can really be . . . Until one day I met a friend . . . Who showed me sympathy . . . Who taught me more than words can say . . . What friendship really means . . . And how it paints the pretty side . . . Of all the passing scenes . . . I saw the glory of defeat . . . The purpose of a pain . . . The sense in every struggle and . . . The reason for the rain . . . I understood the healthiness . . . Of hoping for the best . . . When there appears to be no chance . . . Of finishing the quest . . . And in my heart I came to know . . . How kindness can awake . . . The joy of doing one good deed . . . For someone else's sake.

CHRISTMAS PRAYER IN WARTIME

To You, dear Lord, we give our thanks . . . That we are gathered here . . . To share the Christmas spirit of . . . Good fellowship and cheer . . . We give our thanks to You, dear Lord . . . Who centuries ago . . . Came down to live upon this earth . . . Because You loved us so . . . You were the Star of Bethlehem . . . The three old wise men saw . . . You were the baby beautiful . . . Upon a bed of straw . . . You filled the world with new-born hope . . . You gave us courage true . . . And all You wanted in return . . . Was our belief in You . . . You were the Holy Child Who brought . . . Good will and peace to men . . . We do believe in You, dear Lord . . . Please, bring us peace again!

PROMPT REPLY

I like to get some letters and . . . I very seldom fail . . . To be at least politely prompt . . . In answering my mail . . . And so I naturally expect . . . My friends to do the same . . . Unless they are not well or else . . . Not otherwise to blame . . . But every now and then I get . . . A letter that declares . . . The writer has been occupied . . . With many common cares . . . And then it says, "Now just because . . . I answer tardily . . . I hope you will not take so long . . . In writing back to me" . . . I think that such procedure is . . . Not only impolite . . . But it is sure one way to lose . . . The friends who care to write.

WEATHERMAN

He tells us if the weather will . . . Be miserable or fine . . . And more specifically he tells . . . If it will rain or shine . . . He warns the world of snow and sleet . . . And gales that whip the sea . . . And gives a good idea of what . . . The temperature will be . . . His word is not infallible . . . And now and then it seems . . . He messes up our picnics or . . . Some other pleasant schemes . . . But usually his prophecy . . . Is equal to the day . . . And when he paints a cloudy sky . . . The sun will stay away . . . He simply reads the weather from . . . The omens that appear . . . And how his trusty instruments . . . Survey the atmosphere.

I shall look for you on the farthest hills . . . On the rivers that reach the sea . . . In the cities that rise to the wind-swept skies . . . And the villages small and free . . . I shall watch for you in the crowds that pass . . . And those in the market place . . . I shall sail my way through the ships at bay . . . In search of your beautiful face . . . I shall ask for you in the public square . . . And along the busiest street . . . On the open plains and the lonely lanes . . . Wherever the world may meet . . . I shall long for you when the clouds are gray . . . And the fields are cold with snow . . . When the moon looks down on a sleepy town . . . And only the shadows grow . . . I shall wait for you till the stars go out . . . And the song in my heart is gone . . . Till I know there will be no smile for me . . . And never another dawn.

VERY SPECIAL POEM

I know a certain daddy who . . . Is pleased as he can be . . . With one attractive member of . . . His happy family . . . He sent his love and kisses with . . . A box of candy sweet . . . To give his youngest girl a thrill . . . And something good to eat . . . And when she wrote her note of thanks . . . She took sufficient time . . . To tell him of her gratitude . . . In rhythm and in rhyme . . . It did not sound like Shakespeare or . . . Like Edgar Allan Poe . . . But it had all the sentiment . . . That poetry could show . . . And all the culture in the world . . . That he could find today . . . Would never match the beauty of . . . The words she tried to say.

NO EASY LIFE

We strive to gain perfection and . . . To live an easy life . . . But things are never perfect, as . . . I often tell my wife . . . We have to have some house repairs . . . The radio is dead . . . Or we sit down to breakfast and . . . There is not any bread . . . Kristina needs a pair of shoes . . . The car declines to run . . . And Jimmie wants a dozen things . . . With which to have some fun . . . While Donnie has a list of all . . . He has to have for school . . . And our refrigerator fails . . . To keep its contents cool . . . And so it goes from day to day . . . And I remind my wife . . . There is no true perfection and . . . There is no easy life.

IS THERE A GOD?

How can a man whose sustenance . . . Depends upon the sod
. . . Be fool enough to tell himself . . . There is no God? . . .
Who shaped the soil? Who set the sun . . . And placed the stars
above? . . . Who molded him and lent him breath . . . To live and
love? . . . Who fashioned him a brain to think . . . Put eyes into
his head . . . And gave him hands and feet to earn . . . His daily
bread? . . . Who kept his body out of harm . . . When any night
or day . . . He might have met an accident . . . And passed away?
Who made it possible for him . . . To do as he might please? . . .
These questions are not all—but can . . . He answer these?

HOBBY

It may be said a hobby is . . . A blessing in disguise . . . That
often helps you to become . . . More capable and wise . . . It takes
up idle moments that . . . Might otherwise be spent . . . In less
productive ways of life . . . To bring about content . . . It keeps
you out of trouble but . . . It brings you pleasure too . . . And gives
you relaxation when . . . Your working day is through . . . It may
consist of anything . . . From making useful things . . . To gathering old coins and stamps . . . Or bells and wedding rings . . . But
it is something you should have . . . To while your time away . . .
And fill your hours later on . . . When you are growing gray.

BUTCHER

The butcher is the man to whom . . . We go to get our meat . . .
And who must cut and trim and weigh . . . Whatever kind we eat
. . . He has to know his beef and pork . . . His roast and steak
and chop . . . And when he slices anything . . . He must know
where to stop . . . He handles hot dogs, hamburgers . . . And sau-
sages galore . . . The liver and whatever else . . . We may be looking for . . . His chicken, turkey, goose and duck . . . Fulfill our
every wish . . . Or he can satisfy us with . . . His oysters, shrimp
and fish . . . In time of war and shortages . . . We bow before his
feet . . . But normally he tries to sell . . . More meat than we can
eat.

THE FAITHFUL DEPARTED

The faithful departed are sleeping today . . . In the graves of the land and the sea . . . Where the wandering waves and the winds of May . . . Are keeping them company . . . They sleep in the hills, in the jungle land . . . And under the barren beach . . . Wherever the rows of crosses stand . . . Or the undulant oceans reach . . . They are the heroes, the conquering sons . . . Of America's army and fleet . . . Who faltered and fell and let go of their guns . . . But would never give up or retreat . . . They are the valiant to whom we owe . . . The sum of an endless debt . . . And they are the ones, wherever we go . . . That our hearts will never forget . . . Loyal in duty beyond and above . . . The challenging call to war . . . They are the faithful departed we love . . . And honor for evermore.

CASH CUSTODIANS

I oft deplore the fact that those . . . Who handle cash all day . . . Must be forever on their toes . . . And get so little pay . . . They usually are under bond . . . Which they provide themselves . . . In case they ever should abscond . . . With items on the shelves . . . They make the sales that fill the till . . . And with their friendly smiles . . . They do their part to spread good will . . . Along the business miles . . . They keep a record of the cost . . . Of everything they sell . . . But if a single cent is lost . . . The boss is sure to yell . . . At least there ought to be a way . . . To meet their bonding fee . . . And not require them to pay . . . To prove their honesty.

HOW LONG A VISIT

A visit should be long enough . . . To make the time worth while . . . Not merely something to exchange . . . A handshake and a smile . . . It should endure sufficiently . . . For friendliness and cheer . . . To take possession of the heart . . . And fill the atmosphere . . . There ought to be politeness and . . . A willingness to share . . . The conversation or debate . . . With everybody there . . . And whether it is business or . . . Another social call . . . There should be no display of wrath . . . Or jealousy at all . . . A visit should be measured by . . . The goal it would achieve . . . But visitors should always go . . . When it is time to leave.

PRAYER FOR YOUTH

O Lord, bestow Your blessing on . . . The children of this earth
. . . And let their lives be magic songs . . . Of merriment and
mirth . . . Protect them from the struggles and . . . The cares of
older years . . . Let not their bodies suffer or . . . Their eyes be
filled with tears . . . Show them the beauty of the world . . . And
help them understand . . . The need for love and virtue and . . .
A warm and friendly hand . . . O Lord, inspire them to grow . . .
In goodness and in grace . . . And in the wisdom to attain . . . A
more deserving place . . . From time to time reveal to them . . .
Reality and truth . . . But let them laugh at foolish fears . . . And
always keep their youth.

DINNERTIME

When dinnertime is drawing near . . . Our hungry youngsters
look . . . To see what appetizing dish . . . Their mother plans to
cook . . . And usually I follow them . . . To see if I can tell . . .
What kind of victuals there will be . . . To please my taste and
smell . . . Our visit to the kitchen is . . . The briefest sort of stay
. . . Because she runs out and says . . . That we are in her way . . .
And so I read the paper or . . . I walk around the lawn . . . While
in their playful, merry mood . . . The children carry on . . . But
when their mother calls to us . . . To gather all around . . . The
hungry youngsters and their dad . . . Are nowhere to be found.

ARMY CHAPLAIN

He wears a khaki uniform . . . The same as all the boys . . .
He eats and sleeps and lives with them . . . Through troubles and
through joys . . . He shares their trenches and their tents . . .
And everything they do . . . Including all the dangers of . . . The
battles they go through . . . He brings a smile to lonely eyes . . .
That gaze across the sea . . . By painting pictures of the peace . . .
To follow victory . . . He heals the wounds of heart and soul . . .
Wherever soldiers fight . . . He is their guardian angel in . . . The
hour of their fright . . . He moves among the fallen men . . .
Where darkness draws despair . . . And lights the lamp of faith
in God . . . To guide their lips in prayer.

MY LOVE FOR YOU

I love the moonlight on your hair . . . The shadow at your feet
. . . And all the little flowers fair . . . That bloom along your
street . . . I dream about the moments brief . . . We shared in
years gone by . . . The way you used to look at me . . . That made
me wonder why . . . The songs we sang, the walks we took . . .
At night and in the dawn . . . And how I cried the day I knew
. . . That you were really gone . . . I think of you as fondly as . . .
I ever did before . . . Indeed if that is possible . . . I love you even
more . . . And how could I forget you when . . . You mean so
much to me . . . When you are in my heart and soul . . . And
every memory?

HIS NIGHT OUT

There are some things concerning which . . . I entertain a doubt
. . . And they include the husband's need . . . To have an evening
out . . . I know not why the married man . . . Must have a special
date . . . To wander out at night because . . . He wants to celebrate . . . Of course he should relax himself . . . And every now
and then . . . He ought to have his pleasure in . . . The company
of men . . . But when it happens once a week . . . And sometimes
more than that . . . He ought to find another house . . . In which
to hang his hat . . . His family is not what he . . . Is most concerned about . . . And 10 to one he never gives . . . His wife an
evening out.

WAY OF THE WORLD

If everybody in this world . . . Achieved a real success . . . There
would not be sufficient fame . . . To go around, I guess . . . And
if each person had to have . . . A fortune in his name . . . The
money situation would . . . Be pretty much the same . . . And who
would ever work for whom . . . Or sell the things we need? . . .
And who would ever envy or . . . Applaud another's deed? . . .
It seems there have to be some folks . . . Who never reach the stars
. . . Or even know the luxury . . . Of homes and motor cars . . .
There have to be some people poor . . . Who toil from day to day
. . . While others rise to fame and wealth . . . So they may lead
the way.

WHEN YOU ARE GONE

When you are gone and I am old . . . (If God should so ordain)
. . . I shall remember you each time . . . I hear the gentle rain . . .
I shall remember you when dawn . . . Is lifting up the hills . . .
And when the wind is wandering . . . Among the daffodils . . . I
shall be with you in my thoughts . . . When I behold the sun . . .
And while I watch from wooded paths . . . The way the rivers run
. . . And back in town where people pass . . . Without a smile or
nod . . . I shall be picturing your joy . . . In being there with God
. . . I shall embrace the shadows of . . . The world we lived in
then . . . And I shall long with all my heart . . . To be with you
again.

BLESS EVERYONE

O Lord, be good to all the world . . . This coming Christmas
Day . . . Let everyone be happy in . . . His individual way . . .
Remember all the poor, O Lord . . . Who think so much of You
. . . And bless their perseverance in . . . The things they try to do
. . . Be helpful to the rich, that they . . . May use their worldly
gain . . . For those on earth who otherwise . . . Might struggle on
in vain . . . Bestow Your special grace upon . . . The widespread
middle class . . . That they may serve You well and make . . . The
grade they need to pass . . . Be good to all the world, O Lord . . .
This coming Christmas Day . . . And everyone will praise You in
. . . His individual way.

WE MUST BE PATIENT

This hour is important for . . . The plans we have today . . .
And to that end we should not let . . . The minutes slip away . . .
We should not wander aimlessly . . . Until tomorrow's dawn . . .
And take the chance that what we want . . . May suddenly be gone
. . . And yet we must be patient and . . . We have to understand
. . . That time and opportunity . . . Go slowly hand in hand . . .
We must remember that it takes . . . A share of life to do . . . The
many things by which we hope . . . To make our dreams come
true . . . And so we should be willing now . . . To persevere and
wait . . . Until we gather what we want . . . However small or
great.

SUNSHINE

The world is full of sunshine . . . For those who try to find it . . .
It may be in the open sky . . . Or hiding close behind it . . . It may
be in a sickroom . . . An alley or a hall . . . Or in the conversation
. . . Of friends who come to call . . . It lingers in a letter . . . It
flies across the sea . . . And it is held in every hand . . . That offers
sympathy . . . It is a pass to happiness . . . That's good in any
season . . . It needs no introduction . . . Or any special reason . . .
It is a part of giving . . . The greeting of a friend . . . It goes with
love and laughter . . . And dreams that never end.

WHAT DO I WANT?

What is it that I want from life . . . To make my heart content?
. . . Success and fame, a happy song . . . Or just a compliment?
. . . Do I desire riches and . . . The comforts they can buy . . . Or
is there something more complete . . . To keep my spirit high? . . .
I must admit it puzzles me . . . And there are many days . . .
When I observe my neighbors and . . . I contemplate their ways
. . . I listen to their voices and . . . Behold the things they do . . .
And always I am hoping I . . . Shall come across a clue . . . And
now and then I tell myself . . . I really know the score . . . But
actually I do not know . . . What I am looking for.

HIS FAITH

He knew his time was running out . . . And life would soon be
gone . . . And yet he had the courage and . . . The faith to carry
on . . . The doctors kept on trying but . . . They knew it was
no use . . . And they would not deceive him with . . . A fanciful
excuse . . . And so they told him how it was . . . And like a soldier great . . . He said that he was quite prepared . . . To face his
final fate . . . He told his mother not to cry . . . Or feel forever blue
. . . Because she should not question what . . . The Lord decides
to do . . . And though there were no final words . . . He ever
chose to say . . . He left an inspiration deep . . . For every youth
today.

HOW OLD IS GOD?

How old is God? He is as old . . . As any man on earth . . .
And yet He is as young of heart . . . As every child at birth . . . He
shaped the world in which we live . . . With all its strength and
ills . . . And He is more enduring than . . . The everlasting hills
. . . The years of every century . . . Are vivid in His mind . . .
The struggles and the joys and all . . . The glories left behind
. . . God is as old as time itself . . . For He and time are one . . .
More ancient than the universe . . . The stars, the moon or sun
. . . He was in the beginning and . . . He will forever be . . .
Because He is the God of life . . . And all eternity.

I LOVE

My teacher said I should not say . . . I "love" a lifeless thing . . .
We merely "like" an object for . . . What pleasure it can bring
. . . While love is something deeper, it . . . Is that which can be
spurned . . . Or that which can attract a soul . . . And therefore
be returned . . . And yet I cannot help myself . . . For now I must
confess . . . I love the moon and all the stars . . . A picture and a
dress . . . I love a pair of silver shoes . . . A wisp of golden hair
. . . The flowers in a gay corsage . . . And perfume in the air . . .
I love a garden and a house . . . Upon a certain street . . . I love
the sky, I even love . . . The dust beneath her feet.

IF I MUST LEAVE ○

If I must leave you now, my love . . . Let not your heart be sad
. . . But think of all the happiness . . . That you and I have had
. . . Let not the sunshine disappear . . . Behind a cloud of gray . . .
But live again the dreams we shared . . . When it was yesterday
. . . Remember how we used to walk . . . Among the roses red . . .
The plans we made, the promises . . . The lovings things we said
. . . Remember how we used to gaze . . . Beyond the morning
mist . . . And when the stars came out at night . . . We closed
our eyes and kissed . . . Remember how I told you that . . . No
matter where I go . . . My love for you will always be . . . The only
love I know.

SLEEPY DONNIE

Sometimes when we go out at night . . . And Jimmie is away . . .
We ask young Donnie to remain . . . And help Kristina play
. . . And see that she gets into bed . . . When she is tired out . . .
So we may have one problem less . . . To be concerned about
. . . But Donnie who is 10 years old . . . And soon will be one more
. . . Is hardly quite as active as . . . His sister who is four . . . He
goes to bed real early and . . . He never counts the sheep . . .
Because it is no task for him . . . To topple off to sleep . . . And
so when we get home and when . . . The stars are growing dim
. . . We find Kristina wide awake . . . And watching over him.

MY MEMORY BOOK

I looked into my memory book . . . And saw unfolded there . . .
The places that were beautiful . . . As castles in the air . . . The
garden paths where bloomed my youth . . . The lanes where love
was born . . . The streets whereon I struggled through . . . Each
trial and each dawn . . . I saw the houses where I lived . . . With
windows bright and gay . . . And chimney smoke that long ago
. . . The wild winds blew away . . . I saw the stores and merchants
and . . . Their fascinating wares . . . And life that seemed to suffer
not . . . Or carry any cares . . . And on a special page I found . . .
Where all my dreams came true . . . The page that held the picture
and . . . The loveliness of you.

INDEBTED TO YOU

I only hope you understand . . . How dear you are to me . . .
Because I am in debt to you . . . As deeply as can be . . . You let
me have your faith and hope . . . As well as courage true . . .
And even for the dreams I dream . . . I owe so much to you . . . You
hold a mortgage on my mind . . . And at the very start . . . I
signed a promissory note . . . Supported by my heart . . . Although
I never can repay . . . What you have done for me . . . You may be
sure I never shall . . . Resort to bankruptcy . . . Because whatever
gratitude . . . And kindness I possess . . . Will be a credit to your
name . . . And for your happiness.

Among my books and souvenirs . . . I spend my time with you
. . . And in my silent solitude . . . I see my dreams come true . . .
I know you are not really there . . . And yet you seem to be . . .
Because the very thought of you . . . Is comforting to me . . . I hold
you in my arms again . . . And look into your eyes . . . And all
the words you whisper are . . . The ones I memorize . . . Your
name appears on every page . . . When I attempt to read . . .
And you are every picture of . . . My courage and my creed
. . . You are the music of my mind . . . My happiness of heart . . .
And we are still together though . . . We seem to be apart.

RELIGION

Some people think religion is . . . A church of wide acclaim . . .
Where it is worth their while to have . . . A record of their name
. . . Where they may go in Sunday clothes . . . That captivate the
eye . . . To meet prospective customers . . . Who have the cash to
buy . . . But that is not religion or . . . The reason for a church . . .
And that is not the golden goal . . . For which the faithful search
. . . Religion is that special way . . . In which we study God . . .
And church is where we ask His help . . . Along the path we plod
. . . Religion is the lamp that shines . . . To show the wrong from
right . . . And draw the world from dark design . . . To everlasting light.

NUPTIAL NOTE

Today you will be married and . . . Your life will start anew
. . . And so with all my heart I wish . . . The very best for you . . .
I wish you every happiness . . . That married life can bring
. . . And may you never be in need . . . Or sigh for anything . . .
My only counsel to you now . . . Is that you keep your vows
. . . And be polite and tolerant . . . With your beloved spouse . . .
Forget yourself and what you want . . . And let no task be done
. . . Until it truly benefits . . . Your one and only one . . . And if
you ever disagree . . . Or something is not right . . . Be sure you
have it put away . . . Before you say good-night.

GOOD-BY TO APRIL

/ to say good-by . . . To 30 April days . . . Because
/ happy in . . . So many little ways . . . Somehow they
/ to be . . . The very breath of spring . . . That blows
/inter and . . . Inspires me to sing . . . And whether
/ght and clear . . . Or overweighed with rain . . . They
ma... feel that life is good . . . And dreams are not in vain
. . . They fill my heart with thoughts of love . . . And flowers
everywhere . . . And even when the wind is wild . . . A song is
in the air . . . I never like to say good-by . . . To April atmosphere
. . . Because I know we cannot meet . . . Until another year.

BEGGAR

The beggar is a lowly man . . . As class distinction goes . . . But
what his true condition is . . . His neighbor seldom knows . . .
He may be nothing more than just . . . A plain and simple fraud
. . . Or he may have the honesty . . . That people all applaud . . .
Perhaps he really needs the cash . . . That fills his tattered hat
. . . Or it may be his scheming way . . . Of getting rich and fat
. . . The truth is not apparent to . . . The ordinary glance . . . And
yet I do not have the heart . . . To take the smallest chance . . .
Because when I have passed him up . . . And seen his gray head
nod . . . It makes me wonder whether I . . . Have walked away
from God.

MY FAITHFUL FRIEND

Of all the joys that life on earth . . . Is able to extend . . . I
treasure most the knowledge that . . . You are my faithful friend
. . . The knowledge that you care for me . . . And keep me in your
mind . . . And that your actions always are . . . Considerate and
kind . . . For you have shown in many ways . . . That you are
good and true . . . And that no matter what I need . . . I may
depend on you . . . You have endeared yourself to me . . . Each
time that we have met . . . And blessed me with a memory . . .
I never shall forget . . . And though the world may offer wealth
. . . And pleasures without end . . . I treasure most the knowledge
that . . . You are my faithful friend.

LONG-WINDED CALL

It is a pleasure to be called . . . Upon the telephone . . . Especially in moments free . . . When I am all alone . . . I always like to listen to . . . A stranger or a friend . . . And try to please the person who . . . Is at the other end . . . But every now and then I am . . . Compelled to take a call . . . From one who rambles on and on . . . With no excuse at all . . . Who gossips or who merely wants . . . To pass the time of day . . . With nothing consequential or . . . Enlightening to say . . . I do not yank the wire out . . . Or make a mean retort . . . But I do wish some folks who call . . . Would try to cut it short.

BASKETBALL

In basketball the players jump . . . To hit the ball up high . . . Then hurry down the floor to reach . . . The goal for which they try . . . They dribble and they toss the ball . . . To others on their team . . . And do their best to execute . . . The coach's clever scheme . . . They have to watch their step so they . . . Will not sustain a loss . . . By fouls that allow their foe . . . To take an extra toss . . . The center and the forwards and . . . The guards must do their part . . . And every member of the team . . . Must have a fighting heart . . . But he who keeps the score for them . . . Has nothing much to do . . . For all he has to know is how . . . To add up two and two.

BUSINESS SCHOOL

In business school the student learns . . . To write in shorthand style . . . To type correctly and with speed . . . And how to keep a file . . . To use good English and avoid . . . The tiniest mistake . . . And to correct the ones the boss . . . May be inclined to make . . . The student also learns the need . . . For proper dress and poise . . . And how to do each duty with . . . A minimum of noise . . . The way to keep a set of books . . . And use the dictaphone . . . And how to run the office right . . . Whenever left alone . . . And so the business school prepares . . . The pathway to success . . . And promises employment filled . . . With pride and happiness.

DESERVING WIFE

Whenever any man becomes . . . A great success in life . . . The chances are he owes a lot . . . To his beloved wife . . . He may not know it at the time . . . And very likely he . . . Is blinded by the brillance of . . . His human vanity . . . But if he stops to analyze . . . The cause of his success . . . He soon discovers that his wife . . . Is half his happiness . . . And he observes how much she does . . . With counsel good and true . . . To help him win in everything . . . He undertakes to do . . . Because a wife knows how to take . . . Advantage of the breaks . . . And how to save her husband from . . . His troublesome mistakes.

GLAD TO BE LIVING

However much I have to do . . . However hard I strive . . . I always tell myself that I . . . Am glad to be alive . . . My heart is grateful for the sun . . . That keeps my body warm . . . And for the comforts of this earth . . . Against whatever storm . . . I have my friends to cheer me up . . . And books to read at night . . . With boundless beauty to behold . . . Whenever stars are bright . . . I have enough to eat and drink . . . And clothes enough to wear . . . A normal mind and healthy lungs . . . To breathe the best of air . . . So why should I object when I . . . Have any job to do . . . As long as I have everything . . . To help me see it through?

ALL TO YOUR CREDIT

Each morning of my life becomes . . . More interesting and new . . . Because of all the wonder and . . . The joy of knowing you . . . Whenever I behold the sun . . . That lights another day . . . I tell myself the friendly thoughts . . . That I have heard you say . . . And when the stars surround the moon . . . To decorate the night . . . My dream of you makes everything . . . More beautiful and bright . . . Your very name inspires me . . . To reach a greater goal . . . And that is why I whisper it . . . So often to my soul . . . You are so much a part of me . . . In everything I do . . . That all the credit I receive . . . Belongs at last to you.

SOLDIER'S PRAYER

Dear God, I need Your Help to do . . . My duty in this war
. . . To win the kind of peace that will . . . Endure for evermore . . . Give me the strength to use my gun . . . With steady
aim and true . . . And guide me in all other things . . . A soldier
has to do . . . Let not my eyes grow weary now . . . Let not my
stomach ache . . . And if the going gets too tough . . . Let not
my spirit break . . . Watch over all my loved ones, God . . . While
I am over here . . . See that they never are in want . . . Or have a
single fear . . . And when the air is still once more . . . And we no
longer roam . . . I pray that I may be among . . . The soldiers
going home.

LITTLE COTTAGE

There was a little cottage . . . By the roadside on a hill . . . And
if it has not worn away . . . It must be there still . . . It was not
very elegant . . . But breathed the gentle charm . . . Of flowers on
a balcony . . . Or chickens on a farm . . . Its friendly window-eyes
beheld . . . The peaceful life around . . . And magnified the smiling sun . . . That woke the sleeping ground . . . The chimney on
its sloping roof . . . Blew ribbons at the sky . . . The doors reached
out and welcomed in . . . The traveler passing by . . . And when
the weary, day-worn world . . . In shadows went to hide . . . The
little cottage drews its shades . . . And locked its soul inside.

PUBLIC SERVANTS

We think of public servants as . . . The ones whose time is spent
. . . In executing duties that . . . Pertain to government . . . And
in the strictest sense that term . . . Belongs to them indeed . . .
Who serve their country or their state . . . Or fill some local need
. . . But in another sense it seems . . . It ought to be applied . . .
To everybody everywhere . . . Who wants to keep in stride . . .
Because each citizen is one . . . Who is or ought to be . . . A serv-
ant to the public in . . . His own community . . . He ought to be
unselfish and . . . Contribute all he can . . . To make the world a
better place . . . And help his fellow-man.

GOD BE WITH YOU

May God be always with you, friend . . . May He be good to you . . . And help you to accomplish all . . . That you set out to do . . . May He give comfort to your heart . . . When trouble comes your way . . . And lend whatever strength you need . . . To start another day . . . And when you gain a greater share . . . Of riches or of fame . . . May God inspire you to be . . . Deserving of your name . . . May He protect you from all harm . . . And guide each step you take . . . That you may be as generous . . . For someone else's sake . . . May He bestow upon your soul . . . His blessings without end . . . And when you say good-by to us . . . May God be with you, friend.

RIDING THE BUS

I ride the bus to work each day . . . And I must say I feel . . . That at the very best it is . . . A tiresome ordeal . . . Sometimes I have the fortune good . . . To get myself a seat . . . But usually I make the trip . . . Supported by my feet . . . And yet it is a pleasure to . . . Go back and forth each day . . . Because so many other folks . . . Are traveling that way . . . And I can see their faces and . . . Compare them one by one . . . And figure out the way they live . . . And walk around the sun . . . I hear their conversation and . . . I learn their joys and woes . . . Which makes up for my anguish when . . . They step upon my toes.

＼ MY ONLY ONE

The mountains rise above the mist . . . The sea reflects the sun . . . And all the world is bright because . . . You are my only one . . . You make the flowers lovelier . . . The fields a richer green . . . And in your eyes I find the skies . . . The bluest I have seen . . . You give the snow a whiter touch . . . You fill the rain with song . . . Wherever you decide to go . . . I want to go along . . . Whatever thoughts you ever have . . . Whatever words you say . . . And all the moments of your life . . . Are part of my today . . . You summon forth the silver stars . . . To make my dreams come true . . . And that is why I dedicate . . . My every breath to you.

MAID WANTED

My wife is always asking me . . . To hire her a maid . . . Because the work around the house . . . Requires extra aid . . . And always I agree with her . . . That housework is no fun . . . And she deserves a servant good . . . To help her get it done . . . But every time I find a maid . . . Who seems to be all right . . . My wife declares that after all . . . Our budget is too tight . . . Or else she tries domestics out . . . But never finds a gem . . . Because they are no good unless . . . She stands right over them . . . And so she keeps on working and . . . Complaining every day . . . And I keep looking for a maid . . . Who might be worth her pay.

SORRY SELECTION

I had a special friend one time . . . Who wanted to succeed . . . And who had all the confidence . . . That anyone might need . . . He had the willingness to work . . . And he could take a dare . . . And in the most gigantic job . . . He would perform his share . . . But somehow as he went along . . . He never seemed to see . . . The path that offered him the best . . . Of opportunity . . . And if the chance were given him . . . Or it were his to find . . . His choice would indicate that he . . . Was not a little blind . . . He had the strength to go ahead . . . But when he did decide . . . His own selection gave him cause . . . To be dissatisfied.

LONELY MAN

He must be quite a lonely man . . . As he pursues his way . . . With never any smile or nod . . . And nothing much to say . . . He keeps his troubles to himself . . . If truly he is sad . . . But also he displays no sign . . . Of ever being glad . . . Of course the fact is recognized . . . When all is said and done . . . That he does not disturb the peace . . . Or bother anyone . . . And yet he is not liked or praised . . . Or given a reward . . . And it is doubtful that he has . . . The blessing of The Lord . . . He may have lots of money but . . . He is of little worth . . . Because he does not give himself . . . To others on this earth.

NO SECRET

I have no secret deep that you . . . Do not already know . . .
Unless you do not know how much . . . I love the winds that blow
. . . How much I love a certain girl . . . With certain eyes and
hair . . . A certain one whose name and face . . . Are with me
everywhere . . . How much I think and dream of her . . . Each
hour of the day . . . How much I long to share with her . . . This
life in every way . . . I have no secret deep, unless . . . You do not
know that I . . . Would rather see her smile than all . . . The sunshine in the sky . . . Unless you do not know that she . . . Inspires
all I do . . . Unless you do not understand . . . That certain girl is
you.

GOD'S FAMILY

The family belongs to God . . . In quite a special way . . .
Because it is His own design . . . For living every day . . . He
wants the world to carry on . . . With generations new . . . And
so He planned this noble task . . . For all of us to do . . . He grants
our prayers for children and . . . He helps them grow in grace
. . . That they in turn may help Him to . . . Improve the human
race . . . But He expects us all to do . . . Our fair and equal share
. . . By being parents who bestow . . . Their gentle love and care
. . . Who guide their children faithfully . . . Through hours bright
and dim . . . And teach them to be grateful and . . . Forever
honor Him.

FINDERS KEEPERS?

Some people feel they may retain . . . Whatever things they find
. . . No matter how the article . . . Was lost or left behind . . .
And whether such an item is . . . A penny or a gem . . . They even
think the law declares . . . That it belongs to them . . . But when
they are the losers they . . . Forever wail and weep . . . And
they insist that no one has . . . The right to find and keep . . .
Well, in this latter thought they are . . . As right as they can be
. . . And if they practiced it there would . . . Be no dishonesty . . .
Whatever thing is lost and found . . . Belongs to him at last . . .
Who was its lawful owner in . . . The most immediate past.

OVERSEAS SENTRY

While clouds roll by and strange winds moan . . . As if to rouse
a storm . . . Somewhere out there he stands alone . . . In uniform
. . . His duty called him to the front . . . Where only time goes by
. . . Where orders are precise and blunt . . . And some must
die . . . His gun is ever at his side . . . His helmet on his head . . .
And in his veins the blood of pride . . . Runs deep and red . . . His
work is never at an end . . . His daily meals are brief . . . He cannot slumber or depend . . . Upon relief . . . He watches for the
planes that soar . . . And men who hide and run . . . He only
knows there is a war . . . That must be won.

GET WELL SOON

I am so sorry you are ill . . . And have to stay in bed . . . Indeed
I only wish that I . . . Could be there in your stead . . . It is no
fun for anyone . . . To pass the time away . . . Reclining in seclu-
sion from . . . The beauty of the day . . . I hope however you will
have . . . A visitor or two . . . Whenever you are in the mood
. . . To have them call on you . . . May greeting cards surround
you and . . . May flowers fill your room . . . And may each
moment be untouched . . . By suffering or gloom . . . And most
of all I hope that it . . . Will not be very long . . . Before you are
recovered and . . . Completely well and strong.

HOBO

He wanders on from place to place . . . By boxcar or on foot . . .
But never finds a spot where he . . . Would finally take root
. . . His home is on the dusty plains . . . And in the city street . . .
On river, lake and everywhere . . . His fellow creatures meet . . .
He is not bothered by the wind . . . The rain or anything . . . Nor
does he ponder over what . . . Another day may bring . . . He may
not have the credits for . . . A bachelor's degree . . . But he is most
proficient in . . . Profound philosophy . . . And though he scouts
around for food . . . And has to ride the rods . . . Invariably he
finds a way . . . To overcome the odds.

HOME BOOKKEEPING

I keep a set of books at home . . . In which I try to measure . . .
How much we have for what we need . . . And what is left for
pleasure . . . Each bill we pay, each bond we buy . . . Is entered
as a credit . . . While every show and ice cream cone . . . Becomes
another debit . . . But also, while it may appear . . . Unusual or
funny . . . The books I keep are not made up . . . Entirely of
money . . . Because upon the credit side . . . I post our every blessing . . . While on the debit side I write . . . The things that are
distressing . . . And when I add our blessings up . . . It never
is surprising . . . To see our debits disappear . . . And find our
profits rising.

EASY TO SMILE

A smile is such a simple way . . . Of keeping spirits glad . . .
Why undertake the troubled task . . . Of being blue and sad?
. . . Our tears are never welcome and . . . A look of heavy gloom
. . . Is bound to frighten folks away . . . Like some impending
doom . . . But happiness is catching and . . . A bit of kindly cheer
. . . Will bring us so much closer in . . . A friendly atmosphere . . .
And it will always help to ease . . . The burden we must bear
. . . And overcome the weariness . . . Of every daily care . . .
There is no valid reason for . . . Our fears to get us down . . .
When smiling is much easier . . . Than fostering a frown.

I DREAM OF YOU

I dream of everlasting hills . . . Beyond the purple skies . . .
Where twilight falls and shadow-walls . . . Enclose your wistful
eyes . . . Of sails that touch the distant shore . . . And leave this
world behind . . . Across the seas, where memories . . . Are beautiful and kind . . . I dream of stars that glitter and . . . A moon
that seeks the dawn . . . And of the day I heard you say . . . You
never would be gone . . . And well I know how good and true
. . . This life can really be . . . That now again, the same as then
. . . Your heart belongs to me . . . That you and I divide this
life . . . No matter how it seems . . . And through each night we
share the right . . . To all our endless dreams.

THE BEST IN ME

Dear Lord, as long as I may live . . . I want to do Your will . . .
And overlook no promise I . . . Am able to fulfill . . . I want to
be Your servant in . . . Whatever way I can . . . Especially in
everything . . . For every fellow-man . . . I want to glorify Your
name . . . Wherever I may be . . . By always offering the world
. . . The best there is in me . . . Because I owe so much to You . . .
For what I have today . . . That it is far beyond what I . . . Am
able to repay . . . And so the best that I can do . . . Is not to take
a rest . . . Until I know, dear Lord, that I . . . Have given You my
best.

BACK UP OUR BOYS

Across the wide, blue oceans where . . . The guns are roaring out
. . . Where silence is forgotten and . . . A whisper is a shout . . .
Our boys are fighting gallantly . . . That treachery may cease . . .
That all the world may hold again . . . The happiness of peace
. . . They give their blood, that other blood . . . May never have
to flow . . . They suffer now, that you and I . . . Less suffering
may know . . . And so the least that we can do . . . Is show the
world that we . . . Are backing up our valiant boys . . . Who
fight for victory . . . By doing home defense work and . . . By
buying bonds and stamps . . . And by encouraging the boys . . .
In all our training camps.

GOD'S DAY FOR CHILDREN

Sunday is God's day . . . And after a way . . . Sunday is also
. . . The children's day . . . Healthy and happy . . . And dressed
in their best . . . Shining and smiling . . . To pass every test . . .
Dreaming their dinner . . . Of chicken and cake . . . All the good
dishes . . . Dear mother will make . . . Running and playing . . .
Where breezes blow . . . Getting in line for . . . The picture show
. . . Drinking a soda . . . Or chewing on gum . . . Passing the
time with . . . A favorite chum . . . Home again, tired . . . To
supper and bed . . . Slumber is good for . . . A sleepy head.

CITY EDITOR

The city editor is one . . . Who seems to thrive on noise . . . And adds to it by shouting at . . . The helpless copy boys . . . He sends reporters here and there . . . To get the latest news . . . And then he tells the rewrite men . . . To watch their p's and q's . . . He studies every story for . . . The power it presents . . . To catch the public eye and keep . . . The reader in suspense . . . Expense accounts are his to check . . . The budget his to trim . . . And nobody could do as much . . . As they expect of him . . . He makes a decent living but . . . He gains no public fame . . . And when the slightest thing goes wrong . . . He always gets the blame.

HELPFUL FRIENDS

I hope to keep the friends I have . . . As long as I am here . . . Because they are the treasures that . . . I hold so very dear . . . The rain may drive the sun away . . . The snow may hide the ground . . . But nothing in my heart can change . . . The friends that I have found . . . They lift me up when I am blue . . . Wherever I may be . . . If nothing more than by the touch . . . Of happy memory . . . My friends inspire me to seek . . . The nobler things on earth . . . And by what kindly deeds I do . . . To be of greater worth . . . And yet if they desert me or . . . In silence pass away . . . My having known them makes me try . . . To live a better day.

JOY OF A JOB

I know that when I do a job . . . My energy is taxed . . . And it appears more pleasant to . . . Be idle and relaxed . . . But I have tried the easy way . . . And I have always found . . . That I get mighty tired when . . . I merely lounge around . . . And I have gone about my task . . . With swift and steady step . . . That seemed to lift my spirits up . . . And give me added pep . . . And so I have decided that . . . The wiser thing to do . . . Is just to stay right on the job . . . Until I see it through . . . Because my heart is happy when . . . I know my work is done . . . And then I feel that I have earned . . . My leisure and my fun.

190

BOXING

Among the many sports we have . . . There is the boxing bout . . . In which two men do all they can . . . To knock each other out . . . They face each other with their gloves . . . And bodies all but bare . . . To spar and dance around a ring . . . That actually is square . . . They have to follow certain rules . . . Each time they take a swing . . . But otherwise their hands are free . . . To give it everything . . . For 15 rounds or less they fight . . . To carry off the crown . . . While referees must count to 10 . . . To keep a fellow down . . . The pugilistic contest is . . . A test of strength and skill . . . And many are the purses that . . . The fans are glad to fill.

PROFESSORS

Professors are respected souls . . . Albeit underpaid . . . And not infrequently they are . . . Quite dignified and staid . . . Their learning is attested to . . . By two or three degrees . . . From highly rated colleges . . . Or universities . . . They lecture by the hour and . . . They carefully explain . . . The theories and facts there are . . . To fill the student's brain . . . And in return they only ask . . . Obedience and truth . . . As part of their campaign to build . . . The character of youth . . . Professors are the persons who . . . Are plain and undisguised . . . But whose superb abilities . . . Are seldom recognized.

OUR LOVING THANKS

Dear one, there are so many words . . . That I would like to say . . . This 19th anniversary . . . We celebrate today . . . And all of them are gratitude . . . Of one kind or another . . . For being such a loving wife . . . And such a perfect mother . . . Your faith and your encouragement . . . Have paved the way for me . . . And you have been the guiding light . . . For all the family . . . In sickness and in struggle and . . . In every sort of weather . . . The happiness of having you . . . Has held our hearts together . . . The children want to thank you and . . . With all my heart I say . . . The words of love and gratitude . . . I offer you today.

You never really leave me when . . . You go away from me . . .
Because I feel your presence, dear . . . Wherever I may be . . . Each
time I look up at the sky . . . I see you smiling there . . . And when
the wind disturbs the trees . . . Your kisses fill the air . . . In
every house you move about . . . At every door you stand . . .
Along the winding garden path . . . I take you by the hand . . .
The rain is just your flowing hair . . . That falls against my cheek
. . . And when the radio is on . . . I only hear you speak . . . At
night I always find you in . . . My dreams, and so you see . . . You
never really leave me when . . . You go away from me.

GREEDY MAN

Why does a man who has success . . . And wealth at his command . . . Forever look for ways and means . . . To flourish and
expand? . . . He is not satisfied to hold . . . A fortune in his name
. . . But he is always striving for . . . The goal of greater fame . . .
It is this common attribute . . . Of wanting more and more . . .
That leads to wholesale jealousy . . . And finally to war . . . He
cannot conquer every land . . . Or bridle every sea . . . Nor can he
buy a higher place . . . In God's eternity . . . And yet he reaches
out for gold . . . And glory in each deed . . . To gratify his vanity
. . . And satiate his greed.

YOUR CHILD, O LORD

Dear Lord, I know how much You love . . . The children of this
earth . . . And that Your heart considers them . . . Of everlasting
worth . . . And when I look at them I know . . . Exactly how You
feel . . . For they are all so innocent . . . So honest and so real . . .
And O dear Lord, there was a time . . . When I was just as small
. . . And equally as good, as I . . . Am sure You will recall . . .
But You permitted me to grow . . . According to my way . . . And
foolishly I took the path . . . Where I was bound to stray . . And
now, O Lord, I ask that You . . . Consider me once more . . . As
just a little child who comes . . . To knock upon Your door.

IF YOU KNOW JOE

If you have dough and you know Joe . . . You are a lucky guy
. . . For he can get you anything . . . You ever want to buy . . .
A stove, refrigerator, car . . . A radio or two . . . A grand piano,
nylons or . . . Whatever pleases you . . . However new the article
. . . However hard to get . . . Old Joe will show his friendly
smile . . . And see that you are set . . . In fact if he has known you
long . . . And thinks that you are nice . . . He will arrange for
you to pay . . . Below the standard price . . . Of course it should
not be that way . . . But what is there to do . . . When things are
scarce and good old Joe . . . Can get the stuff for you?

NIGHT WATCHMAN

Each day at sundown when the world . . . Is going home to sleep
. . . He leaves his slumber and begins . . . The vigil he must keep
. . . He takes a trolley or a bus . . . To his appointed place . . . And
there he sits upon a chair . . . Or walks with steady pace . . . His
job is to protect the goods . . . That someone leaves alone . . . As
faithfully and carefully . . . As though they were his own . . . He
has a lot of time to think . . . To study or to write . . . But he must
be prepared for crooks . . . Who operate at night . . . And when
the world wakes up and when . . . The sun is overhead . . . His
lonely job is over and . . . He hurries home to bed.

GREETINGS, U. S. A.!

Birthday greetings, U. S. A. . . . On your Independence Day! . . .
Praise and honor be to you . . . And the red and white and blue . . .
Of your stars and stripes unfurled . . . For the eyes of all the
world . . . Every countryman is proud . . . And his cheers are
long and loud . . . For your glory and your might . . . And the
spirit of your fight . . . In the air, on land and sea . . . For the
sake of liberty . . . All your states united stand . . . As a free-
dom-loving land . . . Where the citizen's consent . . . Is the only
government . . . And the laws with equal weight . . . Rule the
humble and the great . . . Birthday greetings, U. S. A. . . . On your
Independence Day! . . . May your flag forever fly . . . In the
freedom of the sky . . . And may God's good blessing be . . . Yours
for all posterity.

193

FORGETFUL FAME

Some people rise to prominence . . . (Or maybe think they do)
. . . And in the passing of events . . . Forget the friends they
knew . . . They feel their time is worth so much . . . They cannot spare it now . . . To say hello, shake hands and such . . . Or
simply smile and bow . . . They have no time to lunch or dine . . .
With those they used to own . . . To pay a visit, drop a line . . .
Or even telephone . . . They measure their importance by . . . The
glitter of their fame . . . And figure everyone should sigh . . . To
just pronounce their name . . . Well, maybe some day I shall
rate . . . And reach the rainbow's end . . . But may I never be so
great . . . As to forget a friend.

TIME TO PAY

Today we face the deadline for . . . Our tax returns to show . . .
If we have money coming or . . . We are the ones who owe . . . It
is the time when Uncle Sam . . . Insists that we declare . . . How
much in cash we made last year . . . And also how and where . . .
And while we may not like the thought . . . Of paying income
tax . . . We ought to stop a moment and . . . Consider certain facts
. . . Our nickels, dimes and dollars are . . . Collected to be spent
. . . In order to continue to . . . Maintain our government . . . To
serve the public welfare and . . . To answer every call . . . With
liberty and justice and . . . Security for all.

SWIMMER

He dives into the water and . . . He races down a lane . . .
To try to reach in record time . . . The goal that he would
gain . . . Or else he merely flounders in . . . The waves that fall
and rise . . . Or floats upon his back while he . . . Enjoys the
summer skies . . . In any case his muscles grow . . . And he
develops form . . . And water never bothers him . . . Unless there
is a storm . . . He gets a healthy tan when he . . . Relaxes on the
shore . . . Although at first his sunburned skin . . . May be a
little sore . . . He may not make a great big splash . . . But be it
said of him . . . The person who pursues this sport . . . Is always
in the swim.

KRISTINA CALLING

I do not find my daily grind . . . As dull as it might be . . . Because each day by telephone . . . Kristina talks to me . . . She tells
me how she feels and what . . . She dreamed the night before . . .
And all that Mommy plans to buy . . . When they go to the store
. . . She tells me she is washed and dressed . . . And all prepared
to play . . . And she will take her nap when she . . . Has put
her lunch away . . . Of course she always lets me know . . . That
she could use a toy . . . Or that some gum or candy would . . .
Provide a world of joy . . . But I am truly grateful to . . . Kristina
on the phone . . . Because she makes me happy and . . . I never
feel alone.

NEW LIFE

The sun is shining in my heart . . . The sky is clear and blue . . .
And if I make a wish today . . . I know it will come true . . . For
I have blown the clouds away . . . Beyond the golden dawn . . .
And everything of bitterness . . . Is over now and gone . . . The
evergreen is beautiful . . . The field is white with snow . . . And I
enjoy the gentleness . . . Of little winds that blow . . . The river
flows between its banks . . . To join the peaceful sea . . . And
every happy harbinger . . . Is calling out to me . . . The morning
is a melody . . . The world is bright and new . . . And if I make
a wish today . . . I know it will come true.

LOVE LETTERS

They are the words that whisper peace . . . And comfort in the
dawn . . . When someone dear is far away . . . But never really
gone . . . They are the flowery lines that reach . . . Across a paper
page . . . Whose fragance lingers even when . . . The pulp is frail
with age . . . The sentences that sail the seas . . . To new, exotic
lands . . . And have their own familiar way . . . Of joining lonely
hands . . . The paragraphs of pretty prose . . . That paint the
heavens blue . . . And sketch a castle in the clouds . . . Where
happy dreams come true . . . They are the leaves that never fall . . .
The boughs that never bend . . . And all the magic melodies . . .
That never seem to end.

BLESS HER, O LORD

Bless her, O Lord, my loving wife . . . Who now for 18 years . . .
Has walked with me the path of life . . . And shared its smiles and
tears . . . Bless her for all the kindly deeds . . . That she has done
for me . . . And for considering my needs . . . With love and
sympathy . . . She has encouraged me to try . . . Whatever I
would do . . . And she has kept my spirits high . . . To help my
dreams come true . . . Give her, O Lord, a world of wealth . . .
With everlasting smiles . . . And bless her with the best of health
. . . Along the coming miles . . . Let her be happy in her heart
. . . And from all worry free . . . And grant that we may never
part . . . Each other's company.

STINGY MAN

The stingy man is one who saves . . . Beyond the rainy day . . .
And far beyond the point where he . . . Has any time for play
. . . He is the one who never wants . . . To spend a cent at
all . . . Not even once to entertain . . . The friends who come to
call . . . He lets you buy his coffee and . . . His daily dinner too
. . . But he will never use his purse . . . To do the same for you
. . . He always claims that he is broke . . . When in reality . . . He
merely wants to gather up . . . Whatever goods are free . . . And
while he may enjoy the things . . . He gets from day to day . . . He
never knows the greater joy . . . Of giving them away.

WE HONOR THEM

Today we lay aside our work . . . To honor those who fell . . .
Who heard the call to duty and . . . Who served our country well
. . . They are the heroes great and true . . . Who sleep beneath
the sod . . . And who have earned their heritage . . . Of happiness
with God . . . We owe eternal gratitude . . . To each and every son
. . . Whose bravery made possible . . . The victory we won . . .
They gave up all they had to give . . . That we might live in
peace . . . And so that liberty might have . . . An everlasting
lease . . . They are the men who did their best . . . Against the
odds they met . . . And whose supreme unselfishness . . . We
never will forget.

BEFORE WE SAY GOOD-BY

I want to hold you close once more . . . And hear your gentle sigh . . . And kiss your soft, warm lips again . . . Before we say good-by . . . I want to shut tomorrow out . . . For one brief moment here . . . To dream of all the happy days . . . Of every yesteryear . . . To walk among the flowers fair . . . That bloomed when it was spring . . . And feel the breath of autumn winds . . . That blew on everything . . . To gaze upon each street and home . . . The windows and the lights . . . And hear the music and the songs . . . That filled a thousand nights . . . I want to see your smile once more . . . Before you start to cry . . . I want to kiss your soft, warm lips . . . Before we say good-by.

SPOILED

Sometimes although a child is spoiled . . . It will grow up to be . . . A most successful creature in . . . The best community . . . But frequently the family pet . . . Pursues the lesser things . . . With no desire to untie . . . The mother's apron strings . . . And as the child becomes a man . . . It very soon appears . . . That he has been too sheltered from . . . Uncertainties and fears . . . He has to have his comforts and . . . Be coddled every day . . . And he is never satisfied . . . Unless he gets his way . . . And these peculiar facts apply . . . With equal force or more . . . To all the pampered ladies whom . . . Their gentlemen adore.

LET US PRAY

When we were little children we . . . Were taught to kneel and pray . . . If only for protection at . . . The closing of the day . . . We were not hesitant at all . . . In telling God our needs . . . Or asking Him to pardon us . . . For our mischievous deeds . . . But as the years went by and we . . . Began to grow in size . . . We let our thoughts and lips grow lax . . . In keeping up those ties . . . Or maybe we grew bashful when . . . We could not be alone . . . And felt that prayer was something we . . . Had gradually outgrown . . . And yet it is so obvious . . . There is no shame in prayer . . . And we should pray each night and day . . . To show Him that we care.

WE'RE PROUD OF JIMMIE

Our Jimmie brings report cards home . . . That make us really
proud . . . And never do we hesitate . . . To say our praise out
loud . . . Because he sure deserves it and . . . We know from
times gone by . . . He does not boast a bit or let . . . His spirits
soar too high . . . We always give him some reward . . . To make
him happy then . . . And when he hears the school bell ring . . .
He gets to work again . . . Of course there are some pleasant nights
. . . When he would rather play . . . Than struggle with the lessons he . . . Must take to class next day . . . But always he con-
tinues to . . . Excel in every test . . . And always we are proud
of him . . . Because he does his best.

REMEMBERING

When I am old and very gray . . . And hours matter not . . . I
hope that I shall always say . . . That nothing is forgot . . . I hope
I shall remember all . . . The songs of long ago . . . And somewhere in my heart recall . . . The joys I used to know . . . The
friends who came to comfort me . . . When I indulged in tears . . .
And left a kindly memory . . . To carry through the years . . . The
smiling lips, the laughing eyes . . . The letters in the mail . . . The
stars of silver in the skies . . . And all the moonbeams pale . . . But
whether any other view . . . Will draw me to the past . . . I know
I shall remember you . . . However long I last.

OF ALL MY FRIENDS

There are the friends who say hello . . . Wherever we may meet
. . . And those who share my office or . . . Who live across the
street . . . There are the friends who send me cards . . . When they
are out of town . . . And those who ask me now and then . . . If
things are up or down . . . But when I contemplate them all . . .
The only ones worth while . . . Are those who give me courage with
. . . An everlasting smile . . . Who never seem to leave my side . . .
No matter where I go . . . As long as they can help my heart . . .
To understand and grow . . . As long as I attempt to find . . . A
better way to live . . . And share with them the friendship they
. . . Are more than glad to give.

SITUATION WANTED

When I am looking for a job . . . My luck is always slow . . .
And every time they turn me down . . . I feel distinctly low . . . I
pound the pavement constantly . . . I knock on every door . . . And
when the day is done I have . . . Another zero score . . . But when
at last I have success . . . And start to earn my pay . . . A second
offer comes along . . . To add its sunny ray . . . And then a third
and then a fourth . . . Until it seems to me . . . My services are
being sought . . . By every company . . . The fear of being out of
work . . . Would surely be erased . . . If only opportunities . . .
Were somewhat better spaced.

MARBLES

The game of marbles is a game . . . That furnishes a thrill . . .
And in addition it is one . . . That tests a fellow's skill . . . You
have to practice angle shots . . . And how to knuckle down . . .
And you must have a steady hand . . . If you would win renown
. . . The marbles are composed of clay . . . Of porcelain, steel or
glass . . . Except the handsome agate which . . . Is in a separate
class . . . Some youngsters like to play for keeps . . . While others
play for fun . . . But either way it is a sport . . . That pleases
everyone . . . And whether you endure defeat . . . Or you deserve
to rate . . . You learn the more important point . . . Of always
shooting straight.

FINISHING SCHOOL

To get the proper finishing . . . A lady ought to go . . . To some
good school where everything . . . Is just exactly so . . . Where
passing grades depend upon . . . The perfect poise and grace . . .
And how to be polite in all . . . Expressions of the face . . . It may
be difficult to walk . . . Where angels fear to tread . . . And learn
the way to balance books . . . Upon a pretty head . . . But if the
lady perseveres . . . There need be no alarm . . . For she will
surely blossom forth . . . With dignity and charm . . . And at
commencement she will be . . . The loveliest on earth . . . While
dear old dad will be convinced . . . He got his money's worth.

OUR KIND OF HOUSE

I think about the kind of house . . . That I would like to buy . . .
Or one that I would build myself . . . Beneath the golden sky . . .
I know it would be beautiful . . . With many rooms and doors
. . . And gorgeous oriental rugs . . . To cover all the floors . . .
The landscape and the flowers would . . . Be regal as the stars
. . . And my garage could hold at least . . . A half a dozen cars
. . . But then I always think about . . . The friends who call on
me . . . And of the sort of life I live . . . With my dear family . . .
And I decide that we would feel . . . So formal and alone . . .
Without the cozy, humble house . . . That now is all our own.

MY ONLY WISH

I hope this new-born year will be . . . The best I ever spent . . .
And that it will convey to me . . . The fullness of content . . . And
when I say "content" I mean . . . I hope The Lord will bless . . .
My everyday domestic scene . . . With perfect happiness . . . I
mean I want my loving wife . . . Our little girl and boys . . . To
share the beauty of this life . . . And gather all its joys . . . I hope
each hour of each day . . . There will be something new . . . To
keep their hearts forever gay . . . And make their dreams come
true . . . Because if I can just be sure . . . That they have cause
to smile . . . Then anything I may endure . . . Is really worth my
while.

AS LONG AS LIFE

Whatever be the time of year . . . Whatever else I do . . . As
long as I have life to dream . . . My dreams will be of you . . . My
dreams have always been of you . . . Because right from the start
. . . I wanted you and gave you all . . . The love within my heart
. . . I thought of you as something more . . . Than all the stars
above . . . You were my deep devotion and . . . The music of my
love . . . You were the echo of each song . . . The wind beyond
the sea . . . And you were everything that breathed . . . Of happiness for me . . . And so whatever be the place . . . Or yet the
time of year . . . My heart will be remembering . . . And dreaming
of you, dear.

THESE ARE MY WANTS

O Lord, protect my humble home . . . My wife and children three . . . Watch over them each day and night . . . They mean so much to me . . . Help my two boys to grow, O Lord . . . In wisdom and in height . . . That they may be successful men . . . And worthy in Your sight . . . Be good to her, my little girl . . . Who is so sweet and dear . . . And let her blossom forth in time . . . Untouched by any tear . . . Bestow Your richest blessing on . . . My fond and faithful wife . . . Whose love and deep devotion are . . . The fullness of my life . . . And if, O Lord, You do these things . . . You will supply my shelf . . . With everything that I could ask . . . To satisfy myself.

MARCH WIND

They say the wind belongs to March . . . And April owns the rain . . . While flowers are a part of May . . . Along a lovers' lane . . . But I can feel the wind today . . . And it is gentle now . . . It does not break the smallest branch . . . Or even make it bow . . . It is a welcome visitor . . . That takes me by the hand . . . And breathes the quiet beauty of . . . A fragrant, fertile land . . . It has a way of whispering . . . The words I want to hear . . . With eagerness to carry on . . . Another youthful year . . . And April may be filled with rain . . . And May with flowers fair . . . But on this day in March the wind . . . Is gentle everywhere.

WE OWE HIM THANKS

Our country holds the highest place . . . Of glory in the sun . . . For which no little gratitude . . . Belongs to Washington . . . Because his bravery began . . . The struggle to be free . . . That we might live in lasting peace . . . And have prosperity . . . We are indebted to him for . . . His courage and his skill . . . The suffering at Valley Forge . . . The blood of Bunker Hill . . . He saw the need to recognize . . . The human rights we stress . . . Our claim to life and liberty . . . And equal happiness . . . And all throughout the turmoil of . . . A world engulfed in war . . . His noble principles were those . . . That we were fighting for.

DRUGGIST

Long years ago he specialized . . . In tonics, herbs and pills . . .
And making up prescriptions for . . . The people and their ills
. . . But now his duties have increased . . . And he must do much
more . . . To satisfy the young and old . . . Who patronize his
store . . . He has to sell them magazines . . . Perfumes and shav-
ing sets . . . As well as candy bars and gum . . . Cigars and
cigarets . . . He must have greeting cards for all . . . The anniversary dates . . . And he must mix the sodas and . . . Prepare the
luncheon plates . . . So many are his duties and . . . The goods
upon his shelf . . . At times it seems he ought to take . . . Some
headache pills himself.

TRUE FRIENDSHIP

A lasting friendship is a thing . . . That only you can make . . .
But something that a second's time . . . Is all it needs to break . . .
The picture is the same as when . . . We plant an acorn small
. . . And want it to become a tree . . . Magnificent and tall . . .
And then we swing our ax until . . . That one and final stroke
. . . When we discover we have felled . . . The promise of an
oak . . . A lasting friendship is a thing . . . Of delicate design
. . . That needs the rain and sunshine and . . . The silver stars
that shine . . . Indeed it has to have the best . . . Of care that we
can give . . . If we would have it last as long . . . As ever we may
live.

POOR PAY

Some people grumble and complain . . . When they receive their
pay . . . And think they should get twice as much . . . For every
working day . . . And usually their salary . . . Is not what makes
them sore . . . But just the thought that someone else . . . Is getting so much more . . . They figure they produce the same . . .
And far more ably too . . . Than those who draw a higher sum
. . . For what they have to do . . . Of course they do not think
about . . . The money that they make . . . As being neither less
nor more . . . Than they agreed to take . . . They simply know
that someone else . . . Is getting more than they . . . And on that
basis they should get . . . A better rate of pay.

GOING OUT

When we get ready to go out . . . It is not long before . . . My hat is in my hand and I . . . Am standing at the door . . . I call my wife and she declares . . . That she is nearly through . . . And in another minute now . . . She will be ready too . . . So I go out and start the car . . . And get all set to go . . . But after while it seems my spouse . . . Is just a little slow . . . I honk the horn and she replies . . . That it will only be . . . A tiny second more until . . . She will be joining me . . . But seconds pass and minutes fade . . . I feel my patience snap . . . And shutting off the motor I . . . Decide to take a nap.

BASEBALL UMPIRE

Of all the thankless jobs on earth . . . Wherever duty calls . . . The worst is his who must decide . . . Between the strikes and balls . . . Who always has to say at once . . . If it is foul or fair . . . When some determined player hits . . . The horsehide in the air . . . The man whose eyes must rove the field . . . And cover every base . . . And figure if the infield or . . . The runner won the race . . . He is the baseball umpire who . . . Must be prepared to talk . . . When there is any argument . . . About a run or walk . . . But whether crowds stand up and cheer . . . Or impolitely shout . . . He is the one the baseball world . . . Can never do without.

TAKE A REST

It seems to me that life on earth . . . Is brief enough at best . . . So why not set aside the time . . . To take a little rest? . . . Why go on working day and night . . . Without some time for play . . . Instead of thinking how we can . . . Obtain a raise in pay? . . . Of course we all like money and . . . It buys the things we need . . . But if we try to get too much . . . We only foster greed . . . And if we work too hard each day . . . We may impair our health . . . And not be able to enjoy . . . The comfort of our wealth . . . So let us take a little rest . . . And set our cares aside . . . And in the long run we shall be . . . A lot more satisfied.

203

This evening when the sun goes down . . . And skies are red and blue . . . I shall be left with all the dreams . . . I ever shared with you . . . I shall be thinking of the night . . . We kissed and said good-by . . . And how we had to part without . . . The time to wonder why . . . I shall remember all you said . . . And I shall tell myself . . . These things must linger many months . . . Upon a lonely shelf . . . But I shall wait with all my heart . . . However far away . . . To hold you in my arms again . . . Whatever be the day . . . And surely every hour will . . . Be more than worth the while . . . If only we shall meet again . . . And I shall see you smile.

CARELESS PRAYER

I pray each morning and each night . . . But every now and then . . . I say my prayers so quickly I . . . Should say them all again . . . I whisper them mechanically . . . Without sufficient thought . . . Although I realize that is not . . . The way that I was taught . . . It must be either weariness . . . Or laziness of mind . . . Or possibly a goodly share . . . Of both of them combined . . . I know that it is anything . . . But proper and polite . . . To tell The Lord unthinkingly . . . Good morning or good night . . . And so I hope hereafter I . . . Shall say a better prayer . . . Because I want The Lord to know . . . How much I really care.

HAT

A man's conception of a hat . . . Is something he must wear . . . To be presentable and keep . . . His head from looking bare . . . But to the average woman it . . . Is more than merely these . . . And more than just a covering . . . To guard against the breeze . . . It shows that she is quite aware . . . Of how to keep in style . . . And what a certain hat will do . . . To supplement her smile . . . It can be more important than . . . The best of drink or food . . . Because a new one always brings . . . A bright and cheerful mood . . . Unless she sees another hat . . . Exactly like her own . . . And then her feelings are expressed . . . In one despairing groan.

I LOVE MY TEXAS

I love my State of Texas with . . . Her dusty, idle plains . . .
The winds that kiss the cotton and . . . The wild, torrential rains
. . . Her famous, fertile Valley and . . . The Rio Grande too . . .
And I am happy in my heart . . . When all her skies are blue . . .
I love her friendly highways and . . . Her cities tall and clean
. . . Where sun-tanned smiles in silence say . . . What handshakes
really mean . . . I wander in a garden where . . . Blue bonnets
raise their heads . . . And where the roses redolent . . . Are
blooming in their beds . . . And when the Texas stars appear . . .
Wherever cowboys roam . . . My dreams have all come true because . . . I know that I am home.

SONG OF THE WAR WORKER

I shall not look for peaceful skies . . . Around a setting sun . . .
I shall not dream of happiness . . . Until the war is won . . . But
I shall help to hold the ranks . . . That reach across the land . . .
And I shall work with all the might . . . And tools at my command
. . . I shall produce the iron and . . . The copper, steel and tin . . .
The rubber and aluminum . . . We have to have to win . . . I
shall construct the planes and tanks . . . The hand grenades and
guns . . . The submarines and ships we need . . . To help our
fighting sons . . . And I shall be prepared to give . . . The very
blood in me . . . To help our country place the seal . . . On final
victory.

CLOWN

The clown is one who wears a suit . . . Of colors bright and gay
. . . And who does everything he can . . . To make us feel that
way . . . He paints his face peculiarly . . . As though to match
his clothes . . . And more than any other thing . . . He decorates
his nose . . . He wants to make us all forget . . . Our struggle and
our strife . . . And surely he has never missed . . . A circus in his
life . . . His funny face provokes the laughs . . . Of children near
and far . . . And usually at every show . . . He is their favorite star
. . . And if at times he carries tears . . . Inside his human heart . . .
He does not let us know it while . . . He plays his humble part.

LET US BE FRIENDS

Let us be friends in everything . . . Of duty and of play . . . And
in whatever other deeds . . . We do from day to day . . . Let us
be kind and generous . . . To those who cross our path . . . And
not allow ourselves to live . . . In jealousy or wrath . . . Let us
consider what we have . . . And how much we can spare . . . To
spread the sunshine of our hearts . . . To others everywhere . . .
For after all our happiness . . . To some degree depends . . . On
how we go about the task . . . Of comforting our friends . . . So let
us follow friendliness . . . With every step we take . . . And do
some worthy deed each day . . . For someone else's sake.

SALESMAN

The salesman talks persuasively . . . Of quality and price . . .
In order to prevail on us . . . To buy his merchandise . . . He wants
to make his living and . . . He longs to do it well . . . By showing
all the world that he . . . Is competent to sell . . . Of course he
really does believe . . . His product is the best . . . Or else he could
not sponsor it . . . With honesty and zest . . . But it is ethical for
him . . . To boast a little bit . . . And say no other article . . . Is
comparable to it . . . And surely we are not opposed . . . To riding
in his car . . . Or eating lunch and smoking up . . . His 50-cent
cigar.

FOR MY CHILDREN

Throughout the years I worked and saved . . . For what I have
today . . . And many times I sacrificed . . . The chance to rest and
play . . . Because I well remember how . . . My childhood days
were spent . . . And what a warm and friendly home . . . With
parents would have meant . . . And so I struggled constantly . . .
To make my children glad . . . And give them all the comforts and
. . . The joys I never had . . . I did without a lot of things . . . In
order to provide . . . My sons and daughter with a share . . . Of
happiness and pride . . . And while I have some plans for them
. . . That I must still postpone . . . At least I know my children
have . . . A home to call their own.

LIFE IS A SONG

The passing years have taught me that . . . This life is like a song . . . And only that we think it so . . . There is not any wrong . . . There is not any heartache, and . . . There are not any tears . . . Except as we remember them . . . Throughout the passing years . . . There is not any worry or . . . A reason to regret . . . When it is just as easy to . . . Forgive and to forget . . . There is no storm that does not pass . . . And leave a quiet sea . . . Or any day that does not hold . . . Some pleasant memory . . . There is no rain that does not turn . . . To sunshine in the end . . . Or anyone who, if we try . . . We cannot call a friend.

I ASK FOR IT

I used to be afraid to ask . . . For what I hoped to get . . . And I was constantly inclined . . . To worry and to fret . . . A little raise in salary . . . A favor from a friend . . . Or maybe to get back a book . . . I had the grace to lend . . . However much I wanted it . . . And whether great or small . . . I used to be afraid to ask . . . For anything at all . . . Until one day I realized there . . . Was nothing I could lose . . . And life would not be any worse . . . If someone should refuse . . . So now when I want anything . . . That reason will permit . . . I see the proper person and . . . I simply ask for it.

YOU ARE MY LOVE

You are my only love in life . . . You are my dream come true . . . And everything that I possess . . . I want to give to you . . . I want to bring you happiness . . . In every form and way . . . I want you to enjoy yourself . . . And smile from day to day . . . And if I had the power now . . . To give you riches great . . . I would be glad to gather them . . . And leave them at your gate . . . The night is never finished and . . . The day is never done . . . Until my heart repeats again . . . I love you, dearest one . . . And all I ever ask of you . . . Is that you let me see . . . That somewhere in your own dear heart . . . There is a place for me.

THE LORD BESIDE US

We have not seen The Lord, our God . . . As human eyes can see . . . And yet He is no stranger to . . . Our worldly company . . . He is forever at our side . . . Wherever we may go . . . He is the sun, the moon, the stars . . . And all the winds that blow . . . He is the flower at our feet . . . The song that fills the dawn . . . And He is knocking on our door . . . When other friends are gone . . . He does not want us to be shy . . . Or hold His name in fear . . . But He would have us talk to Him . . . And feel that He is near . . . We may not know His voice and yet . . . Our hearts have surely heard . . . The everlasting wisdom of . . . His true and holy word.

TOO MUCH WELCOME

Some people like to entertain . . . And all their comforts share . . . And as their friend you know that you . . . Are always welcome there . . . The door is open day and night . . . And everything is free . . . Their food and drink and every kind . . . Of hospitality . . . And that is truly wonderful . . . And you enjoy it all . . . And many are the moments that . . . You pleasantly recall . . . But when you tell them you would like . . . To give a party too . . . Somehow they never seem to have . . . The time to call on you . . . And while you do appreciate . . . Their generous domain . . . Sometimes you also want to have . . . The chance to entertain.

WAR RINGS THE SCHOOL BELL

This year when classes start again . . . For those in search of knowledge . . . There will not be so many men . . . In high school or in college . . . The halls will not be quite so loud . . . With merry conversation . . . And there will be a smaller crowd . . . To share the recreation . . . For they are legion who have gone . . . To join our fighting forces . . . And now are concentrating on . . . The more important courses . . . Their wisdom will develop from . . . The battles they are learning . . . And some will get degrees and some . . . Will never be returning . . . But all of them will carry through . . . And all will write the story . . . Of scholars and of soldiers true . . . With sacrifice and glory.

TRUCK DRIVER

We seldom think of him who drives . . . A truck by day or night
. . . And even less do most of us . . . Appreciate his plight . . . His
wages may be rather good . . . But he must toil and sweat . . . To
move the load of merchandise . . . That someone wants to get . . .
He has to plow through traffic with . . . His lumbering machine
. . . And somehow grab his coffee and . . . A sandwich in between
. . . He has to find a parking space . . . When there is none to
spare . . . And while he sleeps his life depends . . . Upon a roadside flare . . . In town or on the highway he . . . Must have the
strength it takes . . . Although his eyes grow weary and . . . His
every muscle aches.

TIRESOME TASK

Sometimes I am so tired when . . . I open up my eyes . . . And
realize it is morning and . . . I am compelled to rise . . . I think
about the many tasks . . . There are in store for me . . . And when
at last the day is done . . . How weary I shall be . . . And then it
seems there is no end . . . To what I have to do . . . And even
though I work for years . . . My job is never through . . . I know
I must have food and clothes . . . And I must meet my rent . . .
And I should have some luxuries . . . To keep myself content . . .
And I know too that I must toil . . . To earn my daily pay . . . But
sometimes I would much prefer . . . To stay in bed all day.

I WELCOME YOU

I welcome you with all my heart . . . To come and visit me . . .
And hope you find the better part . . . Of hospitality . . . I may
not have the finest food . . . Or most expensive wine . . . But you
may share in friendly mood . . . Whatever things are mine . . . I
offer you the morning sun . . . With all its golden light . . . And
when the kindly day is done . . . A kindlier good-night . . . My
hours are for you to spend . . . And you are free to stay . . . As
long as I can be your friend . . . And keep you feeling gay . . . I
want to do whatever task . . . You may request of me . . . And in
return I only ask . . . Your friendly company.

EMPTY HOUSE

I saw a wall that seemed to stare . . . (There was no picture hanging there) . . . I saw a floor that was not snug . . . (It did not have a cozy rug) . . . A window likewise something lacked . . . (It had no curtain to attract) . . . The kitchen showed a sorry face . . . (No groceries adorned the place) . . . Each bedroom shed a lonely tear . . . (Not having any bed to cheer) . . . I saw a chimney idly sit . . . (No friendly smoke came out of it) . . . And I beheld a listless swing . . . (I heard no children's laughter ring) . . . I wondered who could bear to own . . . A house so desolate, alone.

KRISTINA'S WORDS

Kristina jabbers all day long . . . In phrases old and new . . . And that is understandable . . . For she is only two . . . She tries to tell us what she wants . . . Of things to eat and drink . . . Or just about the many thoughts . . . A baby has to think . . . She echoes every word she hears . . . As though to try it out . . . And she has all the volume from . . . A whisper to a shout . . . She calls her two big brothers and . . . Informs them how to play . . . And at the table she joins in . . . When we begin to pray . . . While "Mommy" is the special word . . . Her little lips prefer . . . Because she loves her mother and . . . She thinks the world of her.

MONEY-MINDED

Some people like to talk about . . . The money that is theirs . . . And in so many silly ways . . . They try to put on airs . . . They sport the finest clothes they can . . . With jewelry that shines . . . And read the daily stock reports . . . On gold and silver mines . . . They fathom economics and . . . The fate of future years . . . And speak of Wall Street brokers as . . . Their fellow-financiers . . . But when they go to dinner and . . . The waiter brings the bill . . . Their hands are in their pockets . . . And their vocal cords are still . . . And when they are requested to . . . Support a worthy cause . . . They tell the world to turn around . . . And look for Santa Claus.

SHOPPING WORRIES

I do not like to shop for things . . . Regardless of the weather
. . . Because my mind and pocketbook . . . Can never get together
. . . I do not like to shop for things . . . But when I do, I hurry . . .
Because each time I take my time . . . I wonder and I worry . . . I
wonder over what to buy . . . And afterwards I wonder . . . If I
selected properly . . . Or if I made a blunder . . . I wonder if I
bought too much . . . Or bought it out of season . . . And if the
price I paid was fair . . . Or somewhat out of reason . . . I do not
like to telephone . . . Or order things by letter . . . Because I have
a smart, young wife . . . Who does it so much better.

STRANGE BEHAVIOR

I wonder why our children are . . . So well behaved today . . .
And so unusually polite . . . In everything they say . . . They keep
their toys in order and . . . They hang up all their clothes . . . They
brush their teeth and never ask . . . To go to picture shows . . .
They cannot seem to do enough . . . To help around the house . . .
And when we read or talk they are . . . As quiet as a mouse . . . I
hope they are not ill or feel . . . We ought to be ashamed . . . Of all
the times that things went wrong . . . And they were quickly
blamed . . . But wait a minute—now I see . . . It is the time of
year . . . When that old fellow, Santa Claus . . . Will soon be coming here!

IT IS NOT FATE

He is afraid who tells himself . . . Misfortune is his fate . . . And
all he wants is sympathy . . . To soothe his mental state . . . The
chances are it is his fault . . . And had he really tried . . . He would
have been successful in . . . His more courageous stride . . . But
even if he did his best . . . And grief and sorrow came . . . It is not
his prerogative . . . To put aside the blame . . . For only God Almighty knows . . . How deep we are in debt . . . And only God
Himself decides . . . What we deserve to get . . . And whether
there is sunshine or . . . The world is wet with rain . . . No man
on earth has any right . . . To argue or complain.

TAKE ALL OF ME

Take me, my love, take all of me . . . For I belong to you . . . Let
me do everything I can . . . To make your dreams come true . . .
Let me contribute to your joy . . . Whenever you are gay . . . If
only with a smile or with . . . Some little word I say . . . And if
you live in loneliness . . . Or hold the hand of fear . . . I want to
comfort you, my love . . . And be forever near . . . Give me your
faith, your hope, your song . . . To brighten and to blend . . . With
all the longing in my heart . . . To be your constant friend . . .
Take me, my love, for what I am . . . And what I try to be . . . Not
just the good or lesser part . . . But every bit of me.

TURN TO GOD

Tell God about your troubles when . . . They seem too much
to bear . . . And put your faith and confidence . . . In His almighty
care . . . Ask God to be your counsellor . . . And lend His timely
aid . . . And let Him know you need His grace . . . To really
make the grade . . . But always keep in mind that He . . . Expects
some help from you . . . To overcome your problems and . . . To
make your dreams come true . . . God gladly gives encouragement
. . . To those who do their best . . . And whose unfailing trust in
Him . . . Is fervently expressed . . . So let Him know your heartache and . . . The trouble you are in . . . Assure Him of your firm
belief . . . And then go forth and win.

TRAIN

A train is something wonderful . . . For every man and boy . . .
From taking people everywhere . . . To serving as a toy . . . It
carries food and coal and oil . . . And merchandise and mail . . .
No matter what the weather is . . . It gets there without fail . . . A
train is something beautiful . . . When streamlined to a T . . .
With private rooms and every form . . . Of modern luxury . . .
And also it provides a thrill . . . For children near and far . . . Who
hear the whistle and the bell . . . And count each passing car . . .
It takes the people everywhere . . . For business and for fun . . .
And serves the commerce of the land . . . With every scheduled run.

THANKS, SOLDIER

Brave soldier, on your sleeping brow . . . Rests your eternal crown . . . You gave your all for all to know . . . Our flag will not go down . . . You heard the call to duty and . . . You took your place in line . . . Where otherwise it would have been . . . Your neighbor's place or mine . . . Intrepidly you faced the foe . . . On ocean and on land . . . And now you slumber in the soil . . . Where sacred crosses stand . . . You fought unflinchingly for us . . . And for our children too . . . And we can never fully give . . . Our gratitude to you . . . But in our hearts for evermore . . . Your sacrifice will be . . . And we will always keep your faith . . . In life and liberty.

COME BACK TO ME

Each weary day and lonely night . . . I think of you and pray . . . That you will soon come back to me . . . And never go away . . . I miss you every moment, love . . . I call to you and cry . . . But only empty echoes fill . . . The hours passing by . . . The sky is gray all morning and . . . Throughout the afternoon . . . And there is nothing beautiful . . . About the stars or moon . . . I long to find you in my dreams . . . But when I go to bed . . . There is no real or peaceful sleep . . . To keep me comforted . . . Whatever else may happen or . . . My heart may be denied . . . I want you to come back to me . . . And never leave my side.

LAUNDRY MAN

The laundry man is he who takes . . . The laundry from your door . . . And brings it back in better shape . . . Than it was in before . . . He tries to give a clean account . . . Of sheets and shirts and shawls . . . And has the grime and grit removed . . . From crumpled overalls . . . He lets you choose the kind of job . . . That you prefer to get . . . The neatly finished product or . . . The washing that is wet . . . Of course he is not perfect and . . . There are occasions few . . . When you report that you are short . . . A handkerchief or two . . . But all in all he is the one . . . On whom you like to lean . . . To take away your laundry cares . . . And keep you looking clean.

HOW CAN I TELL YOU?

How can I find the words to say . . . That you are in my heart
. . . And I would be so lonely, love . . . If ever we should part? . . .
How can I make it known to you . . . That in your soft caress . . .
There is the only answer to . . . My prayer for happiness? . . . You
are the meaning of my thoughts . . . The purpose of my life . . .
And all the courage and the strength . . . I need to conquer strife
. . . You are the minutes of my day . . . The hours of my night . . .
And only when they shine on you . . . Are stars forever bright . . .
But how can I impart to you . . . This feeling so divine . . . And
make you understand, my love . . . I want you to be mine?

TO BE A FRIEND

You need not grant a great request . . . Or be prepared to lend
. . . In order to convince someone . . . You want to be a friend . . .
You need not send a present or . . . Provide a share of fun . . . Or
exercise your influence . . . To get a favor done . . . But you will be
successful if . . . You merely do your part . . . With friendly smiles
and gentle words . . . To warm a lonely heart . . . A bright and
gay good-morning and . . . A comforting good-night . . . And just
a little sympathy . . . When things are not all right . . . An understanding nature and . . . The hand that you extend . . . Are all you
ever need to show . . . You want to be a friend.

COST

The cost of any article . . . Is not the selling price . . . But
whether and to what extent . . . We make a sacrifice . . . It is not
very high if we . . . Can well afford to pay . . . And it is merely
something that . . . Contributes to our play . . . But if we really
need it and . . . Our cash is rather low . . . The cost appears ex-
orbitant . . . As purchase prices go . . . Of course there is a value
that . . . The market seems to set . . . And that decides to some
degree . . . The treatment that we get . . . But generally the cost
depends . . . On being rich or poor . . . And just how much our
pocketbook . . . Is able to endure.

DREAMS IN ASHES

When I am smoking cigarets . . . The ashes in my tray . . . Are like the remnants of the dreams . . . That I have put away . . . The dreams we dreamed together once . . . When spring was young and new . . . And everything that mattered was . . . My happiness with you . . . We fashioned all the future to . . . A pattern of our own . . . Where neither you nor I would know . . . The meaning of alone . . . And when I kissed your loving lips . . . We promised in the dawn . . . Our love would last as long as we . . . And after we were gone . . . But now I stir the ashes and . . . There is no room for doubt . . . My dreams are only cigarets . . . And I have put them out.

WELCOME HOME

Whenever I go out of town . . . The children always say . . . They hope the time will not be long . . . While daddy is away . . . They hug and kiss me when I leave . . . As though I were a gem . . . And tell me to be sure to bring . . . Some little gifts for them . . . Of course I know they care for me . . . And miss me when I go . . . (All children find it natural . . . To love their parents so) . . . But now and then I wonder what . . . They really have in mind . . . When their affectionate display . . . Is so pronounced and kind . . . Because whenever I come home . . . To my dear family . . . Each youngster looks around and asks . . . "What have you got for me?"

SLEEP

A healthy mind and body are . . . Much easier to keep . . . When we make certain every night . . . To get sufficient sleep . . . Because the human body needs . . . A fair amount of rest . . . If we expect our brain and brawn . . . To do their very best . . . It may be pleasant to ignore . . . How time is passing by . . . And we may like to look upon . . . The ever changing sky . . . But we can only work so long . . . And then we have to quit . . . And too much play by night or day . . . Will not make up for it . . . We have to store up energy . . . For what we want to do . . . And sleep is what we need the most . . . To see our struggles through.

215

PRAYER FOR TODAY

God, give me grace and guide my steps . . . According to Your
way . . . That I may live a better life . . . Than I lived yesterday
. . . Show me the fallacy from which . . . A fool makes his mistake
. . . So I may grow in goodness and . . . In wisdom for Your
sake . . . Let me improve my inner self . . . By learning to subdue
. . . My selfishness and everything . . . Unworthy and untrue . . .
Teach me, O God, to be a friend . . . And walk the kindly path
. . . That I may always be sincere . . . And given not to wrath . . .
Help me to do my duty well . . . According to Your way . . . That
I may live a better life . . . Than I lived yesterday.

SOLDIER'S FAREWELL

They linger shyly as they gaze . . . Into each other's eyes . . .
And strive to find the phrases to . . . Exchange their fond good-bys
. . . This boy in khaki uniform . . . Who stands so straight and
tall . . . And she whose faith inspired him . . . To heed his coun-
try's call . . . They think not of tomorrow, when . . . The bugle's
note will sound . . . Or of the nights when all the leaves . . . Will
sleep upon the ground . . . Nor yet about the winter wind . . .
That sways the lonely tree . . . And lightly shakes its snow upon
. . . The passing cavalry . . . They dream not of the pleasures and
. . . The beauties of the past . . . But only of this hour and . . .
How long it is to last.

PUBLIC SPEAKER

The public speaker is the one . . . Who gets up on the floor . . .
And tells you everything he knows . . . And sometimes even more
. . . He hurries to a luncheon or . . . He keeps a dinner date . . .
And always he is introduced . . . As greater than the great . . . His
message may be serious . . . Or just to entertain . . . Before he
grabs his hat and runs . . . To catch another train . . . Invariably
his schedule calls . . . For many distant tours . . . And so of course
his time is much . . . More valuable than yours . . . His meal is
free, his talk invites . . . Polite applause or cheers . . . And in addition he is paid . . . Wherever he appears.

MY WELCOME FRIENDS

My door is always open to . . . The friends who come to call . . .
They need not ring or knock, for they . . . Are welcome one and all
. . . They fill the house with cheerfulness . . . And every time they
smile . . . They leave another echo that . . . Will last a long, long
while . . . I like to learn about their lives . . . Their travels far and
near . . . And if they sigh I try to lend . . . A sympathetic ear . . .
We usually exchange ideas . . . And analyze our schemes . . . And
over empty coffee cups . . . We talk about our dreams . . . I cherish
their companionship . . . Each moment they can stay . . . And they
are always in my thoughts . . . When they have gone away.

PLANNED ECONOMY

Some ladies look more lovely in . . . The costly things they wear
. . . But my dear wife gives all her clothes . . . A more important
air . . . She makes them really gorgeous by . . . The beauty of her
face . . . When otherwise they would appear . . . Distinctly commonplace . . . At least that is the theory . . . That I expound to
her . . . When she admires jewelry . . . Or something made of fur
. . . I carefully explain to her . . . That there is not much sense . . .
In buying any item of . . . Considerable expense . . . For she can
wear the cheapest thing . . . On sale in any store . . . And give it
the appearance of . . . A million bucks or more.

WHEN I GET UP

Each morning when I leave my bed . . . And rub the sleep away
. . . I wonder what will happen in . . . The hours of the day . . .
I wonder what new happiness . . . Or tears there are in store . . .
And whether I shall get some things . . . I have been waiting for
. . . Which friends will pass and say hello . . . Or stop to talk a
while . . . What new acquaintance I may make . . . To add another smile . . . I wonder how my work will go . . . And what the
boss will do . . . And what will be my pleasure when . . . The
drudgery is through . . . I wonder what exciting things . . . Will
make my life more gay . . . Or if once more I must endure . . . An
ordinary day.

SPRINGTIME AND YOU

I want to wander through the fields . . . And climb the hills with you . . . To share the golden sunshine when . . . The morning sky is new . . . I want to blend my hopes with yours . . . In dreams around the day . . . And keep a careful diary . . . Of everything you say . . . For I am so in love with you . . . And from the very start . . . I have been fondly carrying . . . Your picture in my heart . . . And I have saved your letters from . . . The first one that you wrote . . . Including every postal card . . . And every scribbled note . . . And now that spring is here again . . . And life is young and free . . . I want to know for certain, dear . . . That you belong to me.

WE THANK YOU, LORD

Dear Lord, we thank You with our hearts . . . For this bright Christmas Day . . . When bells of freedom ring again . . . And guns are put away . . . Our gallant sons are homeward bound . . . The seas are calm once more . . . And all the world is joyful that . . . There is an end to war . . . The angels sing in Heaven and . . . The candles glow again . . . For there is peace upon this earth . . . And all good will toward men . . . We are sincerely grateful, Lord . . . That You fulfilled our prayer . . . And faithfully we promise You . . . That we will do our share . . . That we will guard ourselves against . . . Our errors of the past . . . And live our lives in liberty . . . That will be sure to last.

MEMORIES

Memories are all the thoughts . . . That echo from the past . . . To linger in the human heart . . . As long as it may last . . . They are the vision of a day . . . That vanished into night . . . Except for one eternal star . . . Forever clear and bright . . . They are the houses on the street . . . The flowers everywhere . . . And youthful songs of yesteryear . . . Without a single care . . . And memories are diaries . . . Of many moons ago . . . When promises were painted on . . . The whiteness of the snow . . . When everything appeared to have . . . A more enduring name . . . Where now the beauty of it all . . . Is never quite the same.

VICTORY DAY

The bells of freedom ring today . . . The land resounds with
cheers . . . And everywhere along the way . . . We mingle smiles
and tears . . . At last the war is at an end . . . And all the guns
are stilled . . . Our hopes and plans together blend . . . And dreams
become fulfilled . . . Today once more the world is free . . . And
right has proved its worth . . . It is the day of victory . . . The day
of peace on earth . . . We give our gratitude to God . . . For having truly won . . . And with our prayers we kiss the sod . . .
Above each fallen son . . . May we have courage to endure . . . The
aftermath of war . . . And may Old Glory make secure . . . The
peace for evermore.

FRIENDS AT MY SIDE

There are so many friendly songs . . . To fill my heart today . . .
I never stop to look around . . . For any cloud of gray . . . And
if a shadow comes along . . . It does not bother me . . . Because
my spirit is content . . . In kindly company . . . My friends are always at my side . . . To comfort and console . . . And help me find
the faith I need . . . To gain my fondest goal . . . They offer every
service they . . . Can possibly bestow . . . To help me live a better
life . . . Wherever I may go . . . And so I feel I owe them each
. . . An everlasting debt . . . And they may always rest assured
. . . I never shall forget.

ENDEARING DAMAGE

My wife and I object to all . . . The scratches and the stains . . .
That decorate our furniture . . . Our floors and window-panes . . .
We do not like the smudges and . . . The marks the children make
. . . Or getting someone to repair . . . The articles they break . . .
We try to teach our youngsters to . . . Be careful when they play
. . . And not destroy the property . . . For which we have to pay
. . . And yet I guess in later years . . . When they are grown and
gone . . . These things will be the memories . . . That really linger
on . . . And tenderly our hands will touch . . . The places where
they played . . . To treasure all the scratches and . . . The finger-
prints they made.

GOD IS OUR LIGHT

However dark the day may be . . . However deep the night . . .
As long as we belong to God . . . There is sufficient light . . .
There is no need for loneliness . . . Or cause for any fear . . . But
there is consolation and . . . The way is always clear . . . We know
what God expects of us . . . And what we have to do . . . To show
that we are honest and . . . Our loyalty is true . . . We have our
human weaknesses . . . And sometimes they prevail . . . But if we
put our trust in God . . . We cannot ever fail . . . For He is always
at our side . . . To help us in our fight . . . And darkness disappears before . . . His everlasting light.

PHONOGRAPH

A phonograph is something that . . . Is comforting to own . . .
Especially at certain times . . . When we are all alone . . . Because
we have the chance to play . . . The music of our choice . . . And
in the singing of a song . . . We may select the voice . . . From
classical arrangements to . . . The hit that rules the day . . . We
only have to listen to . . . The ones we want to play . . . And if we
think that we can sing . . . Or like the way we laugh . . . Our
efforts can be reproduced . . . Upon the phonograph . . . Although
much better records may . . . Be resting on our shelves . . . At least
it is a simple way . . . Of talking to ourselves.

OUTPOST OF THE AIR

Across the water wide and blue . . . Long miles from anywhere
. . . Our distant shores are guarded by . . . Our navy of the air . . .
Brave lads who soar in silver ships . . . And fly far out to sea . . .
To set their faithful bombsights on . . . The raiding enemy . . .
And those brave lads who stay below . . . To keep the station fit
. . . Who service every plane and wish . . . They could go up in
it . . . They all are good Americans . . . Who know their way
around . . . Who welcome danger while they keep . . . Their feet
upon the ground . . . They are the carefree boys who now . . .
Have grown to sober men . . . With longing for their loved ones
and . . . To see the States again.

I BOUGHT A HOUSE

I bought a little house today . . . And it is really neat . . . And
I am sure that we shall like . . . The neighbors on our street . . .
But what I want to tell you is . . . That when I picked this place
. . . I did not look for stone or brick . . . A lawn or living space
. . . I did not care so much about . . . The fixtures or the fence . . .
And in a way I never was . . . Concerned about expense . . . But
in my mind I saw my wife . . . And wondered whether she . . .
Would be contented in that house . . . With all our family . . . I
wanted to be sure the walls . . . Would echo every day . . . With
all the joy and laughter of . . . Our children at their play.

IN SCHOOL OR OUT

My weary wife is wishing now . . . The summer days were here
. . . Because she figures there would be . . . A lighter atmosphere
. . . She says she would not have to wash . . . And iron shirts and
pants . . . For our two boys to go to school . . . With her approv-
ing glance . . . She would not worry over cash . . . For lunch and
trolley fare . . . And all the other ways in which . . . The youngsters need her care . . . But when the summer days arrive . . . Her
hair begins to gray . . . Because the children disappear . . . When
they go out to play . . . They want some money for a show . . . Or
candy at the store . . . And soon my wife can hardly wait . . . For
school to start once more.

UNWANTED

There are a lot of folks on earth . . . Whom we can do without
. . . Whose loyalty and honesty . . . Are qualities we doubt . . .
Who are inclined to bother us . . . And irritate our nerves . . . By
wanting more of everything . . . Than he or she deserves . . . They
are demanding and they will . . . Insist upon their way . . . Regardless of the kindnesses . . . We give from day to day . . . They
are the ones who have no sense . . . Of self-respect or pride . . .
And who no matter what they get . . . Are never satisfied . . . Who
do not feel the friendly warmth . . . Of being good and true . . .
And who are not concerned about . . . What other people do.

MY ALL FOR YOU

If you could know the part you play . . . In all I try to be . . .
You would begin to understand . . . How much you mean to me
. . . And you would know that everything . . . I ever undertake
. . . Is not for my convenience but . . . For your beloved sake . . .
That I am happy only when . . . I know that what I do . . . Will
ultimately bring about . . . Some happiness for you . . . I never
see the sun begin . . . Or end another day . . . Without I say a
silent prayer . . . To help you on your way . . . You mean so much
to me that I . . . Must honestly confess . . . That everything I ever
do . . . Is for your happiness.

THE LORD IS HERE

When there is sunshine in the dawn . . . And all the skies are
clear . . . My heart is filled with song because . . . I know The
Lord is here . . . And when the clouds are overhead . . . And life
is dull and gray . . . The Lord is present just as much . . . To help
me on my way . . . Whatever be the hour of . . . The passing day
or night . . . He guides me through the labyrinth . . . Of what is
wrong and right . . . He gives me faith and courage strong . . . To
struggle for my goal . . . And every opportunity . . . To sanctify
my soul . . . Whatever be the weather or . . . The season of the
year . . . The Lord is always at my side . . . To help me persevere.

ENGINEER

His hand is on the throttle and . . . His eyes are on the track . . .
As steaming clouds of grayish smoke . . . Come belching from the
stack . . . He blows the whistle, rings the bell . . . The wheels
begin to go . . . While children stand around in awe . . . To watch
the daily show . . . They envy him, the engineer . . . In his ma-
jestic might . . . Who grips the levers as the train . . . Goes roaring
through the night . . . He hauls the freight and passengers . . . Beyond the dusty plain . . . Across the mountains to the sea . . .
Through wind and snow and rain . . . His pride in punctuality
. . . Clear eye and steady hand . . . Have made him a tradition
and . . . A legend of the land.

SIMPLY SPEAKING

I like to listen to a speech . . . By someone who is wise . . . And who has all the gestures and . . . The voice to dramatize . . . But even more I like to hear . . . The average person speak . . . About the common topics of . . . The moment or the week . . . The daily conversation that . . . Reveals our way of life . . . As it affects a man or maid . . . The husband or the wife . . . The ordinary doings of . . . A boy or girl in school . . . And how the old folks feel about . . . Our democratic rule . . . I like the simple subjects of . . . Discussions every day . . . Because I know what people think . . . By what they have to say.

NEED FOR RELIGION

Some people say religion is . . . A literary gem . . . But while it has its value it . . . Was never meant for them . . . They say that it is wonderful . . . For all the common herd . . . But they do not desire it . . . Or need the Holy Word . . . And that is most unfortunate . . . As they pursue their way . . . Becauses they do not understand . . . The foolish thing they say . . . They do not understand that prayer . . . Is just a telephone . . . By which they call on God to help . . . And make their wishes known . . . That only faith in God can keep . . . Their hopes from growing dim . . . And nobody is better than . . . The person next to him.

REAL NEIGHBORS

Real neighbors are the gentle folks . . . Who live next door to you . . . And who display their friendliness . . . In everything they do . . . They say good-morning and good-night . . . And now and then they call . . . To see if they can be of help . . . In any way at all . . . They offer you a ride when they . . . Are driving into town . . . And when they talk they do not run . . . Their other neighbors down . . . Their garden tools are yours to use . . . And they will gladly share . . . The items in their pantry when . . . Your shelf is somewhat bare . . . In manner and in speech they are . . . As friendly as can be . . . But they are always careful to . . . Respect your privacy.

WILL

A will is an expression that . . . Is carefully prepared . . . To designate the way someday . . . We want our money shared . . . A document that tells the world . . . Exactly how we feel . . . We should divide our property . . . Both personal and real . . . It finally unveils the point . . . Where love begins and ends . . . And what we really think about . . . Our relatives and friends . . . A will is something everyone . . . Who is of voting age . . . Should take the time to execute . . . Upon a legal page . . . Some people think they are too young . . . And they decide to wait . . . But some things happen suddenly . . . And then it is too late.

GIVE ME YOUR GRACE

Behold me, Lord, upon my knees . . . Before Your mighty throne . . . I come to You today because . . . I feel so all alone . . . I am discouraged in my heart . . . And lonely in my soul . . . Because I am no nearer to . . . My everlasting goal . . . I stumble on the path of life . . . I hesitate and turn . . . And though I see my sad mistakes . . . I never seem to learn . . . Give me the strength and courage, Lord . . . To carry out Your will . . . That every promise I express . . . I may in time fulfill . . . Give me the grace I need today . . . For what I ought to do . . . And I will really try to show . . . My gratitude to You.

WAVERING WIFE

Whenever I invite my wife . . . To go to some affair . . . She always lets me know that she . . . Is willing to be there . . . But always she insists that she . . . Is giving me a break . . . By doing it entirely . . . For my beloved sake . . . And then I turn to her and say . . . "Of course, my dear, you know . . . I shall not mind if you decide . . . You do not want to go" . . . And thereupon she says, "Oh, well . . . If I am in the way . . . I would much rather stay at home . . . Than spoil your chance to play" . . . Then I announce, "Make up your mind . . . And tell me yes or no" . . . And she replies, "Oh, well, I'm dressed . . . So now I guess I'll go."

THE WAY WE LIVE

The more important thing in life . . . Is neither wealth nor fame
. . . But whether we are honestly . . . Deserving of our name . . .
If we can measure up to all . . . That we profess to be . . . Including whether we possess . . . That true sincerity . . . We may be
wealthy and we may . . . Be very wise indeed . . . But do we
help our neighbor when . . . He seems to be in need? . . . Are we
prepared to sacrifice . . . The comforts we enjoy . . . And overlook
the little things . . . That oftentimes annoy? . . . Because it matters not how much . . . Our own ambition thrives . . . But how we
live and what we do . . . To lighten other lives.

OUR WORTH ON EARTH

We may be very famous and . . . Important in the eyes . . . Of
other people like ourselves . . . Who live beneath the skies . . . But
in the sight of God we are . . . As humans small and frail . . .
Whose worldly gain is empty if . . . They spiritually fail . . . And
often in our glory we . . . Are given to forget . . . That every
blessing we receive . . . Is added to our debt . . . The debt of gratitude we owe . . . For life upon this earth . . . And for the opportunity . . . To demonstrate our worth . . . The chance to be of
service to . . . Our neighbor and our kin . . . And by the kindly
grace of God . . . To stay away from sin.

BELIEVE ME, BELOVED

Believe me, my beloved . . . I mean each word I say . . . I need
you every hour . . . Of every night and day . . . I need you every
minute . . . In pleasure and in pain . . . And whether there is sunshine . . . Or whether there is rain . . . I see you in each flower . . .
The rainbow and the sun . . . I see the stars in heaven . . . And
you in every one . . . I hear you softly singing . . . Wherever
breezes blow . . . I am in love with living . . . Because I love you
so . . . Believe me, my beloved . . . My every word is true . . .
Each minute and each hour . . . My life depends on you.

I TALK TO GOD

I talk to God in my own way . . . And tell Him all my needs . . .
And I apologize to Him . . . For my unfaithful deeds . . . I go to
Him each morning for . . . His counsel and His aid . . . And for
the courage I must have . . . To make a better grade . . . I tell
Him of the task ahead . . . And what is troubling me . . . And ask
Him what I ought to do . . . To earn a victory . . . And when the
shadows shroud the day . . . And I go home again . . . I calculate
the score I made . . . And I present it then . . . And always He
forgives my faults . . . And strives to soothe my soul . . . And gives
me added grace to gain . . . My everlasting goal.

HE WANTS TO SERVE

A friend is one who wants to share . . . The happiness of life . . .
And help you bear the burden of . . . Your struggle and your strife
. . . He wants to walk beside you when . . . The sky is overcast . . .
And show you how to put away . . . The sorrows of the past . . .
He always does his utmost to . . . Encourage you to try . . . And
if you take a different course . . . He never asks you why . . . He
does not hunger for reward . . . But he is satisfied . . . If he can
be the object of . . . Your gratitude and pride . . . In every way he
wants to be . . . A faithful friend and true . . . And more especially
he wants . . . To serve and comfort you.

THIS DAY FOR YOU

Good-morning, love, I offer you . . . My heart and soul today . . .
And promise you I will be true . . . In every little way . . . I want
you to behold the sun . . . In all its golden light . . . Until at last
the day is done . . . And stars adorn the night . . . I shall be doing
everything . . . To make each moment glad . . . Because I want
your heart to sing . . . And never to be sad . . . Wherever I decide
to go . . . My life will be a prayer . . . For you, my love, to let you
know . . . How much I really care . . . I hope that all your dreams
come true . . . And to that happy goal . . . I dedicate this day to
you . . . With all my heart and soul.

DOING A FAVOR

There is no favor great or small . . . I would not undertake . . .
To bring about some happiness . . . For someone else's sake . . .
Because I like to do my share . . . To make the world feel glad
. . . And help my fellow-man forget . . . His reason to be sad . . .
Because there is no greater gift . . . Of virtue on this earth . . .
Than doing deeds of kindness and . . . Of everlasting worth . . .
Because there is no better way . . . Of urging others on . . . Than
giving them a stronger faith . . . To build their hopes upon . . .
And most of all because I know . . . Whatever else may be . . .
Their added joy in life will bring . . . More happiness to me.

LOVE-FILE

I have so many thoughts of you . . . That if I kept a file . . . It
would be just as high and wide . . . And long as any mile . . . And
even then my records would . . . Continually grow . . . And it
would not be long before . . . My file would overflow . . . Because
I have a thought of you . . . Each moment of the day . . . And I
remember you, my love . . . With every word I say . . . Because
wherever I may go . . . And all that I may do . . . Remind me of
my happiness . . . In merely knowing you . . . And in my file the
many things . . . My heart is thinking of . . . Would always find
their place behind . . . The letter L for love.

LORD, LET ME LIVE

O Lord, I hope You let me live . . . Until my hair is gray . . .
Until my limbs are feeble and . . . My work is put away . . . I
hope You let me carry on . . . Until my dreams are spent . . . And
I have given all the world . . . My every sentiment . . . For You
have been so good to me . . . I want to honor You . . . And teach
as many as I can . . . To love and praise You too . . . I want to be
of service, Lord . . . Through every day and night . . . In which
to guide another soul . . . To Your eternal light . . . I want to live
beneath the stars . . . And see the morning sun . . . Until my soul
is satisfied . . . That all my work is done.

UNWELCOME SPRING

I love the sunshine of the spring . . . The freshness of the air . . .
The joyful singing of the birds . . . And beauty everywhere . . .
But spring is not all happiness . . . It has its share of woe . . . In-
cluding what I have to do . . . With spade and fork and hoe . . .
Including blisters on my hands . . . And aches along my back . . .
While weeds look up and leer at me . . . And laugh at my attack
. . . Including too the cleaning of . . . The house where we abide
. . . That never seems to satisfy . . . My wife's domestic pride . . .
Each room and hall must sparkle from . . . The ceiling to the floor
. . . O lucky man in uniform . . . Who merely fights a war!

I DO REMEMBER YOU

I do remember you, my love . . . Not just when skies are bright
. . . But every hour of the day . . . And all throughout the night
. . . Indeed there is no time when I . . . Am ever feeling blue . . .
Because wherever I may be . . . My thoughts are all of you . . . The
rain may come, the wind may blow . . . To tear my plans apart
. . . But in my trying hour you . . . Are always in my heart . . . I
never take a step or stand . . . Beside the fireplace . . . Without I
hold the memory . . . Of your endearing face . . . Yes, I remember
you, my love . . . From years and years gone by . . . And in my
cherished dream of you . . . My faith can never die.

WONDERFUL WORLD

The world is beautiful today . . . The sky is clear and bright . . .
And somehow I am sure there will . . . Be silver stars tonight . . .
There may be disappointments but . . . I think they will be small
. . . And I am certain there will be . . . No bitterness at all . . .
Because my heart is filled with joy . . . And everywhere I go . . . I
try to gather happiness . . . For everyone I know . . . I hope they
will appreciate . . . The blessings that are theirs . . . And find
whatever strength they need . . . To shoulder all their cares . . . Be-
cause the world is wonderful . . . The sky is bright and blue . . .
And there is every prospect that . . . Our dreams will all come true.

MAILMAN

He goes around from house to house . . . And rings the bell or knocks . . . When there is something to be slipped . . . Inside the letter-box . . . His pouch is filled with messages . . . Of happiness and cheer . . . And also those that draw a frown . . . Or possibly a tear . . . He brings the blanks for income tax . . . And statements by the score . . . As well as word from Uncle Sam . . . Of time to go to war . . . He carries papers, magazines . . . And ads of every sort . . . Besides the V-mail letters from . . . The farthest foreign port . . . He is the messenger of love . . . Surprise and tragedy . . . He is the constant courier . . . Of time and memory.

RACE-HORSE

A horse is just an animal . . . Until it starts to run . . . At odds that are 100 high . . . Or merely two to one . . . It prances in a paddock with . . . A jockey on its back . . . And when the starting gun goes off . . . It tears around the track . . . It keeps a certain pace until . . . The rider tugs the rein . . . And whispers magic words to it . . . To make a better gain . . . And if it is the champion . . . On some important date . . . When people by the thousands pay . . . To get beyond the gate . . . A horseshoe made of flowers fair . . . Is placed around its neck . . . While he who owns its lucky hide . . . Receives a handsome check.

THANK YOU, GOD

I thank You, God, with all my heart . . . For what I am today . . . In every deed I try to do . . . And every word I say . . . Except of course my sinful self . . . For which I am to blame . . . And humbly ask forgiveness in . . . The mercy of Your name . . . But what I want to tell You, God, . . . Upon my bended knee . . . Is that I thank You for the fact . . . That You created me . . . That You enabled me to live . . . In pleasure and in pain . . . With equal opportunity . . . In sunshine and in rain . . . I thank You for my heart and soul . . . The freedom of my will . . . And for the hopes and dreams that life . . . Is able to fulfill.

GARRISON RETREAT

Out on a distant, lonely isle . . . The drums beat loud and long
. . . The honor guard comes forward and . . . The bugler sounds
his song . . . The stars and stripes are lowered now . . . By hard
but loving hands . . . And pride and loyalty are one . . . Where
every soldier stands . . . A thousand miles away from home . . .
Or maybe two or three . . . It matters not when men must fight
. . . To keep their country free . . . It is the hour of retreat . . . Just
as the sun goes down . . . When courage comes to life again . . .
To win another crown . . . When smiles and tears and dreams of
home . . . Are things a man can feel . . . Out on a distant, lonely
isle . . . Where God is just as real.

GOD'S DAY

Whatever else I ponder and . . . Wherever I may plod . . . I
must remember in my heart . . . This day belongs to God . . . This
day is meant to honor Him . . . Who understands our cares . . .
And Who is not too occupied . . . To listen to our prayers . . . And
so I try to live my life . . . According to His way . . . Because I
know that Sunday is . . . His very special day . . . These four and
twenty hours are . . . The least that I can give . . . To say my
thanks because He has . . . Enabled me to live . . . And that is why
when Sunday comes . . . I set the day apart . . . And offer God
the gratitude . . . That fills my humble heart.

HIGH SCHOOL

In high school we discover there . . . Is somewhat of a change
. . . And we must study subjects that . . . Are not a little strange
. . . For instance, we have civics and . . . The chemical domain . . .
And in geometry we get . . . The solid and the plane . . . And
many are the courses we . . . May follow or reject . . . As long as
we advance as much . . . As parents may expect . . . But also high
school is a place . . . To gain athletic fame . . . Or in some other
manner to . . . Acquire quite a name . . . And while our graduation seems . . . Just one more stepping-stone . . . We think of college and we feel . . . That we are really grown.

PAINTING THE HOUSE

I went and bought some paint today . . . And bought some brushes too . . . Because the house needs polishing . . . As houses always do . . . I figured up what it would take . . . To make our cottage bright . . . And then I got some turpentine . . . To make the mixture right . . . And so I brought the items home . . . And set them on the floor . . . And made a mental survey of . . . Each window, wall and door . . . I even got an apron and . . . A knife with which to scrape . . . And finally my painting plans . . . Were in the best of shape . . . And now the paint with expert strokes . . . My darling wife applies . . . While I observe and carefully . . . Direct and supervise.

NO RIGHT TO RACE

No trip is so important and . . . No urgency so great . . . That we must drive our auto at . . . A really reckless rate . . . For there are children in the street . . . Who have a right to live . . . And who deserve the fullest care . . . And caution we can give . . . And there are people who are old . . . And those who cannot see . . . As well as folks afflicted with . . . Some worse infirmity . . . We have no right or reason to . . . Be careless at the wheel . . . However much experienced . . . And competent we feel . . . So let us be more careful as . . . We drive our car today . . . That we may cause no injury . . . And take no life away.

TROOPSHIP REVERIE

He stands upon the crowded deck . . . His rifle in his hand . . . His passage booked by Uncle Sam . . . To some unmentioned land . . . He ponders over sunken ships . . . Asleep in sodden graves . . . And wonders what new tragedy . . . Is hidden by the waves . . . But more than that his thoughts go back . . . To all he left behind . . . His town, his home, his parents and . . . His neighbors good and kind . . . And too his dreams go back to her . . . Who stands upon the shore . . . And waits for him and waits for word . . . Of freedom after war . . . Who wants to be with him again . . . But only prays that he . . . Will safely land and bravely keep . . . His date with destiny.

OUR HEARTS ARE ONE

Our hearts are joined because we are . . . Engaged to marry
now . . . We have exchanged a promise that . . . Will soon become
a vow . . . No matter what the future holds . . . Or what the world
may do . . . I know that you belong to me . . . And I belong to
you . . . This little ring that has no end . . . Reflects our lasting
love . . . Eternal as the heavens and . . . The silver stars above . . .
We may be faced from time to time . . . With trouble and with
stress . . . But underneath it all will be . . . Our dream of happiness . . . And just as long as you are mine . . . And I belong to
you . . . I know that we will find a way . . . To make our dream
come true.

THEY WILL BE GOOD

Perhaps I spoil my children by . . . Abstaining from the rod . . .
But I am satisfied as long . . . As they believe in God . . . As long
as they grow up at last . . . To know the right from wrong . . .
And understand their duty and . . . The beauty of a song . . . I
know that there will always be . . . The moments when they stray
. . . And now and then they do not seem . . . So eager to obey . . .
But also I am confident . . . That they know what to do . . . And
that they recognize the worth . . . Of being good and true . . . And
every evening when I see . . . Their heads begin to nod . . . I
know they will be good because . . . They say good-night to God.

FRIENDLY THINGS

The world is filled with friendly things . . . From one end to the
other . . . A fence, a tree, a garden and . . . A kitchen and a
mother . . . The road that winds beyond the hills . . . To where
the sun is rising . . . The letter from the kindly pen . . . Of someone sympathizing . . . The ship that sails across the sea . . . Unmindful of the weather . . . The ring around a finger small . . .
That holds two hearts together . . . A dog, a horse, a flower fair
. . . A dinner invitation . . . The sky, the moon, the stars and all
. . . The beauty of creation . . . The world is filled with friendly
things . . . For those who try to find them . . . Who look for smiles
at every turn . . . And leave their tears behind them.

TOO BUSY FOR LOVE

When you have time to talk to me . . . I want to ask you, dear
. . . If what you told me long ago . . . Was honest and sincere . . .
If actually you meant each word . . . When you declared your love
. . . And promised to be true to me . . . By all the stars above . . .
For you have been so busy I . . . Have had no chance to see . . .
That every day and every night . . . You really think of me . . .
And naturally I wonder if . . . I hold your heart today . . . Or if
I might be just as well . . . A million miles away . . . But maybe
I shall never know . . . The answer you conceal . . . Because you
never have the time . . . To tell me how you feel.

SCHOOL OF LIFE

When all our books and classes are . . . A picture of the past . . .
And we are satisfied we have . . . Degrees enough to last . . . We
find there is another course . . . That we must all attend . . . And
that our education is . . . Not nearly at an end . . . We have to
start in studying . . . At still another school . . . Where we are
taught the principles . . . Of praise and ridicule . . . The school of
real experience . . . Where we are moved about . . . According to
ability . . . And how we stick it out . . . Where we become the
failures and . . . We end up on the rocks . . . Or win because we
have the strength . . . To stand the hardest knocks.

I DREAM AND SIGH

Each lonely hour you are gone . . . I dream of you, my dear . . .
And of the stars that touch the dawn . . . Before they disappear . . .
I dream of daisies dipped in dew . . . The lilac and the rose . . .
And of the day I walked with you . . . Along the path you chose
. . . I look around for yesterday . . . When you were here with
me . . . And I was wishing you would stay . . . And keep me com-
pany . . . But now the sky is overcast . . . Because we are apart
. . . And all the beauty of the past . . . Is calling to my heart . . .
And now I only dream and sigh . . . For what is not my own
. . . And wonder why you said good-by . . . And left me all alone.

WHY NOT FIND OUT?

Why do you look at him like that . . . Without the courage true
. . . Of telling him in simple words . . . How much he means to
you? . . . Why do you keep him in the dark . . . And never let
him know . . . That he is always in your heart . . . And you adore
him so? . . . He will not scold or pity you . . . Or laugh at what
you say . . . And if he loves you in return . . . He will not walk
away . . . He either likes you as a friend . . . And thus is quite
content . . . Or else he thinks the world of you . . . But needs encouragement . . . Then why not take a chance on it . . . And settle
every doubt? . . . If he is not in love with you . . . You may as
well find out.

WHO IS WHO?

Some people when they telephone . . . Invariably will miss . . .
And when I say hello to them . . . They ask me, "Who is this?"
. . . I know we all are human and . . . Inclined to make mistakes
. . . And I have no objection to . . . The little time it takes . . . But
when they want a certain soul . . . Whoever it may be . . . Why do
they ask me to reveal . . . My own identity? . . . Of course I ask
them what they want . . . And whom they have in mind . . . And
just what number in the book . . . They really meant to find . . .
But nothing more effectively . . . Disturbs my peaceful bliss . . .
Than having people ring my phone . . . And ask me, "Who is this?"

I SAY MY PRAYERS

I say my prayers each day and I . . . Repeat them every night . . .
Because I know that when I do . . . My life will be all right . . .
Somehow they seem to comfort me . . . Whenever I have tears
. . . And always they encourage me . . . To overcome my fears . . .
They lend a more enchanting touch . . . To every smile and song
. . . And help me keep a steady stride . . . When anything goes
wrong . . . My prayers inspire me to give . . . The best there is in
me . . . And to consider everyone . . . With love and sympathy
. . . I try to say them slowly and . . . To mean each word I say . . .
Because I want Almighty God . . . To hear me when I pray.

SHOEMAKER

He makes the shoes the people wear . . . At every height and age . . . Including sandals and the kind . . . That tap upon the stage . . . He shapes the pair the baby needs . . . When learning how to walk . . . As well as ladies' footwear that . . . Is all the rage and talk . . . He builds the boots with pointed toes . . . That hold the cowboy's feet . . . And he creates the many styles . . . That grace the city street . . . And then there are the special ones . . . For every type of sport . . . And those G.I. contraptions that . . . Appear too long or short . . . The pauper and the president . . . And merchant prince alike . . . Depend on him to lift them up . . . When they would dance or hike.

PLAN FOR TODAY

Today is just another day . . . And then again it seems . . . It holds the opportunity . . . To carry out my schemes . . . It is the time I have right now . . . To do with as I will . . . And there are hopes that I may be . . . Enabled to fulfill . . . The hours are no longer than . . . The ones of yesterday . . . And they will be no shorter as . . . I go along my way . . . So why should I be waiting for . . . Tomorrow's doubtful dawn . . . When present opportunities . . . May be forever gone? . . . Today may be as commonplace . . . As every other one . . . But I will undertake my plan . . . And try to get it done.

SOMEONE DEAR

The memory of someone dear . . . Is like a thing of gold . . . That never dulls or tarnishes . . . Or grows the least bit old . . . It is a ray of sunshine bright . . . That fills an empty room . . . And it is like a flower fair . . . That never fails to bloom . . . It offers consolation in . . . The face of strife and stress . . . And adds a certain beauty to . . . Each dream of happiness . . . The memory of someone dear . . . However long apart . . . Is like a soothing melody . . . That lingers in the heart . . . It is the perfect picture of . . . A rainbow in the sky . . . It is the portrait of a past . . . That cannot ever die.

235

VACATION PRAYER

Dear Lord, let this vacation trip . . . Turn out to be our best . . .
Our most relaxful outing and . . . By far the happiest . . . Let all
our family enjoy . . . Each moment of each day . . . And help us
keep our worries and . . . Our worldly cares away . . . Give us the
cloudless skies of blue . . . The peaceful wooded streams . . . The
golden sunlight on the hills . . . And stars around our dreams . . .
Protect us on the highways and . . . In unfamiliar beds . . . And
do not let us stumble on . . . The path misfortune treads . . . Dear
Lord, be always at our side . . . Wherever we may roam . . . And
when at last we turn around . . . Please see us safely home.

WHEN YOU ARE MINE

There is no message I may send . . . That ever could express . . .
How much your friendship is a part . . . Of all my happiness . . .
To me you are the sun and moon . . . And all the stars that shine
. . . And when I take you in my arms . . . The whole wide world
is mine . . . You are the darling of my dreams . . . And you in-
spire me . . . To do my best in everything . . . Wherever I may be
. . . I look to you for courage and . . . For faith in every deed . . .
And when I walk beside you there . . . Is nothing that I need . . .
My life is perfect and complete . . . And all the skies are blue . . .
As long as you are part of me . . . And I am part of you.

PORTER

He carries all the bags and trunks . . . He tidies up the floor . . .
And in a dozen ways he is . . . The one you're looking for . . . He
fixes up electric lights . . . And pipes that start to leak . . . And he
is glad to help you get . . . Most anything you seek . . . In sleeping
cars he makes your bed . . . And calls you in the dawn . . . And he
will brush your clothes if you . . . Are not already gone . . . He
takes your laundry, brings it back . . . And shines your dusty shoes
. . . And frequently he is the one . . . Who finds the things you
lose . . . He has a humble station but . . . He takes a certain pride
. . . In giving comfort to the world . . . Where human hearts
abide.

TIME

Time always keeps an even pace . . . But as we live and grow . .
Sometimes in passing by it seems . . . To be too fast or slow . . .
When we are faced with endless fears . . . And all the skies are
gray . . . We often wish the hours would . . . Be quick to pass
away . . . And when our hearts are happy and . . . The time is
ours to spend . . . We wish the clock would falter and . . . The day
would never end . . . But always it appears that time . . . Is slow
when we are sad . . . And that it goes too hurriedly . . . Whenever we are glad . . . And yet we know it never stops . . . And
never tries to race . . . Because each second passes by . . . Without
a change of pace.

RIGHT TO COMPLAIN

Indeed I do not like the one . . . Who constantly complains . . .
Because some little thing goes wrong . . . Or just because it rains
. . . Who frets from morning until night . . . And bothers every-
one . . . As though it were impossible . . . To find a little fun
. . . But I am just as glad at times . . . That there is no restraint
. . . And that I have an equal right . . . To register complaint . . .
That I may speak whatever words . . . I have a mind to say . . .
And nobody may ever take . . . That liberty away . . . I may be
prejudiced or I . . . May have a feeble brain . . . But I am thankful
that I have . . . The privilege to complain.

SLUMBER SHORTAGE

Each morning when I hear the clock . . . I set the night before
. . . I suffer something like the shock . . . Of falling on the floor
. . . I grab the thing, shut off the ring . . . I toss and turn about . . .
And score the rude awakening . . . Of one so tired out . . . I wish
I could remain all day . . . Relaxed in dreams sublime . . . Instead
I have to rush away . . . To get to work on time . . . But on a holi-
day when I . . . May turn the clock around . . . And I am fully free
to lie . . . And rest in slumber sound . . . My eyes are always open
wide . . . My drowsiness has fled . . . I yawn and stretch and soon
decide . . . To tumble out of bed.

THINKING OF YOU

I do not need a birthday or . . . A Christmas bright and new
. . . Or any anniversary . . . To make me think of you . . . For
you are always in my thoughts . . . From morning until night . . .
And then until the smallest star . . . Has faded out of sight . . . I
think of you at work, at home . . . And every place in town
. . . And whether I am happy or . . . My world is upside down . . .
You are the music and the words . . . Of every song I sing . . .
From summer into autumn and . . . From winter into spring
. . . And some day when the sun goes down . . . Beyond the silent
blue . . . I know my parting thought will be . . . Another thought
of you.

WASHING MACHINE

We have a mighty good machine . . . That washes all our clothes
. . . And does them automatically . . . While we enjoy a doze . . .
It cleans the sheet and pillow case . . . The towel and the shirt
. . . And leaves the sox and underwear . . . Without a sign of dirt
. . . It is a great invention and . . . We often wonder who . . .
Possessed the brains to save us all . . . The work that it can do
. . . For it not only cleans the clothes . . . It rinses them as well . . .
And afterwards the laundry has . . . That sweet, refreshing smell
. . . And all we could desire to . . . Improve on its design . . .
Would be to have it take our things . . . And hang them on the
line.

I AM YOUR FRIEND

It does not matter what you think . . . Or what you say or do
. . . You may be confident that I . . . Shall be a friend to you . . .
Because I like you very much . . . And as I always say . . . A
person cannot really be . . . A friend for just a day . . . I want to
be beside you and . . . To serve you here and now . . . As much as
my ability . . . And money will allow . . . I long to share your
struggle and . . . The burden you must bear . . . And in so many
other ways . . . To show you that I care . . . So let me be a friend to
you . . . And add a bit of cheer . . . To every day and every night
. . . Of every coming year.

IMPORTANT PEOPLE

A man's importance in the world . . . Wherever he may go . . .
Is something others should decide . . . And he should never know
. . . He should not think so well about . . . The progress he has
made . . . And he is hardly qualified . . . To elevate his grade . . .
But there are people who declare . . . Or pointedly imply . . . The
height of their ability . . . Is equal to the sky . . . They know the
only answer to . . . The problem of the day . . . And they will
gladly condescend . . . To give advice away . . . And while they
have a right to choose . . . The way they want to feel . . . They
make themselves obnoxious to . . . The people who are real.

OUR BOYS AT HOME

When our two boys are home and we . . . Would like to have
them stay . . . They always want to go outside . . . And concen-
trate on play . . . And always when we need them most . . . And
wish they were around . . . They are the members of our tribe
. . . Who never can be found . . . But when we have some company . . . And long for peace and rest . . . They emphasize their
presence for . . . The eyes of every guest . . . We try to send them
off to bed . . . And keep them out of sight . . . But they are never
satisfied . . . To sleep away the night . . . They want to know
what merriment . . . And words are going on . . . And where the
clock will hold its hands . . . When all the guests are gone.

SECURITY

We used to live from hand to mouth . . . As many people do . . .
And we could hardly wait until . . . My pay check would accrue
. . . And many were the times that I . . . Would borrow here and
there . . . So we would always have enough . . . To eat and drink
and wear . . . But one day we decided we . . . Could not go on that
way . . . For it was too embarrassing . . . To live beyond our pay
. . . And so we forced ourselves to live . . . A life of smaller size
. . . Although we found it mighty tough . . . To thus econo-
mize . . . We struggled and we saved and now . . . We heartily
agree . . . That nothing is more comforting . . . Than planned
security.

WITH ALL MY HEART

There is no creature on this earth . . . So lovable and true . . .
So charming and considerate . . . And wonderful as you . . . You
are the glory of my day . . . The magic of my night . . . And in
your eyes my eyes behold . . . A warm and friendly light . . .
Oh, I could sail the seven seas . . . And wander far and near . . .
And I would never find a soul . . . So helpful and sincere . . . You
are the world and all to me . . . Wherever I may go . . . In valleys
green with clover or . . . On mountain peaks of snow . . . I love
you with my every thought . . . And everything I do . . . And
every hour of my life . . . My heart belongs to you.

HE WATCHES OVER ME

I know God watches over me . . . Because when I am sad . . .
He always has some special way . . . In which to make me glad
. . . When I am weary with my work . . . He takes my cares away
. . . By giving me the silver stars . . . As I complete the day . . .
He follows me at every step . . . Along the streets in town . . . And
if I need His helping hand . . . He never lets me down . . . He
keeps me out of reach of all . . . The speeding cars that pass
. . . And teaches me the way to be . . . Of credit to my class . . .
I know He watches over me . . . Throughout each day and night
. . . As long as I do all I can . . . To stay within His sight.

TENNIS

The game of tennis is a game . . . That calls for speed and skill
. . . In which the player must know how . . . To lob or make a
kill . . . It is an exercise confined . . . To either two or four . . .
And it has its exclusive way . . . Of adding up the score . . . And
yet a game is merely one . . . Of those that make a set . . . And
there must be two sets or three . . . To settle any bet . . . One player
serves the ball and then . . . Another hits it back . . . And victory
depends upon . . . Experience and knack . . . Unless a man and
maid compete . . . And they are thinking of . . . A different sub-
ject when they play . . . A game described as love.

INSURANCE MAN

Somehow he learns about your name . . . And when he calls on
you . . . You think his only purpose is . . . To sign up someone
new . . . Whereas he wants to guard you and . . . To keep you
from despair . . . If suddenly your dearest dreams . . . Should
vanish into air . . . He wants your loving family . . . To be provided for . . . In case you are too old to work . . . Or if you are no
more . . . He helps when you are ill and when . . . An accident
occurs . . . And he protects your home, your car . . . Your jewelry
and furs . . . He educates your children and . . . In every other
way . . . He makes tomorrow easier . . . By what you buy today.

MISUNDERSTOOD

Sometimes we do not say or do . . . Exactly what we mean . . .
And consequently life becomes . . . A rather tragic scene . . . Our
friends are quite convinced that we . . . Intend to do them harm
. . . When actually our thoughts of them . . . Could never cause
alarm . . . Our motive is misunderstood . . . And we are quickly
blamed . . . For something which if it were true . . . Would make
us feel ashamed . . . They never try to analyze . . . What we have
said or done . . . And whether it was serious . . . Or just to have
some fun . . . They merely pout and let us know . . . How much
they are in pain . . . Without affording us the chance . . . To
properly explain.

WORK TO BE DONE

Each morning I behold my desk . . . And see the work piled
high . . . And slowly I sit down and breathe . . . A disconcerting
sigh . . . I feel that I shall never do . . . The task that lies ahead
. . . And silently I make the wish . . . That I were home in bed . . .
But finally I figure that . . . I might as well begin . . . And so I
grab the telephone . . . And make the dial spin . . . I handle correspondence and . . . Record the notes I need . . . And somehow as
I go along . . . I seem to gather speed . . . And somehow when the
clock reflects . . . The setting of the sun . . . My desk is clear of
everything . . . And all my work is done.

TOGETHER, DEAR

Whatever else in life we do . . . From day to month to year . . .
I hope with all my heart we two . . . Grow old together, dear
. . . I pray that we shall never be . . . Beyond each other's sight
. . . Or that for any reason we . . . Shall live a lonely night . . . I
want to look into your eyes . . . And see the laughter there . . .
Assuring me that all your sighs . . . And thoughts are mine to
share . . . I long to hold your gentle hand . . . Along the winding
way . . . And know you really understand . . . Whatever words I
say . . . And when the shadows turn to blue . . . In timeless atmosphere . . . I hope with all my heart we two . . . Go on together,
dear.

GOD IS HERE

There is no loneliness in life . . . As long as God is here . . .
Because His presence is a source . . . Of comfort and of cheer
. . . We do not see Him at our side . . . Or touch His gentle hand
. . . And yet we know that He is here . . . To help and under-
stand . . . And we can hear His loving voice . . . And all He deigns
to say . . . If only we are not disposed . . . To turn our hearts away
. . . Because the words of wisdom He . . . Is eager to impart . . .
Are those that He is whispering . . . Directly to the heart . . . And
so there is no loneliness . . . Or need for any fear . . . As long as
we remind ourselves . . . That God is always here.

LAW STUDENT

No lawyer knows his law so well . . . Or finds it all so clear . . .
As does the eager student who . . . Is in his freshman year . . . But
as semesters slip away . . . And subjects grow intense . . . He is
not quite so confident . . . Of his intelligence . . . For there are
many theories . . . To mystify his brain . . . Including bailment
and the right . . . Of eminent domain . . . Including common car-
riers . . . Insurance, sales and torts . . . As well as what is ethical
. . . In all the different courts . . . And if at last he perseveres . . .
He surely will agree . . . It takes a lot of studying . . . To earn
an LL.B.

OUT OF STEP

In January I incline . . . To thoughts of March and May . . .
And those impatient April winds . . . That blow the rain away
. . . In short, I think about the spring . . . With all its beauty bright
. . . And of the feeling in my heart . . . When there are stars at
night . . . But when the grass is green again . . . And flowers start
to rise . . . I think about the friendliness . . . Of lazy summer skies
. . . And when July and August come . . . I start to look for
fall . . . And in October I would like . . . To wear my winter shawl
. . . Which always makes me feel that I . . . Am never quite in
stride . . . Because there is no time of year . . . When I am satisfied.

GIVE ME YOUR LOVE

Give me this night to kiss your lips . . . And hold you close to
me . . . And let me find a part of you . . . In every memory . . .
Give me the song you used to sing . . . When we were young and
gay . . . And let me walk again with you . . . The paths of yes-
terday . . . For you are all I ever want . . . And all I ever need
. . . To do my daily duty and . . . Eventually succeed . . . Give
me your faith and confidence . . . Your kindness and your smile
. . . And I shall not require rest . . . However long the mile . . .
Give me the promise of your love . . . With all its lasting worth
. . . And I shall be the proudest and . . . The happiest on earth.

FARMER

He is a rough and calloused man . . . With many chores to do
. . . But always in a friendly voice . . . He calls hello to you . . .
He works in dirty overalls . . . And dirt is on his hand . . . But it
is just the healthy soil . . . Of cultivated land . . . He does not have
much money and . . . For him there is no fame . . . But he is rich
in honesty . . . And neighborly acclaim . . . He may not read and
write so well . . . Or add and take away . . . But he has more good
common sense . . . Than many folks display . . . And while his
fences seem to set . . . His premises apart . . . The welcome sign is
on his gate . . . And all around his heart.

243

STORE SERVICE

Whenever I go in a store . . . To merely gaze a bit . . . A dozen clerks pick something up . . . And try to sell me it . . . I never get a moment's peace . . . And I am made to feel . . . That if I make no purchase I . . . Am just another heel . . . But if I go in there to get . . . An article I need . . . And if I choose the item with . . . Extraordinary speed . . . The minutes seem like hours as . . . My eyes look all around . . . Because the clerks who wait on folks . . . Are nowhere to be found . . . I wish the store would serve me when . . . I have a buying craze . . . And let me wander idly when . . . I merely want to gaze.

REMEMBER HIM

He fought on Okinawa and . . . At Iwo Jima too . . . And at Tarawa and Saipan . . . He saw the battles through . . . He was the boy who left your home . . . These many months ago . . . To join the fight for liberty . . . Against a cruel foe . . . He crawled through jungles and he went . . . From shore to shore in ships . . . He entered every battle with . . . A prayer upon his lips . . . He suffered thirst and hunger and . . . He lived with all his fears . . . He burned with fever and he gave . . . His sweat and blood and tears . . . He is the man who fought for you . . . And all his countrymen . . . Give him your thanks and praise and help . . . When he comes home again.

OUR CHOICE

We have the right to choose the way . . . We want to live on earth . . . And so we may pursue a life . . . Of great or little worth . . . We may be very virtuous . . . And loyal to The Lord . . . Or not at all concerned about . . . A heavenly reward . . . But if we take the path of sin . . . We ought to be aware . . . That temporary pleasure is . . . A bubble in the air . . . That it is bound to burst because . . . It is not made to last . . . And nothing we may do can change . . . The color of the past . . . We cannot call the hours back . . . When they are gone away . . . And each tomorrow must depend . . . On what we do today.

COURAGE FROM GOD

The world is full of heroes and . . . The honors we bestow . . . And we are deeply grateful for . . . The bravery they show . . . We recognize their sacrifice . . . And their unyielding will . . . But do we ever think of Him . . . Who made it possible? . . . Do we appreciate that God . . . Has let the world go on . . . And only by His grace do we . . . Begin another dawn? . . . Are we aware that when our lives . . . Are shadowy and dim . . . We carry on with courage strong . . . That emanates from Him? . . . If we are known as heroes in . . . The world in which we live . . . It is because we have the strength . . . That only God can give.

YOU MAY NOT KNOW IT

You may not ever know it but . . . My heart belongs to you . . . Because you are so much a part . . . Of everything I do . . . You wake me in the morning when . . . The sun begins to shine . . . And you remind me everywhere . . . That you are really mine . . . You fill my every afternoon . . . With dreams of days to be . . . In happiness that only God . . . Can give to you and me . . . Because we are together and . . . He made us into one . . . And life is ours from dawn until . . . Another day is done . . . And while you may not realize it . . . As fully as you might . . . I love you more than all the world . . . And all the stars at night.

THE BOSS

He is the pompous gentleman . . . Who rules the girls and boys . . . And tries to keep the office force . . . From making too much noise . . . He checks them in and checks them out . . . And it is his to say . . . If any absence is excused . . . Throughout the working day . . . His countenance is always stern . . . His voice is quite severe . . . And yet there are occasions when . . . He seems to be sincere . . . He tabulates production with . . . A steady hand and true . . . And when a task is done he finds . . . Another job to do . . . He feels important in his post . . . And pulls the puppet strings . . . But underneath he understands . . . The human side of things.

245

STARS TO REMIND ME

There are so many stars tonight . . . I cannot count them all
. . . And yet it seems that every one . . . Is something to recall . . .
Each one is like a memory . . . Of days we used to know . . .
When we enjoyed the seasons from . . . The summer to the snow
. . . When life was so much younger and . . . We had more time
to play . . . And our tomorrow was a song . . . That seemed so
far away . . . But also there are certain stars . . . Reminding me tonight . . . Of all our plans and promises . . . That drifted out of
sight . . . And as I gaze up at the sky . . . I wander everywhere
. . . In search of something to restore . . . The dream we used to
share.

WHEN I AM WEARY

When I am weary of the world . . . And of my daily art . . . I
call upon the happy thoughts . . . I carry in my heart . . . The
thought that you belong to me . . . And I belong to you . . .
And when I look into your eyes . . . The skies are always blue
. . . The thought that you mean more to me . . . Than diamonds
and gold . . . And all the other riches that . . . My hands could
ever hold . . . I think about the countless joys . . . That you have
given me . . . And most of all your boundless faith . . . Your
love and sympathy . . . I think of your encouragement . . . And
how you calm my fears . . . And then the burden of my day . . .
Forever disappears.

CLOSER TO GOD

Whatever we desire and . . . Wherever we may plod . . . We
ought to think a little more . . . Of what we owe to God . . .
We ought to thank Him for this life . . . With all its beauty bright
. . . The sunshine and the flowers and . . . The silver stars at night
. . . The friendships and the pleasures that . . . Are ours to have
and hold . . . And all the other things that turn . . . To memories
of gold . . . And we should try to live our lives . . . According
to His way . . . To glorify and honor Him . . . By what we do and
say . . . We ought to practice virtue and . . . To set our sins apart
. . . And live a little closer to . . . His kind and loving heart.

TICK-TOCK

I like the ticking of a clock . . . However loud it be . . . Because each time I hear it I . . . Can shut my eyes and see . . . A parlor wrapped in coziness . . . Beside a fireplace . . . A rocking chair, a photograph . . . Of some familiar face . . . Or else a kitchen with its stove . . . Its table and its sink . . . Its pots and pans and pantry shelves . . . Of things to eat and drink . . . I see an upstairs bedroom where . . . The sun comes in at dawn . . . And where the stars look in at night . . . Until the shades are drawn . . . The ticking of a clock is such . . . A reassuring sound . . . Especially at times when there . . . Is no one else around.

I GO TO CHURCH

I go to church on Sunday and . . . I say a fervent prayer . . . Because I want The Lord to know . . . How much I really care . . . Because I want to thank Him for . . . The blessings I have gained . . . Not only in the sunshine but . . . Whenever it has rained . . . And also I implore Him to . . . Bestow the grace I need . . . To make myself presentable . . . In thought and word and deed . . . I tell Him I am sorry for . . . The sinful side of me . . . And ask Him to forgive me for . . . My instability . . . I go to church on Sunday for . . . The wonderful reward . . . Of knowing that my heart and soul . . . Are closer to The Lord.

TRACK MAN

The track man practices his stride . . . To keep himself in shape . . . But most of all to be the one . . . Who crashes through the tape . . . Or else he makes a dash and takes . . . The hurdles high and low . . . Or throws the javelin or the disc . . . As far as it will go . . . He puts the shot, he high jumps or . . . He pole vaults into space . . . And then again he does his part . . . To win the relay race . . . He used to choose a certain thing . . . In which to specialize . . . And try to set a record that . . . The world would recognize . . . But nowadays he struggles with . . . His hands and with his feet . . . To capture the majority . . . Of honors at a meet.

KRISTINA'S TIME

Kristina likes each Sunday and . . . She likes each Saturday . . .
Because they are my special time . . . To stay at home and play
. . . She knows I do not go to work . . . But I am there with her
. . . To be a part of any game . . . Her pleasure may prefer . . .
I help her eat her breakfast and . . . Her lunch and dinner too . . .
And she is always interested . . . In everything I do . . . We take
a nap together and . . . Before we close our eyes . . . I tell a fairy
story that . . . She tries to memorize . . . And that is why Kristina
dear . . . Whose age is only three . . . Likes Saturday and Sunday
in . . . Her daddy's company.

PRAYER FOR LIGHT

Sometimes, O Lord, it seems to me . . . The day turns into night
. . . And in the darkness all around . . . I need Your guiding
light . . . I wander in the wilderness . . . Where shadows move
about . . . And in my heart I struggle with . . . My trouble and
my doubt . . . I start to lose my courage and . . . I feel so all alone
. . . And yet I often wonder if . . . The fault is not my own . . .
For if I kept my faith with You . . . I would not be so blind . . .
And I would go ahead instead . . . Of gazing far behind . . . And
so whenever I am sad . . . And conscious of my plight . . . I pray to
You, O Lord, that I . . . May have Your guiding light.

MY SYMPATHY

The grief of sudden tragedy . . . Is poignant as can be . . . And
all that I can offer you . . . Is friendly sympathy . . . But my con-
dolence really comes . . . Directly from the heart . . . Because I
know how sad it is . . . When loved ones have to part . . . I
know you will be lonely as . . . The days and nights go by . . .
And there will be a thousand tears . . . That you will want to cry
. . . And yet we must remember that . . . There is a will divine
. . . And we may never question it . . . Or fathom God's design . . .
And so I grieve with you today . . . And say a fervent prayer
. . . That God will bless and always keep . . . Your loved one in
His care.

REST REQUESTED

My wife is always telling me . . . The things she wants to do . . .
To make our home more beautiful . . . Or build a cottage new
. . . And while I like to listen to . . . Whatever she may say . . .
I am a tired man when I . . . Complete the working day . . . And
anything I figure out . . . For her beloved sake . . . Is only so
much labor for . . . My brain to undertake . . . And so I try to tell
her I . . . Am just another man . . . And when we can afford it I
. . . Will carry out her plan . . . But in the meantime I would
like . . . To rest a little bit . . . So I can do the job she wants . . .
And give my best to it.

WE HAVE TO TRY

We cannot look for better luck . . . In all the winds that blow
. . . Or hope for happiness unless . . . We try to make it so . . .
We have to use our energy . . . And keep our purpose clear . . .
And never be indifferent . . . If we would persevere . . . There is
no good excuse to rest . . . When there is work ahead . . . As long
as we are strong enough . . . To earn our daily bread . . . We
may not always win or get . . . The credit for each deed . . . But
if we do our best we will . . . Eventually succeed . . . We cannot
gain our goal unless . . . We conquer every doubt . . . Or hope to
have our ship come in . . . Unless we send it out.

MY INSPIRATION

If I have any dream tonight . . . It will belong to you . . . Because you are so interested . . . In everything I do . . . Because the
world is wonderful . . . Whenever you are near . . . And there is
never any room . . . For tragedy or tear . . . And that is why I
think of you . . . And dream of you tonight . . . And why the
moon is beautiful . . . And all the stars are bright . . . You are
the inspiration true . . . In every song I sing . . . From summer
into autumn and . . . From winter into spring . . . And every little
minute of . . . Each hour of the day . . . Is just another bit of life
. . . That you are making gay.

249

THANK YOU

I thank you for inviting me . . . To share your evening meal . . .
And for your hospitality . . . So friendly and so real . . . The
dinner was delicious and . . . I surely ate my fill . . . But being in
your company . . . I think was better still . . . You treated me like
one of you . . . And made me feel at ease . . . With never any vain
attempt . . . To honor or to please . . . Why, it was just like
being home . . . With folks and friends of old . . . Where happy
hours slip away . . . And memories unfold . . . So please accept my
heartfelt thanks . . . And I do hope some day . . . I may return
your favor in . . . The same unselfish way.

GOD BLESS OUR FLAG

God bless our flag, the stars and stripes . . . And see it safely
through . . . God bless and keep our colors all . . . The red, the
white, the blue . . . In every war that we have fought . . . Our
flag has led the way . . . On battlefield, among the clouds . . .
Beyond and in the bay . . . In all our fights for human rights
. . . Our banner bright has flown . . . And we Americans are
proud . . . To claim it for our own . . . Its folds have rested on
the graves . . . Of heroes near and far . . . A colony in every stripe
. . . A state in every star . . . And now it guides us on our way
. . . To triumph great and new . . . God bless our flag, the stars
and stripes . . . And see it safely through!

IN LATER YEARS

In later years I hope they find . . . Some mark upon this earth
. . . For everything I leave behind . . . However small its worth
. . . I hope my every word and deed . . . Will touch some kindred
soul . . . And in the hour of its need . . . Give guidance to its goal
. . . I pray that I may use my time . . . To do the greatest good . . .
And in the song of every rhyme . . . Be rightly understood
. . . And if I do some foolish thing . . . I do not mean to do . . . I
only ask that it will bring . . . Some helpful lesson too . . . In later
years I hope they share . . . All I attempt to be . . . And surely I
shall never care . . . If they remember me.